TEXAS
Chronicles

Photo Research
by Teri Davis Greenberg

Produced in Cooperation with
the Texas Chamber of Commerce

Jostens Publishing Group, Inc./
Cherbo Publishing Group, Inc.
Encino, California

TEXAS
Chronicles

THE HERITAGE AND ENTERPRISE *of the* LONE STAR STATE

by Darwin Payne

Jostens Publishing Group, Inc.
Book Division
Editorial Director *Karen Story*
Production Director *James Burke*

Staff for *Texas Chronicles*
Senior Editor
Teri Davis Greenberg
Designer
Ellen Ifrah
Editorial Assistant
Kathy B. Peyser
Project Coordinator
Merle Gratton

JPG

Jostens Publishing Group, Inc.
under the management of Cherbo Publishing Group, Inc.
Jack C. Cherbo, President

Library of Congress Catalog Card Number: 94-075767

ISBN: 1-882933-04-4

Published 1994
Printed in the United States of America
First Edition

Credits for photos appearing in the "articles" sections of the book may be found under "Additional Photo Credits" on page 189. All other photos are credited in their corresponding captions.

Frontispiece: San Antonio was one of only a handful of towns that existed when Mexico took over "Tejas." This view depicts the west side of San Antonio's main plaza as it appeared in 1849. Courtesy, San Antonio Museum Association

Above: Meet "The Big Texan," a bit of Texas kitsch on a grand scale. Photo by Michael D. Sullivan/ TexaStock

CONTENTS

PREFACE

While the recent history of the Texas Chamber of Commerce reaches back only to its formation six years ago, most who read this book will not be aware that from 1918 to 1924 there was a Texas Chamber of Commerce.

It was dissolved for what were, at the time, very valid reasons. In the early 1900s the issues facing business and communities were very regional in nature—for example, where were highways, schools and universities, penal institutions, dams, and other developing infrastructure going to be located?

Those issues, or, in some instances, battlegrounds, were very regional in nature, and it was very reasonable to decide to form regional chambers of commerce in East, South, and West Texas. As a result of the decision to dissolve the Texas Chamber, the state's business community had no major presence in Austin for decades.

By the 1970s and 1980s it became obvious to the volunteer leadership of the regional chambers and to the executives of local Texas chambers that something needed to be done. The regional mission had disappeared and Texas business needed an Austin presence.

In the late 1980s one single dynamic occurred that made the reconstitution of a state chamber a practical possibility. At the same point in time, heading their regional chambers of commerce as chief volunteers were Dr. Nancy Speck of Nacogdoches, E.W. "Bubba" Wehman, Jr., of Pleasonton, and F.L. "Steve" Stephens of San Angelo. These three individuals led the effort to establish the Texas Chamber and successfully brought about the marriage between the East, South, and West Texas chambers.

Open for business in 1988, the Texas Chamber of Commerce has increased from 1,500 members to around 4,000; and it has managed some important successes along the way. Its first legislative year was marked by the historic reforms in workers' compensation laws in the state; and this last legislative session marked outstanding successes in health care reform, lawsuit abuse, and trucking reform. Along with its commitment to impact legislative decisions on budget and taxation, public education, criminal justice, economic development, and the environment, the short history of the Texas Chamber of Commerce is no less distinguished than the many exciting tales you will enjoy in this book.

Under the watchful guidance of previous chairs Steve Stephens, Glenn Biggs of San Antonio, Jerry Farrington of Dallas, Don Jordan of Houston, Dr. Don Carlton of Austin, and Allan Shivers, Jr., of Austin, the Texas Chamber of Commerce is proud of its contribution to the dynamics that have made the history of this great state so remarkable.

The images portrayed in the pages you are to read lend toward a better understanding of why our state is so unique and so wonderful. The Texas Chamber of Commerce is delighted to have played a part in bringing them to you.

Texas Chamber of Commerce

Bob Lane	James M. Windham, Jr.	Bruce Gibson
Dallas	*Houston*	*Austin*
Chairman	*Chairman-Elect*	*President and CEO*

FOREWORD

This is the story of Texas as it might have been chronicled by a newspaper reporter who either personally observed an historic event taking place or who—as is more frequently the journalistic case—interviewed those persons who were privileged to witness or to participate in the event. The advantage of such an approach, in addition to its uniqueness, is to create a history that follows some of the basic tenets of journalism—an account that is readable, concise, relevant, and interesting. It is intended to be the type of book that a reader may pick up at odd, spare moments for brief sessions, put down, then pick up again without losing his or her train of thought.

The topics chosen in *Texas Chronicles* are intended to be suggestive of the state's rich history in its many aspects, and especially to trace its evolution from raw frontier to urban and technological base. Actually, of course, many of the episodes related here are by no means confined to the boundaries of Texas, because they hold great significance for the nation and the world. Some of the stories included are intended to reflect sweeping changes—barbed wire's impact on the cattle kingdom, the ushering in of the modern petroleum industry with Spindletop, the significance of a Texas company's development of the transistor. Others reflect less significant but nonetheless highly colorful or intriguing episodes—the failed attempt to introduce camels as a means of transportation in arid West Texas, the career of Judge Roy Bean and his practice of "law west of the Pecos," and the adoption of the pecan as the official state tree.

Because it is the nature of most news stories to deal with specific moments in time rather than with long-term trends, a central question concerned when to pick the moment. For instance, if the moment involves the first use of barbed wire to enclose a cattle ranch, it is awkward to attempt to project the overall impact of barbed wire into the future in a news story intended to be contemporary. As a result of such considerations, the strategy frequently employed here was to select a related event occurring at a later date so that a fuller treatment could be given without assuming the role of a seer in forecasting the future. Sometimes, when focusing on an individual and his or her achievements, only an obituary seemed appropriate as a vehicle for providing the full story. Sam Houston, Oliver Loving, and J. Frank Dobie are examples. Some huge topics, of course, required more than one story.

The topic selection process, or the exercising of "news judgment" for the entirety of Texas' history, was endlessly fascinating in itself. Opinions always vary in such matters, and I'm certain that no one would agree with all the choices I have made nor in my emphasis.

The reader may notice that certain ethnic and racial terms now considered "politically incorrect" such as "Negro" instead of "African American" or "Chinaman" instead of "Asian American" have been used in the stories. Employing the language used at the time in which the story took place was done to heighten the reality of the story and in no way should be considered derogatory or offensive.

Most of my research for this book was conducted within the friendly confines of Fondren Library at Southern Methodist University, where I am a journalism faculty member. Of special use to me were editions of the *Texas Almanac,* a reference work on Texas first published in 1857, and the invaluable *Handbook of Texas.* They are cited along with other works in the bibliography that appears at the end of this volume.

I would also like to acknowledge my appreciation for the fine people at Jostens Publishing Group, especially the editor and photo researcher of this volume, Teri Davis Greenberg.

Darwin Payne
Dallas, Texas

CHAPTER ONE

New Land, New Opportunities, New People

1821-1861

W*hat was true for the American nation was true for Texas. The frontier was the determining factor in shaping its character, culture, and institutions; and no part of the American nation played a larger, more central role as a frontier than that of the land once referred to as the "great kingdom of the Tejas."*

The frontier signified opportunity. It was an opportunity for those people ambitious enough to come to shed the old for the new—to create new lives, new wealth, new educational and cultural institutions, new resources, and new business ventures. Texas and opportunity were synonymous. This has been true from the time that Spaniards first set foot on Texas soil in the early 1500s and began sending back glowing reports to their sovereignty. *It was a new, varied, vast land awaiting entrepreneurs to organize and develop it.*

The Spaniards laid claim to the land for some 300 years, leaving an indelible imprint on Texas culture and institutions through Spanish place names, land titles, religion, and architecture.

By the time Spain lost Mexico through revolution in 1821, though, the territory Mexico claimed as part of its bounty north of the Rio Grande—Texas—still lacked almost all civilizing influences. Exceptions were the very notable Spanish missions and a handful of small towns: San Antonio, Goliad, and Nacogdoches.

Here was a vast, unpopulated, promising terrain crying out for settlement and development by those with the wit and resources to do so. Those willing to meet these huge and important challenges were entrepreneurs, bold people with vision. They were early political leaders who sought to organize Texas through government. They were settlers and farmers who raised vast amounts of wheat, cotton, corn, and other food products not just for fellow Texans but, ultimately, for export as well. They were cattlemen who created ranches and new techniques of ranching that still exist today. They were businessmen who arranged for the products and services essential to the development of any growing population. They were miners who invested money and energy to discover and utilize mineral and raw resources, most importantly oil. They were inventors and engineers who introduced the Industrial Age to Texas.

Texas held the kind of opportunity that Americans, imbued with the concept of manifest destiny, were eager to seize. Even before Mexican independence, they had been casting hungry glances in its direction. Filibusters such as Philip Nolan were crossing into the land from Louisiana, and squatters were beginning to settle.

The Mexican authorities were far from ignorant concerning the potential of Texas. Their opportunity to speed up the civilizing process there in a formal, official way presented itself through the person of Moses Austin, who, in 1821, won a Mexican commission to bring American settlers into a colony along the rich agricultural lands on the lower Brazos River.

The new colony, which upon Austin's death was led by his son Stephen F., created a foothold Americans had been seeking for years. They were Americans, not adopted Mexicans. The ultimate result was conflict with the Mexican authorities, a declaration of independence, the epochal massacre at the Alamo, the surprising victory at San Jacinto over Santa Anna, and the creation in 1836 of a new nation—the Republic of Texas.

The flow of American emigrants eager to share in the development of this new nation and enticed by generous offers of land reached immense proportions in the next few years. Although the Republic of Texas obviously held untold potential for these new settlers, the difficulties of organizing from scratch and of financing government operations were overwhelming. The temptation to solve those problems by becoming part of the United States (from whence the vast majority of Texas settlers came) was great.

When the American political climate changed (evidenced through the election of James K. Polk in 1844), this permitted the annexation of Texas to the United States on December 29, 1845.

Mexico, however, was not yet ready to relinquish its claims. As a result, President Polk ordered General Zachary Taylor to assemble a large contingent of armed forces at Corpus Christi to secure Texas and especially the disputed land between the Nueces River and the Rio Grande. When Taylor's army moved southward to the Rio Grande and confronted Mexican troops, hostilities erupted.

The American triumph in the War with Mexico secured the state of Texas and its Rio Grande boundary as a recognized part of the United States. Additionally, the Treaty of Guadalupe Hidalgo, signed on February 2, 1848, gave the United States its greatest land acquisition in history. Now the United States of America stretched all the way to the Pacific Coast off California.

There was trouble within the American nation, though. This was the same trouble that had made Texas' annexation politically impossible for years—slavery.

Texas, with an agricultural base already firmly seated in cotton, automatically assumed status as an integral part of the South. Prosperous Texas settlers who had come from Alabama, Georgia, and other slave states had brought large numbers of slaves with them. In 1860, by the eve of the Civil War, the state's slave population was nearly half that of the white population and growing at a faster rate.

Town building had also been taking place. By 1860 San Antonio, with 8,235 residents, was the state's largest city. Galveston, on the coast, was second with a population of 4,177. Next came Houston, and Austin was fourth.

The period of the Republic and early statehood was characterized by building. Texans constructed railroads, founded colleges and universities, established churches, improved waterways, started businesses, created military posts, and published newspapers.

Then, as Southern states began seceding from the Union after Abraham Lincoln's election, a new era was beginning. Despite the pleadings of Sam Houston, Texas quit the Union to become one of the Confederate States of America

Facing page: The Battle of San Jacinto resulted in the capture of Santa Anna, victory for the Americans, and independence from Mexican rule. This painting depicts Santa Anna surrendering to the wounded Sam Houston. Courtesy, Archives Division—Texas State Library; photo by Eric Beggs

Top: Before the Spaniards set foot on Texas soil in the early 1500s, the Lipans (depicted here) and other Native Americans occupied the land. Courtesy, San Antonio Museum Association

Above: By 1821, when Mexico won from Spain the territory that would later be known as Texas, the Spanish missions were almost the only symbol of civilization in the vast, unpopulated region. Pictured here is the Mission of Conception in San Antonio. Courtesy, Amon Carter Museum, Fort Worth; Gift of Mrs. Natalie K. Shastid

Right: The Fall of the Alamo or *Crockett's Last Stand* depicts the legendary 1836 battle between the Americans and Mexicans. Courtesy, Friends of the Governor's Mansion, Austin

Top: In late April 1836, just six weeks after the massacre at the Alamo, Sam Houston's men surprised a force of Mexicans at San Jacinto. Courtesy, Archives Division—Texas State Library; photo by Eric Beggs

Above: Filibuster Philip Nolan and others like him settled the area long before Mexican rule. Here Spanish soldiers approach Nolan and a companion in 1801. Painting by Bruce Marshall. Courtesy, Institute of Texan Cultures

Right: **By about 1860 San Antonio boasted 8,235 residents, making it the largest city in Texas. Courtesy, Amon Carter Museum, Fort Worth**

Below: **As is evident from this broadside posted in Austin in December 1860, not all Texans were in favor of seceding from the Union. Courtesy, The Center for American History, The University of Texas at Austin, Broadsides Collection**

PROGRAMME
OF THE
UNION DEMONSTRATION
SATURDAY, DEC. 22, '60.

THE PROCESSION
Will form at 11 o'clock, A. M., on Pecan Street, at its junction with Congress Avenue, in the following

ORDER
1. Band of Music.
2. Citizens on Foot.
3. Citizens in Carriages.
4. Citizens on Horseback.

The procession will then march down Pecan street to Brazos, thence down Brazos to Pine street, thence up Pine to Congress Avenue, thence up Congress Avenue to the Capitol, from the steps of which ADDRESSES will be delivered upon the subject of **Maintaining Our Rights in the Union.**

GEO. H. GRAY,
AMOS MORRILL,
Marshals.

Austin, Dec. 21, '60.

Right: **This 1840 ad offers a $200 reward for the return of a slave named John to Austin resident John H. Harry. Prosperous Texans from southern states brought their slaves with them when they moved to Texas. Courtesy, The Center for American History, The University of Texas at Austin, Texas Newspaper Collection**

$200 IN GOLD OR SILVER will be given for the del very to me in the city of Austin of my negro boy Joh he left about the 1st February. Said negro is very dark in his con plexion, and of a heavy build,—stands about 5 ft. 8 inches, is abo 24 years of age, and smiles when he is conversed with; he was ca tured by a detachment of the 1st Regiment Regular Infantry. Wh he left he carried with him a new plain-stocked rifle—calabre 60 the pound, percussion lock, a pouch made and fringed with buckski and a powder horn; on the pouch srap there was a pecan handl knife, with three copper rivets. One half of the above reward wi be paid to any person lodging said negro in any jail in the Republi and all expenses paid.

Feb. 24, 1840-16:12m JOHN H. HARRY.

Alamo (1850)
Mission de la Concepcion
E BEXAR.

Moses Austin Receives Grant to Settle Texas

(1821, January) The Spanish government has granted a man from Missouri, Moses Austin, the right to settle 300 families in the huge, largely unpopulated province of Texas north of the Rio Grande.

Under terms of the grant, Austin will be permitted to bring the families to an area covering 200,000 acres.

The grant, a difficult one to obtain, was achieved through a combination of persistence and good fortune. Austin, whose once-lucrative holdings in the lead-mining area of southeastern Missouri had turned to ruin, traveled to San Antonio de Bexar in Texas in December 1820 for an audience with Spanish Governor Antonio Maria Martinez.

At first Martinez refused to hear Austin and ordered him to leave Texas, but before departing, Austin encountered an old friend, the Baron de Bastrop, who interceded and persuaded Martinez to give the 59-year-old American an audience. The result was a favorable recommendation from Martinez, who forwarded Austin's petition to the chief civil and military commandant of Texas in Monterrey, about 175 miles south of the Rio Grande. The commandant, General Joaquin de

Moses Austin

Arredondo, approved the request.

Many details about the grant remain unclear. For one thing, its location is uncertain, and there is no word as to how much property the settlers will be entitled to claim. Nevertheless, Austin has returned to Missouri to organize a group of settlers to travel to Texas and begin their new lives in this undeveloped land of great promise.

Austin, a Connecticut native born in October 1761, worked with his brother Stephen for some years in a merchandising business in Philadelphia. Later he opened a branch of the firm at Richmond, Virginia. In 1791 he moved to Wythe County in southwestern Virginia and became involved in developing the lead mines there. Afterward he moved to southeastern Missouri, where, having obtained a league of land from Spain, he earned a fortune in the lead mines.

When Austin's fortunes declined after the War of 1812 and in the Panic of 1819, he was generally considered to be financially ruined. It was at this point that he looked to Texas to regain his fortune. Evidently, Moses Austin has done so with promising results.

First Settlers Arrive in Austin's Texas Colony

(Late 1821-Early 1822) The first of an anticipated 300 American settlers have begun to arrive along the Brazos River to begin their new lives in the colony approved January 1821 by the Spanish government.

In a tragic turn of events, however, Moses Austin died shortly after winning permission to bring the settlers to Texas. His son, Stephen F. Austin, now heads the settlers.

The younger Austin, just 27 years old, had been sworn in as a circuit judge in Arkansas when his father's death occurred. To assume his late father's obligations, he had to

Right: Stephen F. Austin and Texas colonists

give up that position.

Despite his youth, Austin is said to be a highly qualified individual, having been blessed with a good temperament and having served five years in the Missouri legislature.

The younger Austin negotiated with Spanish authorities to obtain specifics of the broad agreement his father had obtained for settlement. These details include the offer of 640 acres of land to each head of a family, 320 acres for his wife, 320 acres for each child, and 80 acres for each slave.

Austin also was able to gain a desirable geographical designation for the colony along the lower Brazos and Colorado rivers.

Andrew Robinson, the first of the settlers to arrive, camped with his family west of the Brazos River near the La Bahia Road crossing in November 1821. Joining Robinson and his family a few days later were the Kuykendall brothers and their families. Others began to arrive, including Jared E. Groce, an Alabama planter who brought his family, 50 wagons, and 90 slaves.

These and other settlers were attracted by Austin's promotional work in Natchitoches and New Orleans in Louisiana, where he had published the terms of the land provisions and invited colonists to join him. The depression and Panic of 1819 prompted many settlers to eagerly take advantage of the opportunity to acquire substantial homesteads in an unsettled land of good climate and bright agricultural prospects. When Austin arrived in Natchitoches after a trip to San Antonio, he checked his mail and found more than 100 letters from interested persons.

Some colonists are arriving by land; others are coming by sea.

First Cotton Planter Now Builds Cotton Gin in Texas

(1828) Jared E. Groce, the pioneer settler who planted the first cotton crop in Stephen F. Austin's colony, now has constructed a cotton gin to process his crops as well as those of his neighbors.

The growth of cotton among Austin's colonists already has proven to be quite successful. It promises to be a significant cash crop, no less so than in the southern parts of the United States from where so many of the colonists came.

Groce arrived in Texas from Alabama with his son Leonard in 1822. The Groces brought with them a large number of possessions—50 wagon loads of goods, 90 slaves, and a herd of livestock. The family settled on a high bluff on the east bank of the Brazos.

Groce immediately became the leading citizen of the area. He erected his large, wooden gin at the tiny settlement named for him—Groce's Retreat. He planted his first cottonseed shortly after arriving in Texas and, soon, with the help of son Leonard, began exporting the product. Before finding a ready market in New Orleans (where he now sends his cotton), Groce transported his first cotton crops on the backs of pack mules to Mexico, where he traded cotton for coffee, tea, clothing, and Mexican silver dollars.

Eventually Groce built a landing near his plantation, permitting cotton to be floated on flatboats down the Brazos to be put on schooners bound for New Orleans.

Groce's cotton gin, which son Leonard brought from New Orleans, is expected to make a significant contribution to farmers in the area, who have found that the soil is very accommodating to the crop. Groce's is the second gin to be constructed in Texas. (John Cartwright built the first one in East Texas in about 1822.)

Groce, who was born on a Virginia plantation in 1782, migrated to Georgia at the age of 22. Ten years later he moved to Alabama.

Success as a planter permitted Groce to accumulate the large number of slaves and other property he brought with him to Texas. His 90 slaves entitled Groce to claim 80 acres for each one of them, and the Mexican government granted him 10 *sitios* of land.

Groce's land holdings, for which he obtained title in 1824, have expanded even farther since then.

"Bowie" Knife Becomes Popular Over Frontier

(Early 1830s) The sturdy knife that James "Jim" Bowie popularized and which took his name has been widely adopted by frontiersmen throughout North America, especially in the Southwest, but also as far away as England.

Jim Bowie's brother, Rezin, forged the knife for its namesake from a file he designed and had shaped by his plantation blacksmith.

James Bowie, whose name was given to the new, popular knife

The Bowie knife has the proportions of a short butcher knife with more curve on the blade near the point than at the handle, but it has a heavier handle. It is so well balanced that it can be thrown a considerable distance with deadly effect.

The knife is economical and practical for skinning, cutting meat, eating, fighting duels, and for performing a variety of other purposes. Frequently it is carried in a leather sheath.

Jim Bowie was born at Elliot Springs, Tennessee,

in 1795. A formidable frontier figure, he was connected for a while with the James Long expedition. Since then his wide variety of activities has included land speculation, slave smuggling, and various enterprises with Jean Lafitte.

Bowie was given the specially designed knife while recovering from wounds suffered in a duel near Natchez, Mississippi.

Bowie came to Texas in 1828, was baptized in the Catholic Church, spent time searching for lost treasure mines in the San Saba River area, and was elected a colonel in the Texas Rangers in 1830.

Sam Houston Elected Republic's First President

(1836) Sam Houston, the military hero who only four months ago led the Texan forces in their decisive victory over Santa Anna's Mexican army, has been elected the first president of the Republic of Texas.

Houston, a native of Virginia who is more closely identified with Tennessee by virtue of having served there as governor before coming to Texas, will take the oath of office on October 3 at Columbia. He was elected by a resounding majority, receiving some 80 percent of the nearly 6,000 votes cast in the new nation.

In the same election voters overwhelmingly accepted the new constitution for Texas and elected Mirabeau B. Lamar vice president.

The first congress for Texas will assemble at Columbia at the same time that Houston takes the oath of office.

The 43-year-old Houston was a delegate from Nacogdoches to the recent Convention of 1836. He had settled in Nacogdoches upon moving to Texas in 1833.

Houston, who is widely known to be a close confidante of U.S. President Andrew Jackson, came to Texas ostensibly to be an agent of the Cherokee Indians and a representative of a New York firm with an interest in the rapidly developing area of Texas. Many have speculated, however, that his true interest in Texas is as an agent of President Jackson's.

Sam Houston

Whatever the case may be, Houston clearly won the popular support of Texans after taking charge of a rag-tag army as commander-in-chief, then holding that army together as it retreated across Texas from Santa Anna's invasion. Then he surprised all by the resounding victory over the Mexican forces at the Battle of San Jacinto.

One of Houston's key appointments as president is expected to be that of Stephen F. Austin as secretary of state.

An essential, surely overriding task of Houston and the new Texas Republic will be in devising an appropriate land policy for dispensing the vast amount of public lands to the settlers, who are certain to come from the bordering United States.

Telegraph Resumes Publication

(1836) Publication of the *Telegraph and Texas Register,* the first regularly issued newspaper in Texas, has resumed in Columbia after interruptions by hostile Mexican forces who, after their resounding defeat at San Jacinto, no longer pose a threat.

The newspaper, which first began publishing on October 10, 1835, at San Felipe de Austin, became the official organ of the Republic of Texas when it was organized. Its circulation soon reached as high as 500.

Soon after this promising start, however, the newspaper was forced to suspend publication when the Mexican army headed by Antonio Lopez de Santa Anna approached the area in its sweep across Texas following the brutal massacre of patriot forces at the Alamo.

Under this military threat, the press was moved to Harrisburg. On April 14 the first issue was ready for publication at this location when, once again, the Mexican forces interrupted, capturing the printers and throwing the press into Buffalo Bayou.

A new press was obtained from Cincinnati this summer by Gail E. Borden, who had founded the paper with Thomas H. Borden and Joseph Baker. It was set up at Columbia, where the Congress of the Texas Republic soon met.

The first issue published in Columbia appeared on August 2 and immediately found wide acceptance for reprinting the text of the new Constitution of the Republic. Until its publication in the new *Telegraph,* the wording of the Constitution had been available to very few Texans.

The press is useful to the new government in another important way as well—it will serve as the public printer.

General Land Office Opens in Houston

(1837) The General Land Office of the Republic of Texas opened its doors in Houston on October 1, 1837.

The office, headed by Commissioner John P. Borden, has the duty to "superintend, execute, and perform all acts touching or respecting the public lands of Texas." Thus the office is charged with one of the most important duties of the new government—that of making the new nation a land of homesteaders whose work will civilize it and bring to it a prosperous economy.

The General Land Office's functions will be at least twofold. It will translate, record, and locate all the Spanish and Mexican land grants made prior to the independence of Texas (because the Constitution of 1836 recognizes all these transactions as being legitimate), and it will follow the Constitution's provisions regarding land disbursement. Heads of families living in the Republic on March 2, 1836, will be given a league and labor of land (4,605 acres), while single men older than 17 years of age will be given one third of a league. Heads of families who arrived after March 2, 1836, but before October 1, 1837, will be given 1,280 acres, and single men will be entitled to 640 acres. (Details are still being worked out for those families arriving after October 1, 1837.)

Veterans of the Texas army also will be given generous land grants. Volunteers who arrived before August 1, 1836, are being given the same amount of land as the original colonists.

New Capital Chosen on Edge of Frontier

(1839) Republic of Texas government officials arrived in October in the small town of Austin, a community that only recently was chosen as the new capital.

Located on the edge of the frontier on the Colorado River, Austin is the young Republic's third capital. (Both Columbia and Houston preceded it.)

Formerly known as Waterloo, Austin was chosen as the site for the new capital in 1839 by a commission appointed by President Mirabeau B. Lamar. Construction of government buildings was begun in May of that year.

Congress will be seated in a one-story frame capitol surrounded by an eight-foot stockade to guard against Indian attacks.

The town's population is approximately 800, but it is growing rapidly. Edwin Waller surveyed the town site and sold 306 lots in August.

Some have criticized the location of the new capital because it is situated far beyond the frontier of Anglo settlement (approximately 75 miles north of San Antonio), and Comanches are a menace.

At the time the commission chose Austin as the Republic's new capital, it was populated by only four families.

Citizens in Houston have expressed bitter disappointment at the removal

Top: The capitol at Austin

Right: Panorama of Austin, the capital of Texas

of the seat of government from their city. The editor of the *Houston Morning Star* has complained that costs for moving the government offices and personnel will be inordinately high. He also contends that the selection commission acted in an illegal manner, and that the only reason to move was for "making speculation." He further complained that the new site lacks wood, water, and accessibility.

Some in Houston fear that the move will have a negative impact on their city, but the *Morning Star* editor maintains an optimistic view: "We will have a great city, in spite of them, and it they dont [sic] behave very well up there in Austin, we will cut off their supplies, and throw them upon corn bread and beef."

Many legislators had expressed great dissatisfaction with the Houston location. "I find this the most miserable place in the world," wrote Kelsey H. Douglass to his wife in 1837. He and others complained of bad weather, mud, sickness, and general discomfort.

Texan Santa Fe Expedition Fails

(1841) The effort to divert some of the lucrative trade between the United States and Santa Fe to Texas and to establish Texan jurisdiction over the huge New Mexico area on the east side of the upper Rio Grande has failed.

The expedition of 270 volunteer soldiers and some 50 civilians, organized at the bequest of President Mirabeau B. Lamar, was captured on arrival in New Mexico after a long and arduous journey over the arid western parts of Texas. They never got as far as Santa Fe.

Mexican forces took the Texans without firing a shot. The rag-tag force had arrived in an exhausted state after a brutal journey of 1,300 miles across the scorched prairies and rocky canyons of west Texas.

Texas' territorial claims over the Santa Fe area, announced in an ambitious act passed on December 19, 1836, thus remain nothing more than that—claims.

President Lamar and others had believed that the New Mexican people were eager to come under Texas jurisdiction and would welcome Texas forces with open arms, but such was not the case. The skeptical Texas Congress had refused to authorize the expedition, so President Lamar took responsibility for raising and equipping the party.

Lamar, however, eager to act because of the Republic's desperate financial straits and his eagerness to extend jurisdiction over the territory, persisted. (The Texas public debt now stands at more than $7 million, and the interest on this debt is $400,000 a year. Annual income for the new Republic just about equals required payments for interest.)

The Texans, known officially as the Santa Fe Pioneers, departed on June 19 from a point about 20 miles north of Austin. Their journey carried them in a northwestern course toward New Mexico, but they unfortunately took a wrong route when they mistook the Wichita River for the Red River. The expedition followed the Wichita River for 12 days before it realized the mistake.

On the journey the party also suffered from lack of provisions, a scarcity of water, and raids from Kiowa Indians. Some 30 members of the expedition were lost en route.

When the exhausted force arrived at last in New Mexico, its members were greeted not with open arms, but, rather, with the hostile Mexican military detachment. The Texans surrendered on October 5.

Last reports indicated that the prisoners were enduring yet another forced march—this one some 2,000 miles across arid lands under an armed escort to imprisonment in Mexico City.

The Texans, commanded by Hugh McLeod, had with them 21 ox-drawn wagons containing more than $200,000 worth of supplies and merchandise from traders.

With this tragic ending to the ambitious venture, it appears unlikely that the Texas Republic will be able to confirm its claims on the New Mexico lands nor be able to establish a much-needed source for trade.

Texas President Mirabeau B. Lamar, who ordered the expedition to Santa Fe

Houston City Council Establishes Port of Houston

(1841) Houston's city council has voted to create an entity called the Port of Houston, establishing municipal control over all the wharves, landings, slips, and roads along Buffalo and White Oak bayous.

The decision follows a long series of events that has brought navigation to Houston via the Buffalo Bayou, thus linking the city to the Gulf of Mexico with all the great port cities of the Atlantic Ocean and other waters.

Only last year (1840) the Texas Congress authorized the City of Houston to build and maintain wharves. The previous year (1839) a group of the city's businessmen formed the Buffalo Bayou Company, assuming responsibility for clearing the bayou and making it navigable. Members of that company collected money from various merchants to pay for clearing five miles of the channel from Harrisburg to allow boats to travel from there without danger of hitting snags.

Still, despite such ongoing work to keep the bayou clear, snags and overhangs continue to be a problem. Last year two ships, the *Emblem* and the *Brighton*, both hit snags and sank, partially blocking the channel. The *Brighton* was salvaged after a public subscription and rechristened the *Sam Houston*. Before another year was over, however, it sank again.

Although Houston's founding fathers, the Allens, advertised the new settlement's location as the "head of navigation," that description was admittedly an exaggeration. Navigating the bayou had been a torturous venture, and before recent improvements only small steam vessels could manage it.

A reporter for the *Telegraph and Texas Register*, who was taken to the new city via Buffalo Bayou in 1837, described the waterway in these words: "The principal objection to this place is the difficulty of access by water; the bayou above Harrisburg being so narrow, so serpentine and blocked up with snags and overhanging trees, that immense improvements will be required to render the navigation convenient for large steamboats."

The same writer predicted that while Houston was "merely a city in embryo," the industry, enterprise, and amount of capital being spent toward its greatness soon would "elevate it to a prominent rank among the cities of older countries."

Republic Signs Contracts with Land Agents

(1842) To speed up the process of settling the vast amount of public lands in Texas, government officials have signed contracts this year with several empresarios.

These contractors have been assigned huge areas of unappropriated public domain and given the responsibility of recruiting settlers.

While their contracts differ in detail, basically each empresario is awarded 10 premium sections of land as payment for every 100 families that settle. Additional compensations are possible through survey costs, fees, erection of cabins, and other such things.

Contracts, authorized by acts of Congress, have been signed with W.S. Peters and Associates (also known as the Texas Emigration and Land Company), Charles F. Mercer, and Henri Castro.

The Peters Colony, which measures more than 16,000 square miles, extends through North Texas in the Three Forks area of the Trinity River.

Mercer's contract calls for settlements in a huge area south and east of Peters Colony.

Castro, a Frenchman, has been assigned two areas now overrun with Indians. One of them is just west of San Antonio; the other is along the Rio Grande. Castro is advertising his colony extensively in Europe and intends to lead a large group of Europeans toward settlement in Texas.

Mier Expedition Prisoners Executed

(1843) Word has arrived that 17 members of the Texan forces captured by Mexican forces at Mier on the Rio Grande have been executed.

Those shot to death by a firing squad constituted one out of every 10 soldiers captured during their unsuccessful punitive expedition into Mexico. After their initial capture, they enraged Mexican authorities by escaping and fleeing toward Texas, only to be recaptured.

Mexican authorities selected the doomed victims by forcing all 176 Texans to reach into a bag of beans in which 17 of them were black. Those drawing black beans were shot to death.

The surviving Texans have been imprisoned in the Perote Prison in Mexico City, which they reached after a forced march accompanied by forced labor on the roads.

The Mier expedition stemmed from the Republic of Texas' decision to send several raiding expeditions into the disputed area south of the Nueces River.

Those captured were part of a rump group who defied the orders of their leader, General Alexander Somervell, to return to the settled parts of Texas. They preferred to stay behind to seize and plunder. Their commander was Captain William S. Fisher.

Nearly all the men were political opponents of Sam Houston, who had ordered their return in an effort to avoid war with Mexico.

The group's effort to plunder the town of Mier precipitated their capture. They were surprised by a much larger force of Mexican troops, who arrived and defeated the Texans in a battle. The victory was a costly one for the Mexicans, who lost some 600 men in the process. The Texans, by contrast, suffered only 30 deaths. The surrender occurred on December 19, 1842.

The 17 Texans being executed at El Salado, Mexico

Bryan's Town—Dallas—Surveyed by Dumas

(1844) This small North Texas settlement, founded by Tennessean John Neely Bryan in the Three Forks area of the Trinity River, has been surveyed into a proper, half-mile square town.

Bryan, who boasts that the town he founded in 1841 is destined to be the head of navigation on the Trinity with boats eventually arriving with loads of cargo from Galveston Bay, persuaded surveyor J.P. Dumas to move to Dallas from the Falls of the Brazos in Central Texas.

Dumas arrived in January 1844, bringing with him his wife, 12 men, a hundred head of cattle, and a wagon filled with corn.

In surveying the town, Dumas marked off one block for a courthouse square. (Bryan says he intends to donate it for that use if the occasion should arise.)

Dallas is in an area already recognized for its rich agricultural land. The largest town in the immediate area, Farmers Branch, was so named because of the proliferation of farmers. (Farmers Branch is where the Peters Colony field office is located.)

Another nearby settlement, Cedar Springs, is just three and a half miles away.

Bird's Fort, the first settlement in the area, is located about 15 miles west of Dallas. Bryan was able to attract a number of residents from Bird's Fort to join him in Dallas. The future of that outpost is uncertain, for it has not been improved since it was constructed.

Dumas laid off Dallas' streets in a grid adjacent to the Trinity River, which makes an ox-bow bend at the site of the settlement. Some of the major streets are named Main, Commerce, Elm, Water, Broadway, and Houston.

The founder of Dallas, John Neely Bryan, and Margaret Beeman Bryan, his wife

Texas Voters Approve Annexation by United States

(1845) The decades-old question of whether Texas should be a part of the United States of America has been settled.

The Republic of Texas will give up its sovereignty to become a state of the union.

Voters in Texas approved annexation in the October 13 election by a wide margin of 4,254 votes to 257. At the same time they approved a state constitution.

In February the United States Congress, prompted by President John Tyler's initiative, adopted a joint resolution offering statehood to Texas. This followed Democrat James K. Polk's election to the presidency. (Polk had campaigned on a pro-annexation platform.) Tyler, still in office, accepted the election as a mandate for annexation and presented the subject before Congress.

The United States had acted with some sense of urgency because Great Britain (and France) did not favor annexation. Great Britain preferred to see Texas act as an obstacle to further westward expansion of the United States and hoped to reap commercial advantages from Texas trade.

Efforts by both nations to induce Texas President Anson Jones not to proceed with plans for acting on the matter failed. After a lengthy series of negotiations, Jones had called for a special convention on July 4 to consider two questions: whether or not to accept an offer of annexation by the United States or whether to accept a peace treaty with Mexico that acknowledged the independence of Texas.

The same questions had been submitted earlier to the Texas Congress; both bodies had voted for annexation.

President Polk and the U.S. Congress are expected to act on the matter before the end of the year, at which time Texas will become one of the United States of America.

In September 1836, when Texas had gained its independence, its residents had voted in favor of annexation. Martin Van Buren, then President of the United States, refused to consider the matter. Anti-slavery sentiment as well as a fear of war with Mexico seemed to be overriding factors at the time.

Richardson Becomes New Owner of *Galveston News*

(1845) Willard Richardson has assumed sole ownership of the *Galveston News.*

Samuel Bangs, a man with extensive printing experience in Galveston and Mexico, had founded the newspaper on April 11, 1842. Then, less than a year after the first issue was published, Richardson, a native of Marblehead, Massachusetts, became the paper's editor.

Forty-year-old Richardson, who is a close friend of former President Mirabeau B. Lamar, worked as a surveyor for some years during Lamar's presidency. Afterward, he operated a school for young men in Houston.

A major gateway for the Republic of Texas, the city of Galveston is located on an island of the same name. (Pirate Jean Lafitte settled the same island in 1817.)

Galveston is the largest town in the Republic of Texas. Its population had reached more than 3,000 by 1840.

Hostilities with Mexico Commence at Fort Brown

(1846) Mexican troops attacked the earthen fort near the mouth of the Rio Grande and across the river from the Mexican town of Matamoros, and Major Jacob Brown, the fort's commander, was killed in the bombardment.

This appears to be the beginning of war. U.S. General Zachary Taylor, commander of the large contingent of American forces in the disputed territory between the Nueces River and Rio Grande, contends that the attack amounts to overt aggression on the part of Mexico on American soil. He has notified Washington by packet that "hostilities may now be considered as commenced."

President Polk is expected to ask at once for a declaration of war.

An initial skirmish occurred away from the earthen embankment when 60 of Taylor's dragoons, on patrol, stumbled into a Mexican cavalry unit. Two other battles followed later as Americans sought to bring supplies from Port Isabel (the battles of Palo Alto and Resaca de la Palma, fought on May 8 and 9).

Units commanded by Major Brown within the fort underwent artillery attacks from the Mexicans across the river in Matamoros. Brown, a native of Massachusetts who had enlisted in the U.S. Army as a private in the War of 1812, was fatally wounded in these attacks. After the major was buried within the fortifications on May 17, the post was named Fort Brown in his honor.

The American forces originally stationed themselves in July 1845 at Corpus Christi on the Nueces River, an area the Mexicans claimed as their own northern boundary. General Taylor, acting under orders from President James K. Polk, kept his army at Corpus Christi for some nine months before marching to the Rio Grande in April 1846. He settled at a bend of the river directly across from Matamoros, where a large contingent of Mexican forces was located. The earthen fort now known as Fort Brown was built with a perimeter of 800 yards, walls more than 9 feet high, a parapet of 15 feet, and a moat 15 feet deep and 20 feet wide.

Baylor University Opens for Classes

(1846) A new Baptist college, Baylor University, opened its doors this year in Independence. Chartered by the Republic on February 1, 1845, it is Texas' fifth institution of higher learning.

Professor Henry F. Gillette, a former Houston schoolteacher, will head Baylor until the new president, Henry Lea Graves, arrives. A 33-year-old North Carolina native and former professor at Wake Forest College, Graves will also serve as pastor of the Baptist church at Independence.

Baylor's origins may be traced to three men—-Judge Robert E.B. Baylor, James Huckins, and William Milton Tryon—who organized an education society in the Texas Union Baptist Association in 1841 with the idea of ultimately founding a Baptist university.

Baptists in Texas have been very aggressive in their work, concentrating on evangelism and stressing the need for education.

The man for whom Baylor is named, Judge Baylor, was born in Kentucky in 1793. He served in that state's legislature before going to Alabama to practice law. In Alabama he also was elected to the state legislature and then to the United States Congress. He was ordained a Baptist minister in 1839 before coming to Texas two years later and being elected a judge of the third judicial district and an associate justice of the Supreme Court.

Though Baylor University is not the Republic's first institution of higher learning, with so many Baptists in Texas, it is expected to become one of the leading colleges.

Methodists first established Rutersville College with preparatory and female departments near LaGrange in 1840. The following year the college expanded to include a collegiate department. Rutersville, like Baylor, was chartered by the Republic.

The University of San Augustine was opened in 1842 in East Texas; McKenzie College, located near Clarksville in Northeast Texas, was founded in 1841.

Tryon Hall, the university's main building

Legislature Authorizes County Named Tarrant

(1849) Texas' third legislature, encouraged by the settlements that are growing around the military establishment of Fort Worth on the West Fork of the Trinity River, has established a new county for the area to be named for General Edward H. Tarrant. It will be carved out of the existing Navarro County.

Fort Worth came into being earlier this year when an Army company headed by Major Ripley A. Arnold chose the location on a bluff overlooking the river as a westward outpost to protect settlers against Indians.

When the soldiers located themselves on the bluff, they found a family of settlers already living there. Press Farmer and his wife Jane had chosen the area themselves as a site for their tent. Their baby daughter, Susan Ann, also resided with them.

Major Arnold, the only officer in the company, has 42 men under his command. He arranged for Farmer to be the sutler for the fort, supplying the soldiers with food and other items.

Fort Worth is named for General William Jenkins Worth, a former commandant at West Point who served under generals Winfield Scott and Zachary Taylor in the War with Mexico. General Worth's military career was cut short tragically when he died of cholera earlier this year. Named commander of the Texas forces, Worth caught the disease upon his arrival and died on May 7, 1849.

Railroad Begins Service; Revival Seen for Harrisburg

(1853) For the first time in Texas, a railroad line has been completed and trains are running up and down its steel tracks.

The line, 20 miles long and extending from Harrisburg to Stafford's Point, began operation on September 7, 1853. It is owned and operated by the Buffalo Bayou, Brazos, and Colorado Railway Company, which was chartered on February 10, 1850, by the state legislature and was authorized eventually to reach all the way to Austin and beyond.

The 13-ton engine pulling the railroad cars was unloaded at Galveston.

Sidney Sherman, the man responsible for starting the railroad, has an interesting background. A native of Massachusetts who was orphaned at the age of 12, he had established a successful career in making cotton bagging at the time of the Texas Revolution. He sold his plant and used the money to equip a company of 52 volunteers to come to Texas via steamer. He and his volunteers were serving with General Sam Houston when they routed the Mexicans at San Jacinto to win independence.

Sherman assembled a group of Massachusetts capitalists to help fund the new railroad, although a number of Texans, including William M. Rice, participated in the project.

Construction of the railroad cost $18,400 per mile.

Some wagoners, critical of the notion of railroads, have argued that nothing could travel as fast as proponents of trains say.

There is evident rivalry among the towns in this part of the state. Advertisements for the railroad appearing in the *Telegraph and Texas Register* have claimed that Harrisburg is the head of navigation on the Buffalo Bayou, not Houston. The completion of the railroad certainly makes Harrisburg the first railroad terminal in Texas, and its steamship connections with Galveston promise to make it a formidable town. Some people in Houston fear that the new railroad may take business away from their city and restore the once-promising, but recently declining, town of Harrisburg.

Since 1836 Texans have looked to railroads as a promising new means of transportation. The Texas Republic Legislature chartered four railroad companies, but for various reasons, none of them succeeded.

Telegraph Service Begins in Texas

(1854) The wonders of the modern age have brought instant communications between the prosperous East Texas town of Marshall and cities such as Shreveport and Alexandria in Louisiana and Natchez in Mississippi. They have arrived in the form of the state's first telegraph line, which was established by the Texas and Red River Telegraph Company. Chartered on January 5, 1854, the company lost little time in commencing service, which began on February 14, 1854.

The line already is in the process of being extended to towns such as Henderson, Rusk, Crockett, Montgomery, Houston, and Galveston. Wires have been strung somewhat precariously along treetops. When high winds and swaying limbs break the lines, telegraph operators frequently have to close their offices and ride the lines themselves to locate and repair the breaks.

It is little wonder that Marshall claims the honor of being the first city in the state to have a telegraph line. The town is the county seat of Harrison County and one of the largest and most prosperous. Settled in 1839, it is sometimes referred to as the "Athens of East Texas" because of its cultural amenities. Even before 1850 the Methodist, Baptist, and Presbyterian churches were organized. The town is also the site of Marshall University, chartered in 1842, and the Masonic Female Institute, which separated from Marshall University in 1850.

Troops Establish New Fort

(1854) Lieutenant Colonel Washington Seawell and his six companies from the 8th Infantry, after skirmishes with Indians, have arrived to establish a fort in a canyon of the Davis Mountains in that arid area of West Texas.

They have named their encampment Fort Davis in honor of Secretary of War Jefferson Davis. It was Davis who ordered the establishment of the military post at a "suitable location" in the region to assist the area's settlers and also travelers, notably gold seekers en route to California.

The site of this new fort was chosen "because of the salubrious climate and pure water," according to Army reports. It has an elevation of approximately 4,700 feet and is located midway between San Antonio and Presidio del Norte in a particularly picturesque setting surrounded by mountains.

Lieutenant Colonel Seawell and his troops arrived in the area on October 7 after departing from Fort Ringgold in Starr County along the Rio Grande. Before selecting the name Fort Davis, they temporarily named the site "Painted Comanche Camp."

Comanche and Apache Indians continue to menace the troops, but the fort is expected to be a central crossroads for the wagon trains traveling to and from Mexico or westward to Presidio del Norte and California.

Houston Entrepreneurs Change Name of Railroad

(1856) The Galveston and Red River Railway Company, which was chartered on March 11, 1848, to build the first rail link all the way across the state from Galveston to the Red River, has a new name.

The newly named Houston and Texas Central Railway Company is the state's major hope for tying its vast regions together with a modern and rapid transportation facility.

The railroad's new name

Camels Introduced into West Texas

(1856) The continuing dilemma of how best to cope with transportation in the dry frontier of West Texas may have been solved.

Secretary of War Jefferson Davis' dream of introducing camels is now a reality. Thirty-two camels purchased along the North African coast at a price of $12,000 arrived at the coastal town of Indianola on April 29, 1859. Accompanying these peculiar beasts of burden were three Arabian and two Turkish handlers. The party of camels was augmented during the sea journey by the births of two calves.

Davis, appointed Secretary of War by President Franklin Pierce, long had pondered the problem of coping with Indians and transportation in Texas. At his insistence, the Congress authorized the expenditure of $30,000 for the purchase and importation of dromedaries into Texas to be used for "military purposes."

Major H.C. Wayne was given the assignment of finding suitable camels, which he did along the North African coast.

Upon arriving at Indianola, Major Wayne and his troops began moving westward, stopping near the town of Victoria long enough for the animals to be clipped. A

resident there, Mrs. Mary A. Shirkey, used the clippings to spin and knit a pair of camel-pile socks for President Pierce.

The animals are being kept at Camp Verde, where experiments are being conducted concerning their utility in carrying burdens across the land and also for a more frightening purpose—that of being ridden to pursue marauding Indians.

One camel trek already has been made to the unexplored area of the Big Bend on the border of Texas and Mexico. At least one more group of camels will be brought to Texas, and still more if the experiment warrants it.

Thomas W. House, businessman and former Houston mayor, helped secure the H&TC for Houston

better reflects its precise goal and the success of Houston residents in energizing the ambitious project. After four years of inactivity in Galveston, a number of Houston residents successfully convinced the Texas Legislature to change the charter to permit the railroad to emanate from their city rather than from Galveston. Thus, Houston citizens such as Cornelius Ennis, T.W. House, W.J. Hutchins, W.M. Rice, Augustus C. and John K. Allen, and Francis and Ebenezer Allen assumed leading roles in the enterprise.

By October 1856 the railroad had already placed 25 miles of rail into operation between Houston and Cypress.

The ultimate goal remains to link the populous Houston and South Texas areas with the growing regions of Central and North Texas, where citizens are clamoring for a transportation link to the rest of the state.

While the Houston and Texas Central has an ambitious goal, it is not the state's first railroad. That honor went to the Buffalo Bayou, Brazos, and Colorado Railway Company. Construction of its rails began in 1852, and the next year a 20-mile route was in operation between Harrisburg and Stafford's Point. Though its ultimate goal is to reach Austin, progress has been slow.

Fort Worth Becomes County Seat

(1856) Tarrant County voters, by a margin of seven votes, have chosen Fort Worth as their new county seat.

Fort Worth will replace Birdville, a smaller town in the eastern part of the county, which has been the county seat since Tarrant County was organized in 1849.

In that same year, with the establishment of the military encampment of Fort Worth, a civilian settlement of the same name sprang up, and in the past several years its business activity has just about equaled that of Birdville, which has a slightly larger population.

Believing that the county seat had to be theirs for their town to reach its full potential, Fort Worth residents persuaded the Texas Legislature to call for the special election.

On election day Fort Worth boosters conceived of a perhaps ignoble stunt to attract voters. Barrels of whiskey with dippers for all to enjoy were placed in front of the two mercantile stores, and a large number of fun-seeking settlers showed up. Naturally, they were predisposed to vote for Fort Worth.

Birdville leaders had much the same idea, but Fort Worth men sneaked into the town on the eve of the election and siphoned Birdville whiskey into their own barrel. Thus Birdville was left without a lure for the voters.

Fort Worth further aided its cause by sending riders throughout the county to persuade friendly voters to make their ways to the polls.

Polling places in Tarrant County were located at Birdville, Fort Worth, and Johnson Station.

With the decision made, Fort Worth now will be obliged to build a courthouse.

Birdville residents, keenly disappointed over the results, have indicated that the matter is not finished, and that another election likely will be called.

Lieutenant Colonel Robert E. Lee Takes Command in San Antonio

(1860) Lieutenant Colonel Robert E. Lee of the U.S. Army has arrived in San Antonio to take command of the Department of Texas. Lee, who reached this destination in February, replaces Colonel Albert Sidney Johnston.

Recently Lee was involved in sensational news as the commander of the forces that captured the radical John Brown and his abolitionist group at Harper's Ferry.

Robert E. Lee's generous monetary contribution made possible the completion of San Antonio's St. Mark's Episcopal Church.

Lee's headquarters in San Antonio, a town of some 8,000 residents, is in the two-story, stone building erected by John and William Vance at the corner of Houston and St. Mary's.

The Southern gentleman has already endeared himself to residents, especially the town's Episcopalians for his monetary contributions toward the new St. Mark's Episcopal Church, the building of which has been under progress for several years.

The new commanding officer has extensive military experience, beginning with his graduation as second in his class at the United States Military Academy in 1829.

In addition, he is no stranger to Texas or to San Antonio because during the War with Mexico, he served with General John Wool's army in its march from San Antonio to Buena Vista and, later in the war, served as chief of staff for General Winfield Scott. In the latter capacity Lee distinguished himself with conspicuous gallantry on the field, winning three brevets—major, lieutenant colonel, and colonel.

In 1856 and 1857 Lee was commander at Camp Cooper of two squadrons on the Comanche Indian reservation north of Albany, Texas.

Lee, a family man with seven children, is married to Mary Custis of Arlington, Virginia, a descendant of George Washington.

King Acquires Ranching Partner

(1860) Richard King, who in 1852 started his huge ranch by purchasing 75,000 acres of land in Nueces County on Santa Gertrudis Creek, has taken in a partner.

A former steamboat business associate and friend, Mifflin Kennedy, has purchased half interest in the vast ranch.

The two men have a long history of business ventures in partnership. They first met while serving on an army steamboat during the Seminole War in Florida. Afterward they became partners in a steamboat

Galveston Island Connected by Rail

(1860) The first train has arrived in the island city of Galveston, a feat noted by the celebratory boom of a cannon.

The train arrived from Houston in January via the Galveston, Houston and Henderson (GH&H) Railroad, which has been working toward this goal since 1853 when it was chartered and construction of the track began. Completion of the railroad links Galveston to Houston by rail for the first time.

Galveston residents assured the railroad link by voting $100,000 in bonds to finance a wooden trestle bridge across the bay, and the GH&H was backed by French loans and state land donations. In addition, the company received 610,500 acres of land from the state, which it sold for $87,316.

Because of the heat and severity of the work, the builders used the slaves of plantation owners along the Brazos as well as Irish laborers to grade and lay the track. The Irish laborers received part of their pay in whiskey.

The rails of the track were imported from Great Britain.

Galveston, the major port on the Texas Gulf Coast

business that carried men and supplies to Mexico for General Zachary Taylor. Upon the conclusion of the war, they remained in southern Texas to operate a steamboat business along the coast and on the Rio Grande.

King, who was born in New York City in 1825, was apprenticed to a jeweler, but became disenchanted with that line of work and stowed away on a ship before landing in Mobile, Alabama, and ultimately serving on an army steamboat in the Seminole War.

Kennedy, a Pennsylvanian born in 1818, worked very briefly as a teacher before giving up that occupation for entrepreneurship. He operated steamers on the Ohio and Mississippi rivers. After the War with Mexico, he began raising sheep in Hidalgo County.

Kennedy and King will operate the huge ranch together.

George Kelly Takes Control of Plow Company

(1860) Following the death of John A. Stewart, George A. Kelly has become sole owner of the prominent Kelly and Stewart plow manufacturing company in East Texas.

Stewart founded the plow factory in 1843 to serve the farmers in the area. At the time he was making crude plows in a blacksmith shop.

Kelly, a native of Tennessee born in 1832, joined the company in 1852 after arriving in nearby Jefferson as a mate on a steamship. His first job at the plow company was as foreman over the slaves who worked in its iron foundry.

Under Kelly's encouragement, the firm started making cowbells and country hollowware. Kelly studied methods of manufacturing and brazing the bells on a trip to Louisville, Kentucky, in 1854. The improved methods of manufacturing instituted upon his return led to a constant demand for the firm's fine, sandy land plows.

Kelly was named a partner in 1858 when the prosperous firm moved into a larger building and added cast-iron stoves, cooking utensils, machinery castings, and andirons to its line of products.

Now Kelly has developed a product that has been widely accepted—the Blue Kelly Plow.

Butterfield Mail Route Brings World to Texas

(1861) Texas' connections via semiweekly mail and passenger service to a large section of the United States have been made secure through the continued prosperity and success of the still-new Butterfield Overland Mail Route.

The route, established in September 1858, passes through the entire northern part of the state from Franklin at El Paso del Norte to just eight miles east of Preston on the Red River in Northeast Texas. Sherman, located near Preston, has been designated a distribution point through which postal service extends into the interior of Texas.

The Butterfield stagecoaches travel between St. Louis, Missouri, and Memphis, Tennessee, to San Francisco, California. There are, as well, certain extensions, such as the one between San Francisco to Los Angeles. The 2,795-mile distance between St. Louis and San Francisco makes this the longest such route in the history of the United States.

The journey is always completed in fewer than 25 days, and stagecoach stops have been constructed at intervals of about 20 miles. At these points passengers are able to purchase meals while the horses or mules are exchanged.

The Butterfield service was authorized by an act of Congress in 1857 that called for the conveyance of letter mail twice a week in both directions in four-horse coaches or wagons suitable for carrying passengers as well.

John Butterfield and Associates won the contract, which provides for compensation of $600,000 a year in addition to receipts for passengers and express.

Butterfield uses the Concord coach, which accommodates as many as five or six passengers, to make the journeys.

Fares average about $200 for a one-way trip (not including meals), and passengers may carry baggage weighing up to 40 pounds.

The trip is not without its dangers or discomforts. Passengers must sit up throughout the trip, and they generally carry firearms in case of attack by Indians.

The Butterfield service provides countless Texas towns with twice-a-week connections with the outside world, and it inevitably brings economic gain to all the towns on the route.

Despite the service's many benefits, with the stormy political climate now facing the nation as tension between the North and South grows, the future of the service is highly questionable.

DuPont and Texas

DUPONT

Founded: 1802
Texas Employees: 9,000

In August 1838, two years after Texas declared independence from Mexico, Samuel M. Williams was appointed Texas naval commissioner. Authorized to purchase ships and provisions for the Texas Navy, Williams found a steam packet that was refitted for war and rechristened the *Zavala*.

In 1839 Williams contracted with E.I. Du Pont de Nemours and Company to supply munitions for the *Zavala*. The purchase order for 100 rounds of powder for each of the guns remains in company archives.

That purchase order marked the beginning of a long relationship between the company and the state. Today DuPont and its energy subsidiary, Conoco, together employ more than 9,000 people throughout Texas. DuPont has plants in Beaumont, Orange, LaPorte, Victoria, Corpus Christi, Round Rock, and Pasadena. Conoco's headquarters west of Houston employs more than 2,000 people, and other Conoco employees work at a variety of sites throughout the state.

DuPont is an active corporate citizen, contributing to its communities in many ways. The company's talented employees are encouraged to be involved in civic activities, giving time and energy to the community. In addition, DuPont contributes to a variety of organizations that improve quality of life, from the Boy Scouts, Girl Scouts, and United Way, to funding for the arts, to significant contributions for scholarships and educational programs.

DuPont environmental professionals coordinate shipment of the drums around them to provide for safe transportation and environmentally sound disposal of waste. ©1990 Janice Rubin

Perhaps the most important aspect of DuPont's dedication to the community is its commitment to the environment. The company's five major plants in the state are members of Clean Texas 2000, a voluntary waste-minimization program that commits its members to going beyond state and federal environmental requirements.

In 1994 DuPont's LaPorte plant received a Clean Texas 2000 Award from Texas Governor Ann Richards for the plant's employees' outstanding pollution prevention actions.

Respect for the environment is a top priority for DuPont, a long-standing commitment that was evident even in 1938, when the first statement of environmental responsibility was issued. A resolution identifying pollution abatement as a key issue was adopted, and an engineer was assigned to the job of managing pollution control.

The company continues to operate under its long-standing policy that it will not "make, sell, transport, or dispose of a product" unless it can be done in a safe and environmentally sound manner. This policy applies to all DuPont employees at all sites around the world.

DuPont practices include regular review of products and operations to assess environmental quality and to determine the potential for improvement. DuPont openly communicates with employees and the public about plant products and processes. And the company devotes significant resources to pollution prevention and to protecting communities through extensive safety systems and emergency response programs and training.

DuPont's goal is to be the world's most environmentally sound manufacturing company. That commitment to the future includes goals to reduce any carcinogenic air emissions by 90 percent and, ultimately, to eliminate them altogether. DuPont aims to

eliminate disposal by underground injection, or to render nonhazardous all waste disposed of in this manner.

In 1983 DuPont implemented a program with the goal of managing 1,000 square miles of company land for wildlife enhancement, with a particular emphasis on wetlands. Since then, DuPont facilities across the country, including Texas, have initiated projects to support this objective.

Major DuPont plants in Texas are located along the Gulf Coast, starting with the site in Orange, Texas. The plant employs more than 1,800 people, making intermediate chemicals for nylon fibers, engineering plastics, specialty packaging, and industrial polymers, plus solvents and other chemicals for diverse markets. The plant works closely with local educators, particularly on the company's sponsorship of an annual environmental and science fair for students in about 32 schools in Orange County.

In nearby Beaumont, DuPont employs more than 1,000 people at a plant that produces plastics, two synthetic rubbers, and a range of intermediate products to make everything from agricultural products to plastics. The site holds the world record for off-job safety, achieving over three years with no lost-time accident. At a wildlife habitat on plant property, efforts such as planting grains and providing nesting areas have resulted in a significantly increased wildlife population. The area is home and haven to ducks, cranes, purple gallinule, turtles, alligators, turkey, pheasant, and various fish and migratory birds.

Near Houston, the LaPorte plant employs about 1,000 people to produce crop protection chemicals and intermediates for items such as textile fibers, automotive safety glass, and refrigerants. This site's successful pollution prevention efforts have been recognized by the State of Texas as an example for industry to follow.

In Victoria, DuPont employs more than 1,200 people, who make 21 products for use as solvents, additives, and intermediates for fibers, plastics, and agricultural products. Environmental personnel at this plant recently developed an important new environmental technology for use in groundwater and soil remediation.

The company's plant in Ingleside sits across the bay from Corpus Christi, and employs 250 people to make refrigerants, foam blowing agents, and cleaning agents for high-tech electronics. It is the site of the first facility with world-scale production of non-ozone-depleting CFC alternatives.

DuPont's early link to Texas is not surprising when you consider the company's long history since 1802, when it was founded on the banks of the Brandywine River in Delaware to manufacture black powder. Headquartered in Wilmington, Delaware, DuPont employs 140,000 people, makes products in about 40 countries, and markets them in more than 150 countries. DuPont is a diversified company with interests in petroleum and petrochemicals, agricultural products, fibers, electronics, imaging systems, plastics, and specialty chemicals.

The DuPont Sabine River Works, located in Orange, Texas, employs more than 1,800 people. The plant is active in the community, particularly in its support to local education programs.

A Burgeoning Economy

1862-1899

For Texas the last four decades of the nineteenth century were days when innocent youth gave way to promising adolescence. The unfocused pioneering days ended abruptly and tragically with the War Between the States and the difficult years of Reconstruction. After this interregnum, though, industries, institutions, and associations of great importance were founded, and population trends were established that would continue well into the next century.

It was a time, too, when images of Texas and Texans were created that would leave indelible images soon to be spread throughout the world. Cattle and cotton jumped into the fore of economic activities. And while the oil industry would wait until the next century before becoming dominant, a tiny foreshadowing of its role could be seen in a mini-boom occurring in the little town of Corsicana.

The impulse of so many to leave familiar surroundings and strike out for the promises of Texas, so evident in the area's first days of settlement, resumed vigorously after the Civil War era. During the decade of the 1860s the population gain was just over 200,000, but the next decade saw a jump to about 775,000. Thereafter, that larger pace continued to the end of the century when the state's total population had grown from 604,000 to just over 3 million.

The people of Texas predominantly lived in rural areas, although urban centers certainly were thriving in cities such as Houston and Dallas, which were surpassing the older settlements of Galveston and San Antonio. From an average of 2.3 persons per square mile within the state, the population density climbed to 11.6 per square mile in 1900. Houston, Dallas, and other growing urban areas found most of their prosperity, though, in serving as marketing centers for the rich agricultural lands around them.

While Texans fought enthusiastically in the Civil War, not all of them were eager to leave the Union. This included such notables as Sam Houston, governor at the time, whose office was declared vacant when he refused to take the oath of allegiance to the

Confederacy, and also David G. Burnet, E.M. Pease, and J.W. Throckmorton. Settlers of German origin in the Hill Country of Texas also were notably reluctant to withdraw from the Union. Yet Texas, overall, favored secession, voting better than 3 to 1 to do so.

The state escaped major conflict during the war, although Union ships blockaded the coast and Union forces occupied a number of port cities such as Brownsville and Corpus Christi.

At the end of the war, farmers who had relied on slave labor to work their fields of cotton were in a bind. Securing labor was difficult; the value of cotton dropped from 31 cents a pound in 1866 to 13 cents a pound in 1875; production declined; farmers found themselves land-poor; and their economic status was perilous. Then their situation improved, especially when farmers in the North Central Texas area found that the rich black land there was ideally suited for growing cotton. By 1900 Texas was producing one-fourth of all the cotton grown in the world.

The cattle kingdom, having started south of San Antonio as an industry utilizing the great, unfenced expanses of Texas plains, both matured and evolved rapidly during these decades. Just after the Civil War a few pioneering ranchers and their colorful "cowboys" drove herds of cattle north across Texas, Oklahoma, and into Kansas, where they sold their animals at far superior prices. A new phenomenon that became romanticized in story and film was born—the Texas cattle drive.

Even the arrival of closer railheads in Texas didn't halt the drives to Kansas, for the prices there continued to make the effort worthwhile.

Finally, the barbed wire fence was invented and widely adopted in Texas. The fabled cattle drives ended, but the business of ranching was greatly improved.

The immense distances of Texas insured a certain remoteness for tiny settlements everywhere. Towns such as Dallas chafed endlessly for years about their isolation, and before they could escape it through connections by railroad, Dallas and other towns in North Texas had to wait until 1872 when the Houston & Texas Central finally arrived.

At the end of the Civil War the state had just over 300 miles of railroad track (less than in 1860 on the eve of the war). Most of the early track was concentrated in the more heavily populated areas around Houston. By 1900, however, the state had just under 10,000 miles of track. Truly, the last decades of the nineteenth century constituted the age of the railroads.

The desire to connect the various parts of the state by rail was so great that Texas offered generous inducements to railroads, usually 16 sections of land for every mile of road constructed. Under this plan the Texas & Pacific Railway received 5.1 million acres of land from the state, and overall the state gave to railroads 32.1 million acres of land (an area as big as all of Alabama).

As was true throughout the nation, the power of the railroads engendered great resentments and accusations of abusive practices. This growing feeling altered the political situation and was evidenced in Texas by the rise of Jim Hogg to the governorship and the creation of the Railroad Commission to regulate the industry. Not until the next century did the commission develop another more important function—that of regulating the oil industry.

All these elements together—the Civil War, cattle, cotton, railroad building, and reform—were major components of the 1860-1900 era, but not the only ones, of course. The state wrote a new constitution in 1876 that has lasted to this day; the Farmers Alliance was founded in Texas and spread throughout the nation; in the pine forests of East Texas emerged a growing timber industry; state universities were founded; a new capitol was constructed in Austin; and sheep-raising became an important enterprise.

Here was the nation's biggest state laying the groundwork for the arrival of 1900 and its first full century of existence.

Facing page: These cotton-filled wagons line Dallas' Elm Street. Texas/Dallas History and Archive Division, Dallas Public Library

In the years following the Civil War, Galveston gained popularity as a vacation spot for residents of Houston. The Beach Hotel (seen here) catered to the busy tourist trade. Courtesy, Rosenberg Library

Left: The billowing smoke stacks in this 1891 view of Fort Worth symbolize the prosperity of the town at the time. Courtesy, Amon Carter Museum, Fort Worth

Right: While urban centers such as Houston and Dallas were bustling with activity in the late nineteenth century, towns such as San Antonio still retained the slow-paced yet colorful atmosphere of an earlier era. *Market Plaza, San Antonio* (seen here) was painted by Thomas Allen in about 1879. Courtesy, San Antonio Museum Association

Houston, Texas (Looking South), 1891 depicts a growing urban center. Courtesy, Amon Carter Museum, Fort Worth

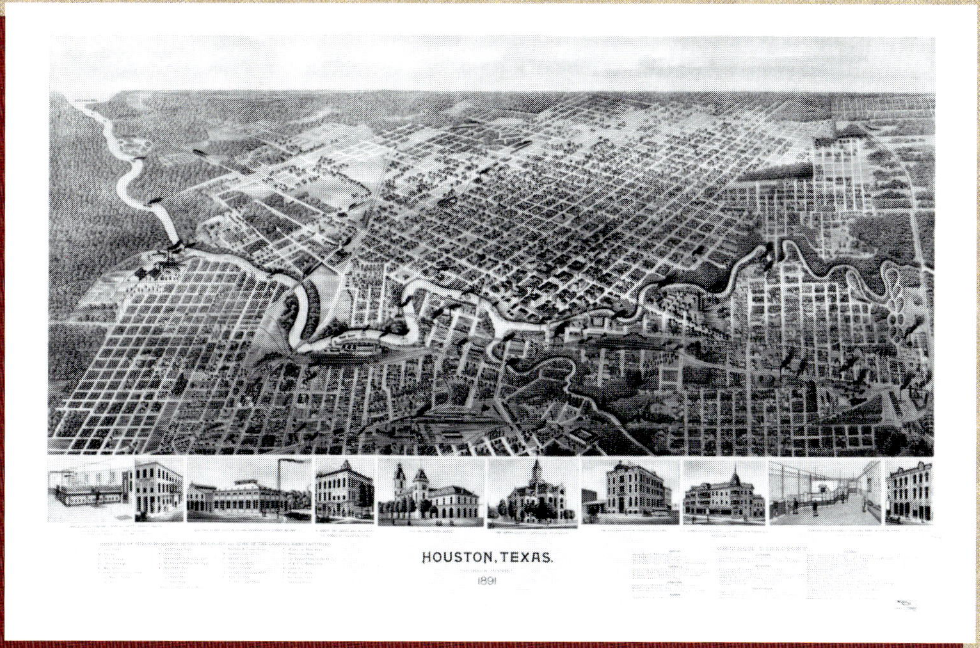

David G. Burnet (above) and Elisha M. Pease (right) were among the prominent Texans who did not favor seceding from the Union. Burnet—From Cirker, *Dictionary of American Portraits,* Dover; Pease—Courtesy, Archives Division—Texas State Library

Frank Reaugh's *Watering the Herd* depicts a cowboy keeping watch over his cattle. Courtesy, Panhandle-Plains Historical Museum, Canyon, Texas

Ranch hands from the LS Ranch in Amarillo take a break from their labors to chow down at the chuckwagon in 1895. Courtesy, Panhandle-Plains Historical Museum, Canyon, Texas

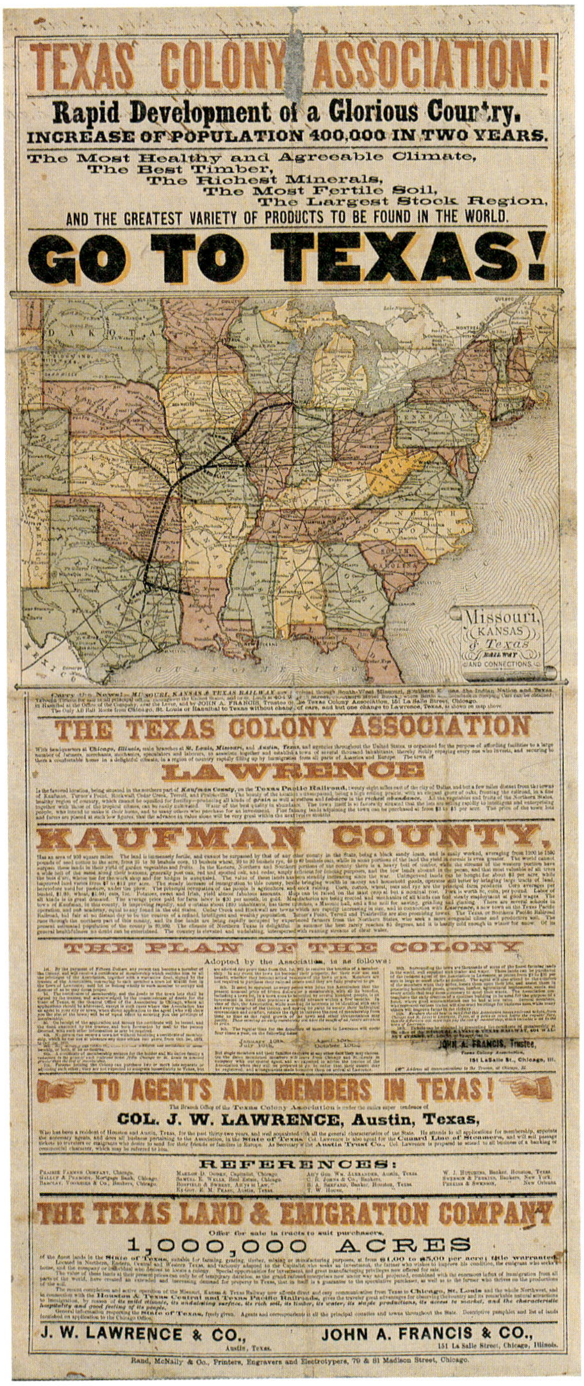

In 1871 the Texas Colony Association posted this broadside in New Orleans in hopes of enticing people to come to Texas. Courtesy, Archives Division—Texas State Library

When the Texas State Capitol was constructed in the 1880s, it was the largest state capitol in the nation. Architect Elijah E. Meyers designed the structure and drew this rendering of the building. Courtesy, The Center for American History, The University of Texas at Austin, Prints & Photographs Collection

Sam Houston Dies; An Era in Texas Over

(1863, July 26) Sam Houston, the Texas hero who led the revolutionary forces to victory over the invading Mexican forces of Santa Anna and then served two separate terms as president of the Republic of Texas, is dead. Houston died July 26 on his farm near Huntsville. He was 73 years of age.

Although a hero for so many decades, in recent times Houston had fallen from popular favor because of his pronounced opposition to secession and his vigorous campaigning to keep Texas out of the Confederacy. However, even as governor of the state, he was powerless to defy the popular vote, which favored secession from the Union.

Sam Houston in his later years

After secession Houston contended that Texas was not a member of the Confederacy, but once again an independent nation. He declined to take the oath of allegiance to the Confederate government, and Lieutenant Governor Edward Clark took his place.

Houston then decided to retire to his farm outside Huntsville.

His colorful political career included the governorship of Tennessee, two terms as president of the Republic of Texas, 14 years of service as a U.S. senator from Texas, and one term as governor of Texas.

As for his military career, he served with Andrew Jackson in the Indian battle at Horseshoe Bend in Alabama and commanded the Texas Army during the revolution against Mexico. His victory at San Jacinto assured his place in history.

Houston's first marriage to a Tennessee woman was of short duration. It ended under somewhat mysterious terms. Houston, evidently despondent, spent the next six years in Indian country, where he allegedly took a Cherokee wife. Soon afterward he moved to Texas (some said as a secret emissary of President Andrew Jackson, whose eye was on Texas).

In 1840 Houston married Margaret Moffette Lea of Alabama, who was 26 years younger. By all accounts their marriage was a happy one. They had eight children.

Union Effort to Invade Texas Foiled at Sabine Pass

(1863, September 8) An invasion force of 5,000 Union soldiers that attempted to land at Sabine Pass has been turned back by the heroic actions of a small Confederate force of Texans led by former saloonkeeper Dick Dowling.

The assault, consisting of four U.S. gunboats and a flotilla of 20 transports carrying Union soldiers, was ordered by Union General Nathaniel P. Banks. Its ultimate object was to capture Houston, Beaumont, and Galveston.

Dowling's repulse of the would-be invaders was nothing less than sensational. Fort Sabine, from

A Confederate ship blows up a federal gunboat in 1863.

whence the brave Texans defied the Union forces, is nothing more than earthwork. Dowling and his 42-man force had six cannons.

Before approaching Fort Sabine, three Union gunboats, the *Clifton,* the *Arizona,* and the *Sachem,* bombarded the site for an hour and a half. The results were insignificant. As all four gunboats next moved toward the fort, Dowling ordered his defenders to hold their fire until the attackers drew within easy range. That distance turned out to be some 1,200 yards from the fort.

At this point Dowling's men unleashed a terrific attack by cannon. The *Clifton* and *Sachem* both were knocked out of action; the other two boats retreated. The entire force of 5,000 would-be invaders, waiting offshore on their transports pending the results of the naval battle, returned to New Orleans.

The Federal casualties numbered 19 dead, 9 wounded, 37 missing, and 315 prisoners.

Ironically, Confederate General John G. Magruder, thinking Fort Sabine to be vulnerable, had ordered Dowling to render his cannons inoperative in anticipation of the almost-certain takeover by enemy forces. But Dowling declined to do so. To help prepare for the forthcoming assault, he used rails from a nearby railroad to reinforce the earthen fort.

The hero of the hour, Richard W. (Dick) Dowling is a native of Ireland who moved to New Orleans with his sister at the age of 10 in 1848. Later he migrated to Houston, where he owned a saloon named "The Finish."

The battle at Sabine Pass was not his first military adventure. On January 1, 1863, he participated in the Confederate recapture of Galveston from Union forces.

The Union sea blockade has effectively curtailed the export of cotton and other products from these and other ports via the Gulf of Mexico, but these port cities and other parts of Texas continue in their support of the Confederacy.

Cattleman Oliver Loving, Noted Trail Driver, Dies

(1867) Rancher Oliver Loving, who with his partner Charles Goodnight, established the cattle trail known as the Goodnight-Loving Trail, has died from wounds suffered in an attack by Indians.

Loving was en route to Fort Sumner, New Mexico, on his new trail with a herd of cattle when, riding ahead of the herd with another man, he was wounded in the Indian attack. Rescued by a party of Mexicans, Loving was taken to Fort Sumner, where Army physicians treated him. Three weeks later, however, though seemingly on the road to recovery after having his arm amputated, he died from gangrene.

His partner, Goodnight, says he intends to return the body to Texas for burial at Weatherford. "Take me back to Texas," Loving told Goodnight before his death. "Don't leave me in foreign soil." Goodnight accordingly pledged to do so.

Loving, born in Kentucky in 1812, had taken his herds of cattle from Collin County, Texas, in 1855 to Palo Pinto County. Three years later, seeking a good market for his animals, he drove a herd of steers to Chicago. This was the first instance on record of a herd of Texas cattle being driven straight to market.

Producing Oil Well Dug Near Melrose

(1866, September) For the first time in the state's history, a producing oil well has been dug.

The entrepreneur who decided to capitalize on this black, sticky substance is Lyne Taliaferro Barret, a resident of Nacogdoches County. His well is located 12 miles southeast of Nacogdoches near Oil Springs.

The nation's fledgling oil industry first started in Pennsylvania in 1859, but the fact of oil's existence in Texas has been known since the sixteenth century when the explorer Moscoso caulked the bottoms of his boats with the substance. Most of the time, though, oil has been considered a nuisance because it infiltrates water wells and renders the water unfit for drinking.

Barret, whose friends call him "Tol," had intended to drill for oil in the area in early 1859, but a lack of machinery caused him to postpone his plans until after the Civil War. Otherwise, he would have drilled the world's first producing well instead of the Pennsylvanians.

To reach the oil Barret utilized steam power and crude tools made by a blacksmith. Using a rotary principle, he bore into the ground with an eight-inch auger fastened to a joint of pipe. He rotated the pipe downward with a steam engine, and he used a mule to pull out the pipe. When he reached 106 feet, water, oil, and gas began gushing up.

He estimates production to be about 10 barrels a day.

The market for this substance is expected to be limited, however, because its chief value is in lubricating the axles of wagon wheels. (Some of the Indians in East Texas have bathed in "oil springs" to relieve aches, pains, cuts, and burns, while some even drink it as a medicine.)

Associates in Barret's Melrose Petroleum Oil Company are Charles A. Hamilton, John T. Flint, John B. Earle, and Benjamin F. Hollingsworth.

Barret plans to go to Pennsylvania this winter in an effort to secure financing to drill an additional well.

Barret was born in Virginia on November 1, 1832, but by the time he was 18 years of age, he was clerking in a Nacogdoches store.

The next year in 1859 he drove a herd of cattle to Colorado.

In 1867, working with his new partner, Goodnight, he drove two herds of cattle to Colorado via Fort Sumner, overcoming an 80-mile stretch that offered no water and caused great suffering among the animals. The result, though, was a highly profitable sale at Fort Sumner.

He was returning there a third time when the attack occurred. The cattle industry in Texas is growing rapidly, having been started in earnest after the War with Mexico. The cattleman's domain has been extending gradually westward from North Texas, although trouble with hostile Indians has proven to be a menace.

The Civil War also slowed down the westward movement.

A persistent problem has been in finding ready markets in Texas, but the trail pioneered by Loving and Goodnight has inspired intense interest in the possibility of driving herds north and selling them at railroad heads.

The northern market is much greater, and with some time to feed on the rich prairie lands, the cattle are fattened quite easily.

[Goodnight lived up to his promise to return Loving's body to Texas. He exhumed the body in 1868 and carried it by wagon to Weatherford, an event that inspired a famous episode in Larry McMurtry's novel, *Lonesome Dove*.]

Physicians of Texas Form New Association

(1869) What formerly was known as the Medical Association of Texas has been reorganized and given a new name—The Texas State Medical Association.

The organization intends to continue to emphasize its goals of raising the standards of the medical profession.

Annual meetings are expected to be held, and transactions for these meetings will be published.

The organization originally was founded on January 17,1853, with an initial membership of 35. Pioneer doctors Ashbel Smith, George Cupples, and J.W. Throckmorton were leading lights, and Joseph Taylor served as the first president.

Texas now has its own medical school—Galveston Medical College—which was established in 1865 with an enrollment of 21 students.

Ashbel Smith, one of the founders of the Medical Association of Texas

Texas Cattlemen Find New Markets in Kansas

(1870) Scores of Texas cattlemen have been driving their herds of cattle to several new markets in Kansas, where the animals are sold for delivery to northern markets via the rail outlets there.

The towns that seem to be attracting the most business are Wichita, Abilene, Newton, and Caldwell.

Most of these cattle are driven along what is commonly called the Chisholm Trail, which in truth is a number of different routes extending from as far south as the Rio Grande near its mouth at the Gulf of Mexico, crossing the Red River into Indian Territory at either Preston or Red River Station, and then proceeding across Indian Territory into Kansas.

The original Chisholm Trail was laid out by an Indian trader and guide named Jesse Chisholm, who originated it by driving a wagon train bearing goods from Fort Leavenworth to Council Grove in Oklahoma in 1865. His tracks soon were followed by drovers from Texas in search of the Kansas market, who extended the trail from various points in their state.

The trail was more clearly marked in 1867 when Joseph G. McCoy, the entrepreneur who is largely responsible for establishing the Kansas settlements as "cattle towns," persuaded Tim F. Hersey to mark it

H&TC Railroad Reaches Dallas

(1872, July 16) Citizens in this north central Texas area roared with jubilation with the arrival in Dallas of the first train over the just-completed Houston & Texas Central Railway tracks.

Some 5,000 to 6,000 spectators, far more than live in Dallas, gathered to greet the train.

A huge barbecue was held at the county fairgrounds, and the founder of the city, John Neely Bryan, sat on the wooden platform as a special guest of honor.

The H&TC arrived in Dallas only after great difficulty. Dallas residents, desperate to find a transportation outlet from their interior city, had induced the railroad to pass through town with a gift of 115 acres of land, free right-of-way through the city, and a cash gift of $5,000.

The railroad, chartered in 1848, started from Houston, but construction was slow at the beginning, and during the Civil War it was totally halted. But after the war it was the first Texas railroad to resume construction. It reached Bryan in 1867, Hearne in

This map shows "The Best and Shortest Cattle Trail from Texas."

southward from Abilene, Kansas.

Chisholm himself was born in Tennessee. His mother was a Cherokee Indian and his father of Scotch ancestry.

The cattle drives from Texas are colorful affairs. The large herds of cattle are pushed along by cowboys on horseback. Sometimes the herds number as many as 5,000 cattle. Ten cowboys can drive as many as 2,000 cattle.

Texas cattlemen have learned that it is cheaper to drive the cattle to Kansas than to ship them from Texas by rail.

Unfortunately, the man for whom the trail was named, Chisholm, died in 1868. Cause of death was said to be cholera morbus contracted from eating bear's grease poisoned by being melted in a brass kettle.

The H&TC Station, Dallas

1868, Bremond in 1870, and Corsicana in 1871.

The first train into Dallas was a special one, bearing a passenger car with important guests and also several freight cars.

So that the first train would not be late, a number of prisoners volunteered to help lay track on the previous Sunday.

For many citizens, and for almost all the children of the town, the train was the first one they had ever seen.

Dallas residents were especially excited at the train's arrival because of their unsuccessful efforts in the past to make the Trinity River navigable. The area is a bountiful one, but farmers have been frustrated by a lack of transportation outlets for their products.

A&M College Opens for Classes Near Bryan

(1876, October) After a rocky start, the Agricultural and Mechanical College of Texas, authorized by the State of Texas five years ago in 1871, has opened its doors for classes.

The original starting date, September 17, had to be postponed because only six students enrolled. On the new date for opening, October 4, approximately 40 men enrolled.

The campus is located on a 2,416-acre site near Bryan in Brazos County. It has a faculty of six in addition to its president, Thomas S. Gathright. Gathright, a native of Mississippi, was recommended for the job by Jefferson Davis.

On the campus are two college buildings and five homes for faculty members.

A&M is the first institution of higher education to be sponsored by the state, having been authorized on April 17, 1871, under terms of the Morrill Act of 1862, passed at a time when Texas was in rebellion. The college was endowed by a federal grant of 180,000 acres of land that were sold for $156,000.

The legislature's intent is to create at the lowest possible cost a facility for liberal and practical education. Its main emphasis will be on the agricultural and mechanical arts, although questions already have been raised concerning the qualifications of the faculty members in this regard. With the exception of General Hamilton P. Bee, who is steward and superintendent of the farm, the faculty has been trained in the classics. Their specialties include such subjects as pure math, applied math, ancient languages and literature, chemistry, and modern languages.

While the legislature specified that A&M would be a branch of the "University of Texas," the representatives have yet to establish that institution.

Farmers' Group, Grange, Showing Rapid Growth

(1876) Since the first Grange in the state was organized in Salado in July 1873 and the Texas State Grange shortly after in Dallas in October 1873, the movement has shown remarkable growth and strength.

Farmers from the Red River to the Rio Grande have been establishing their own lodges, and now it is estimated that there are 40,000 members in 1,275 lodges across the state and in the Indian Territory.

Members of the Grange have shown unusual power, especially as evidenced by the state constitutional convention which met recently to write the new 1876 constitution. More than half of the delegates were members of the Grange.

Politically, Grangers oppose the growing power of the railroads as well as alleged abuses by other businesses. They believe government controls should be instituted to keep them in check.

Some of their goals achieved in the constitution included protection of homesteads from seizure for debt and a general retrenchment on the powers of government.

What has inspired the Grange movement (or Patrons of Husbandry as they sometimes are known) is a desire to improve farm conditions. This includes not only economic and political improvement, but more educational opportunities, more social contacts, and better home lives as well.

Grangers typically meet twice a month, where they sing songs, read essays, and listen to speakers. They have been especially important in working toward the improvement of community schools.

Their latest venture, accomplished last year in Marion County, was to form the Texas Grange Manufacturing Association to process iron and farm equipment.

Colonel Belo Gets State's First Telephone

(1878, March 18) Colonel Alfred Horatio Belo, the publisher of the state's outstanding newspaper, the *Galveston News,* has installed Texas' first telephone.

This unusual new communications instrument, invented just two years ago by Alexander Graham Bell, has been installed at Belo's office at the newspaper and his home in Galveston. The two telephones are connected, of course, by a line that permits individuals to talk to one another.

Belo was inspired to install the telephones upon visiting the Philadelphia Centennial Exposition, where he saw Bell's exhibit.

[One year later, the first commercial telephone exchange in the state was opened in Galveston. The subscriber with telephone number 1 was George Dealey, the tea and coffee merchant, whose son helped establish the *Dallas Morning News* and served as its publisher for many years.]

Alfred Horatio Belo

Farmer Pipes Natural Gas into Home in Washington County

(1879) What began as an unfortunate, even bizarre, accident has been converted by a farmer in Greenvine, southwestern Washington County, into a bonanza for his home.

The fortuitous discovery was made while the farmer, William Seidell, was boring a well in hopes of finding water. When he reached a depth of 106 feet, he was startled by a strange upward rush of "air." Seidell and his two helpers, puzzled, summoned a passing farmer to come and investigate. The farmer leaned over to see what he could, and to the surprise of all his lit pipe ignited the gas and caused an explosion. Luckily, no one was injured.

Seidell decided to pipe the gas into his home, where he is now using it for fuel.

This is the first known instance of gas in Washington County, though it had already been discovered in Nacogdoches and Young counties.

The growing town of El Paso

El Paso Blossoming After Railroad Arrival

(1883, January) Texas' latest boom town is El Paso, the once-tiny settlement that lies where the Rio Grande slices through two mountain ranges at the border with Mexico.

The cause for the population explosion was the arrival of the Southern Pacific Railroad on May 26, 1881, followed before the end of the year by the arrival of three more, the Santa Fe, the Galveston, Harrisburg, and San Antonio, and the Texas and Pacific. Then during 1882 the Mexican Central Railroad arrived.

Until the first railroad came, El Paso was a sleepy little village of some 800 souls without a single church. Since then the city now can boast of four churches, two banks, a street railway, three newspapers, and the largest hotel in the state.

There are also some other matters commonly associated with boom towns—saloons, dance halls, and gambling parlors. Nearly every corner has a saloon, and in them one may play roulette, faro, sweat, craps, or keno.

Some say that because of its strategic location, El Paso is destined to be the most important city between Kansas City and the Pacific Coast, possibly excluding Denver.

The city definitely has an even greater international flavor than one might suspect. In addition to the Americans and the Mexicans, there is a considerable Chinese population. Many of the Chinese came to work on the railroad, then settled to open restaurants and laundries.

El Paso's new municipal government has before it problems that sometimes seem overwhelming: law enforcement, fire protection, health and sanitation, public transportation, utilities such as water, flood control and drainage, and streets and sidewalks.

Signs of El Paso's new power are seen already in the fact that its residents are demanding an election to determine whether the county seat should be moved from Ysleta to El Paso. It is expected that the election will be held later this year, and it is also expected that El Paso will become the new county seat of El Paso County.

Texas Gets a State University at Last

(1883, September 15) The notion of establishing a great public university has been around since 1839 when, at the request of President Mirabeau B. Lamar, the Republic of Texas allocated 50 leagues of land to establish it.

But not until September 15 did that dream come true. On that day in Austin, students attended classes at their new University of Texas for the first time.

The first wing of the university's planned main building is still under construction. It is located just north of the capitol on a 40-acre site.

The cornerstone was laid in a ceremony on November 17, 1882, with keynote speaker Dr. Ashbel Smith saying, "Smite the rocks with the rod of knowledge, and fountains of unstinted wealth will gush forth."

Dr. Smith was elected president of the eight-man board of regents, which is charged with setting policy.

While the building is being completed, students are attending classes in the temporary capitol.

The faculty consists of eight professors, four assistants, and the proctor. A total of 221 students has enrolled.

Austin was chosen as the site of the university in a

Above: Architect's rendering of Old Main by Oscar Ruffini

Left: A crowd of more than 3,000 turned out for the laying of the cornerstone for Old Main on November 17, 1882.

statewide election, receiving 30,913 votes to Galveston's 20,741 and Tyler's 18,794.

The delay in establishing the university was caused by many factors—the end of the Republic and the beginning of statehood, the Civil War, and, in what perhaps was a sign of priorities, the opening of the Agricultural and Mechanical College 12 years ago in 1871 as an institution devoted to agriculture and the mechanical arts.

While the event has been long-awaited, the notion of creating a state university has not been favored by all. Sam Houston, for instance, opposed it because he felt it would be "a project for favoring the rich at the expense of the poor."

Houston Post *Result of Merger*

(1885, April 5) Two Houston newspapers, the *Morning Chronicle* and the *Evening Journal,* have combined forces to create a new periodical, the *Houston Post.* The last issues of the *Chronicle* and *Journal* appeared on April 4. The first issue of the *Post,* published by the united staffs, appeared the next day.

Colonel Rienzi Melville Johnston will be editor of the paper; Julius L. Watson will be business manager.

This will not be the first *Post* for Houston, for in 1880 Gail Borden Johnson began publishing a newspaper under that name. He combined it in 1881 with the *Houston Telegraph,* but in 1884 the publication failed.

Johnston's keen interest in newspapers has been exhibited since he was a printer's devil as a boy. He left that job to be a drummer boy in the Confederate Army. Later, he served as Austin correspondent for the old *Post.*

Watson's past also is remarkably colorful. He has been an advance man for a spiritual medium, a door-to-door book agent, and a Brenham, Texas, newspaperman. He came to the *Post* after a term as treasurer and manager of Houston's Pillot Opera House.

Dallas Morning News *Begins Publication*

(1885, October 1) A new daily newspaper, the *Dallas Morning News,* has begun publication as the North Texas branch of the *Galveston News.* Circulation of the first issue was just under 5,000.

The newspaper is being printed with the most modern equipment in a new, modern, three-story brick building on Commerce Street.

The *Morning News* and its parent in Galveston are connected by a special leased telegraph wire. This is believed to be the first effort in the state of Texas to establish a branch newspaper connected by wire.

A.H. Belo, owner of the *Galveston News,* established the branch newspaper in order to have a presence in the rapidly growing north central area of Texas. To select a site, he had a trusted employee, George B. Dealey, visit the area and inspect scores of towns over a period of several months. Dealey recommended Dallas, which already was a crossing point for five railroads. Dealey, a native of Manchester, England, has been named business manager of the newspaper.

The *Dallas Herald,* which had served the area since 1849, will face stiff competition. Some say the *News* is seeking to acquire it and shut it down. [This happened on December 1.]

The *Herald* has emphasized local news coverage and circulation. As a result, the dominant newspapers in the North Texas area have been those published in St. Louis. But the *News* intends to provide coverage for the entire state of Texas, and it is expected to seek to supplant the St. Louis newspapers in the area.

This bold ambition has met with some skepticism. The *San Antonio Express* noted that the claim of covering the entire state amounts to "brazen effrontery" and "arrogance and assumption." Other newspapers, however, have hailed the goal as a step forward.

As to its editorial policies, the *Dallas Morning News* promises to be fiercely independent.

Dallas has a population of 18,000 residents, most of whom have arrived there only recently.

In the days before refrigeration, some Texas farmers used windmills to hang meat out of the reach of animals.

Windmills Solve Problems for Many in Texas

(mid-1880s) The windmill and barbed wire are revolutionizing the way of life for Texas ranchers. The developments are tied together.

The old days of free and open ranges permitted cattle to move about as they pleased in search of that vital necessity—water. Barbed-wire fences are rapidly ending that aspect of ranch life. And yet, a supply of water is absolutely mandatory for livestock. And that's where the windmill comes into play.

Ranchers throughout the state have been drilling wells to locate water, then building windmills to pump up the water for their stock.

Some of this activity came as a desperation move when ranchers in back lands found that new fences had cut off their access to sources of water. Not only did they retaliate in some instances by cutting the fences and fighting, they began drilling wells and experimenting with windmills as well.

The first Texas industry to make good use of windmills, though, was the railroad industry. In 1860 the Houston Tap and Brazoria Railroad obtained the right to build windmills along its right-of-way from Houston to Wharton as a way to provide water for the steam engines.

Small towns and small farms next began using windmills.

And, now, after the introduction of barbed wire in 1879, the gadgets are becoming familiar across the state.

The first American windmill was constructed in Connecticut in 1854 by Daniel Halladay. Texas cattlemen added to the windmill a vane or "tail" to help position the wheel into the wind.

State Fair of Texas Formed by Merger

(1887, February) The two feuding groups in Dallas who put on not one but two state fairs last year have resolved their differences and have agreed to put on a single exposition this year. It will be known as the Texas State Fair and Exposition.

After negotiations, both

factions agreed to cooperate with a new fair in East Dallas near the site used last year by the Dallas State Fair and Exposition Association. This new site, further east along the Texas & Pacific tracks, will contain 80 acres.

The two factions split last year after a fierce debate over an appropriate site. A group headed by several farm implement men, including C.A. Keating and O.P. Bowser, complained that the property selected was "the worst kind of a hog wallow" and not suitable for displaying their equipment.

They thus split from the group and put on their own Texas State Fair on property north of town owned by J.H. Cole.

The other fair was headed by such prominent citizens as Colonel J.B. Simpson, Sydney Smith, W.H. Gaston, and Thomas L. Marsalis.

Although both fairs competed with one another last October, both drew large crowds and claimed success.

The site to be used this fall is on land formerly owned by William H. Gaston and located on the south side of the Texas & Pacific railway tracks.

The city's new newspaper, the *Dallas Morning News,* had urged the two factions to come together. "Differences, estrangements, and misunderstandings must be obliterated," the newspaper editorialized.

James Moroney will be president of the new united fair. Governor Sul Ross will be asked to attend the fair when it opens in October.

Charles Goodnight Divides Ranch

(1887) The JA Ranch, usually referred to as the "Goodnight Ranch," has been divided between Charles Goodnight and the widow of his Irish co-founder, Mrs. John G. Adair.

Charles Goodnight

Mrs. Adair has maintained the Palo Duro and Tule divisions of the ranch, and Goodnight retains the Quitaque division.

At one time the JA Ranch ran 100,000 cattle over one million acres of land. It has been widely recognized not only as one of the largest, but also one of the most scientifically managed ranches in the land.

Goodnight introduced Hereford bulls to his herds and created some of the finest cattle around.

Goodnight also was one of the founders of the Panhandle Stockmen's Association, an organization that not only led to improved breeding methods, but also rid the entire North Texas area of outlaws and cattle thieves.

The JA Ranch was founded shortly after Goodnight met Irishman John George Adair in Colorado. Adair aspired to enter the cattle business in Texas.

Adair provided the money and Goodnight found the property. The two men agreed to use the brand, "J A," and property and profits were split—two-thirds for Adair and one-third for Goodnight.

The first land, 12,000 acres, was purchased in the Palo Duro Canyon after both men visited the area.

Goodnight established an early reputation in Texas by driving herds of cattle into Colorado and establishing the Goodnight-Loving Trail. Before entering ranching, he was a ranger and Indian scout, and he also served as a scout and guide for a frontier regiment in the Civil War.

Adair, who died in 1885, had an equally colorful background. An Irishman trained for the diplomatic service, he established his own brokerage firm in New York in 1866. Thereafter he began dividing his time between Ireland and America.

In 1874 he and his wife went on a buffalo hunt on the Kansas prairies. Adair failed to slaughter any buffalo, but he did shoot his own horse in the head, killing him, and almost killing himself in the process. But he so liked the West that he moved his brokerage firm to Denver, Colorado, in 1875, and after meeting Goodnight, he gave up his firm to enter the cattle business.

Thurber Coal Mines Reopened by Texas Pacific

(1888) The abandoned mines at Thurber, Erath County, where the state's largest single source of coal is located, soon will be in production again.

Texas Pacific Coal Company has purchased the property from the Johnson Coal Company. The latter firm closed the operations earlier this year after miners struck when the company failed to meet its payroll obligations.

Mining operations began at the site in the fall of 1886.

Coal mining is a new industry for the state of Texas. Not until 1884 was the product mined in any meaningful quantity. That year 125,000 tons were mined.

However, a map of Texas published in 1818 in Paris, France, shows a coal mine in East Texas and, in 1839, Dr. J.L. Riddell described brown coal he found on the banks of the Trinity River.

Production and use of coal in Texas began about 1850 according to published reports.

Prairie View Normal School Established

(1889) Prairie View State Normal School has a new name and a new curriculum.

The new name, compliments of the Texas legislature, is much longer: Prairie View State Normal and Industrial College. The new curriculum will permit students to obtain teaching certificates, to study military science and nursing, and take courses leading to qualifications for various trades.

This college for Negroes, founded in 1876 by the legislature as a branch of the Agricultural and Mechanical College of Texas, was first called Alta Vista Agricultural College. When no students enrolled, the college failed.

In 1879, at the suggestion of Governor O.M. Roberts, the college was reestablished as an institution for instruction in trades and agricultural subjects. Its name was then changed to Prairie View State Normal School.

Prairie View College is located one mile north of the town of Prairie View and five miles east of Hempstead.

The first college for Negroes west of the Mississippi—Wiley College—was established in 1873 in Marshall, Texas, by the Freedman's Aid Society of the Methodist Episcopal Church.

Barbed Wire Changing Ranchers' Way of Life

(1880s) The cattlemen's old way of letting their herds range freely over the plains is rapidly becoming a thing of the past. The once-proud ranges are becoming enclosed pastures. The reason? The introduction of barbed-wire fences.

Since barbed wire was first sold in the state late in 1879, the open ranges are quickly being hemmed in. The familiar trail drives to Kansas and other states up north no longer are possible.

The placing of barbed-wire fences around ranches permits the cowmen to control the breeding of their cattle, leading to improved strains. It also eliminates the need for large numbers of cowboys to establish camps on various sides of the property and their need to make daily patrols to hold in the cattle.

While wooden fences would provide the same services, Texas ranches simply are too vast for the use of wood.

The desire of so many ranchers and farmers to put barbed-wire fences

Above: Joseph F. Glidden, the inventor of barbed wire

Right: This wagon filled with barbed wire is stopped in front of a hotel in Channing, Texas.

around their homesteads has brought with it not a little turbulence.

It has been the bigger ranchers who have generally recognized the value of fencing in their vast acreages. Some of the smaller ranchers, finding themselves cut out of favorite watering holes or no longer able to conduct trail drives, have resorted to tearing down or cutting the fences. And some ranchers, owning no land at all, fenced off several thousands of acres of lands for which they held no title.

New laws have been passed, however, which make these actions felonies.

The most famous of the barbed wire salesmen has been John W. "Bet-a-Million" Gates, who is the Texas representative for a wire and manufacturing company.

Gates used an ingenious

scheme to demonstrate the efficacy of the new kind of fence. He built a barbed-wire corral on San Antonio's Main Plaza and bet ranchers that his wire would hold a herd of longhorn steers. He won his bet, and the orders began pouring in.

In 1880 Gates next organized his own company, the Southern Wire Company, and then in 1882 he started the Braddock Wire Company.

Born near Chicago in 1855, Gates went on to become a traveling salesman for a wire and manufacturing company in 1873.

Almost as well known as Gates is his partner, Henry B. Sanborn, who formerly lived with the inventor of barbed wire, J.F. Glidden. Sanborn came to Texas in 1875, and in that year sold his first barbed wire—10 reels—at Gainesville.

In 1881 Sanborn and Glidden established the Frying Pan Ranch in Potter and Randall counties in the Panhandle. The next year they fenced in the entire 120,000-acre ranch with four strands of wire.

Also in 1881 Charles Goodnight began fencing in his huge JA Ranch in the Panhandle.

Railroad Commission Adopted by State

(1891, April) Governor James Stephen Hogg's longtime goal to begin regulation of railroads in Texas because of their alleged abuses, discrimination, and distortion has become a reality.

Following Hogg's election, the Texas Legislature has enacted legislation creating a railroad commission and giving it the power to fix rates and fares and otherwise to generally regulate activities of the railroads. The legislation declares railroads to be public highways and common carriers.

Railroads have been powerful in all of the nation's states, but especially in Texas because of its immense size and the many miles of track required for transportation. There are more than 8,000 miles of track in the state.

The railroads have amassed even more power and wealth because of vast amounts of public lands given them as an incentive for laying track. The Texas & Pacific alone was given 5.1 million acres of land.

Under the new legislation railroads will be

James Stephen Hogg

required to maintain offices where their books will be open for inspection; they will be forbidden to consolidate with competing lines; and they will be subject to other regulations.

Efforts to regulate railroads have been made as early as 1875 by the Grange, and then by its successor, the Farmers' Alliance.

As the state's youthful attorney general, Hogg had worked diligently to secure effective railroad regulation. He had prosecuted a number of railroads successfully, but he had failed to get a commission established. However, after his election last year to be the state's governor on a pro-commission and reform platform, the legislature now has given him what he wants.

The railroad commission will be headed by three officials to be appointed by the governor.

Opponents of the new legislation claim that the commission's actions will amount to an unconstitutional infringement on the rights of the railroads. They say they will pursue this matter in the courts.

Hogg is a formidable political opponent for the railroads. The state's first native-born governor, Hogg was born in Rusk in 1851, the son of a brigadier general in the Civil War who died at the head of his command in 1862. The following year, Hogg's mother died. Hogg, two of his brothers, and two older sisters were left to run the family plantation.

In his first race for public office in 1876, he was defeated in a bid for the Texas Legislature, but he became county attorney of Wood County in 1878 and remained in office until 1884. He was elected attorney general of the state in 1886.

The Texas & Pacific Railway received 5.1 million acres of land from the State of Texas.

Corsicana Oil Field Continues to Prosper

(1898) The frenzy over oil that began in this central Texas city of Corsicana in 1894 shows no signs of letting up.

The town is experiencing a boom much like that of a gold-mining town in Colorado or California. Oil well derricks spike up from practically every block in the city, from front and back yards, from gardens, and from horse lots.

Investors and speculators from throughout the country have arrived.

The frenzy started when the city of Corsicana was drilling for an artesian well but found, to its dismay, oil instead of water.

The first signs of oil appeared at 1,035 feet. The drillers continued until the well was completed at 2,480 feet, but the presence of oil persisted. Three water wells were drilled, but the oleaginous substance kept rising up through the pipes and soaking the surrounding ground.

Spectators were attracted to the scene, and their carelessness was such that fires were started and three derricks burned down.

While the drilling contractors were disappointed at the nuisance of the oil, others saw promise in it. Several citizens organized a partnership the next year, named it the Corsicana Oil Development Co., and began drilling for oil just 200 feet from the city's water well.

Joseph Cullinan, organizer of the first pipeline and refinery in Corsicana (the first efficient oil refinery in Texas)

The result was a well that began producing two and a half barrels a day. Yet another well came in the next year, also well within the city limits.

The discovery of oil caused almost every parcel of property in the town and around it to be leased for exploration.

In 1896 five wells were completed and 1,450 barrels of oil produced; and in 1897 50 of 57 wells completed were producing oil. Production in 1897 was amazing: 65,975 barrels!

Production has been so steady that a refinery has been built by J.S. Cullinan and Company. Cullinan came from Pennsylvania at the invitation of Corsicana's mayor to build the refinery. It is one of the first refineries in Texas, and surely the first efficient one. (The first one was built in Nacogdoches in 1888.) The refinery has six stills and a tank capacity of about 1,000 barrels. It cost $150,000 to build.

Now, well into the year 1898, there are 287 producers in the Corsicana field.

Until now Corsicana has been a sleepy little town, although it had served as a wholesale and retail center for the surrounding agricultural territory.

Joseph Stephen Cullinan, organizer of the company bearing his name, has introduced a new use for oil other than that of lubricating axles. He persuaded Corsicana city officials to spread it on the streets as a dust-settling agent to keep the dust from blowing. He and his brother also have devised a mechanism that will enable railway locomotives to burn oil.

While oil has been known to exist in Texas, the amounts discovered have been so small that they have failed to be of commercial significance. The abundance of oil in Corsicana has changed that.

Texas Leads Nation in Production of Cotton

(1899) In this concluding year of the nineteenth century, there is no doubt about one thing: Texas dominates the nation as a cotton producer. Its 1899 crop more than doubled that of its closest competitor, Georgia. Texas produced 2.6 million bales as compared to Georgia's 1.29 million bales.

In fact, the state produces annually just more than one third of the entire American cotton crop. And, on an even bigger scale, Texas produces about one-fourth of all the cotton grown in the world. Moreover, Texas' production shows absolutely no signs of abating.

The counties that are neck-and-neck for producing the most cotton are Ellis, just south of Dallas, and Williamson, just north of Austin.

The part of the state particularly suited for the growing of this product is a belt of rich land extending in a northeasterly direction from Travis County, near the center of the state, toward the Red River to Grayson, Fannin, and Lamar counties.

There are more than 3,000 cotton gins in the state, more than five times as many as existed in 1890 when there were just 572.

One happy consequence of Texas' prowess in growing cotton is its leadership in a concomitant industry—cottonseed-oil products. Texas ranks first in this, too. About 25 percent of all cottonseed oil produced in the nation comes from Texas. Large quantities of the oil are shipped from Galveston to ports in the Mediterranean.

Cottonseed oil is used for fertilizer and also as food for cattle.

Lumber Industry Now Most Important

(1899) Texas' lumber industry is now neck-and-neck with that of flour milling and cottonseed oil extraction as the leading enterprise in the entire state. It also is one of the leading states in the nation in the industry.

Lumbering activities, which center between the Sabine and Trinity rivers in deep East Texas where the piney woods thrive, picked up enormously with the arrival of the railroads after the Civil War, and they have shown no signs of slowing down.

The railroads made possible the shipping of the tall trees even when there was no water outlet available. Six years ago, in 1893, a study showed that more than a third of the cargo handled by trains in Texas, nearly 3 million tons, was lumber.

Moreover, the railroads themselves required enormous numbers of ties as their tracks were being extended across Texas and the nation, as well as depots, section houses, repair shops, and wooden water towers.

In 1890 there were 314 manufacturing establishments in the industry, and lumber products were valued at $11.9 million. Now there are more than 600 establishments with products valued at about $16 million annually.

Even before the last few decades, though, lumbering had been an important industry (though largely locally based) in East Texas settlements. As early as 1825 a horse-powered sawmill was being used in San Augustine. Another one operated in Nacogdoches as early as the 1820s.

An interesting story from the Texas Revolution shows how intimately the

Right: Logs await loading at an East Texas lumber mill.

Below: Steves Lumber Company in San Antonio, part of the state's $16-million lumber industry.

timber industry has been tied to Texas history. Not long before the Battle of San Jacinto a messenger appeared in haste at a new sawmill under construction six miles northwest of Orange. Santa Anna and his men were approaching; all hands were being pressed into service with the Texas army. The men, seeing the desperateness of the situation, threw down their tools, picked up their flint-lock rifles, and headed for the front. After participating in the victory at San Jacinto, they returned to their work at the sawmill, completed a dam, and cut several thousand feet of lumber with a sash saw before winter.

The piney woods provided much of the timber for construction in Texas for several decades before the Civil War. Logs were floated downstream via the Neches and Sabine rivers to the population centers of Beaumont and Orange.

One of the most important lumbermen is John Henry Kirby, who has acquired millions of acres of pine and hardwood forests and built a sawmill at Silsbee in 1896.

Developing New Ways of Teaching

HOLT, RINEHART AND WINSTON, INC.

Founder: Henry Holt
Founded: 1866 in New York City
Principal: Bill Talkington, president
Current Owner: Harcourt General

Behind the doors at Holt, Rinehart and Winston, editors and professional educators dedicate themselves to developing and designing instructional materials for the 1990s and beyond. Holt, Rinehart and Winston is a company with a rich heritage and has numbered among its distinguished authors Robert Frost. In more recent times, HRW has been identified by its distinctive owl trademark and noted as a premier publisher of textbooks. Now, as the world changes with the electronic age and the coming of the information highway, HRW is going through the transition into a more diverse company.

"Books are the heart of what we do, but it's really not that simple anymore. We are, in fact, developers of 'instructional materials,' whatever the format," says Bill Talkington, president of Holt, Rinehart and Winston.

Today HRW is developing new ways to teach middle and high school students with computer software, video, laser discs, CD-ROM, and other tools unimaginable when the company was founded in the wake of the Civil War.

The year was 1866 when a young Yale graduate named Henry Holt approached publisher Frederick Leypolt to buy his translation of a foreign work. Soon, Leypolt and Holt formed a new publishing house unique in its time. The two devoted themselves to publishing, without operating bookstores or printing presses as other publishers did. Leypolt withdrew from the company after a few years, but Henry Holt remained active until his death in 1926.

Originally founded to provide Americans with good translations of the best European writers, Henry Holt & Co. later began publishing American works, and a rich literary tradition was born that lasts to this day. Henry Holt was an innovator in the publishing industry and that spirit of innovation and delivery of exceptional works continues to live under the watchful owl trademark.

Robert Frost was one of the company's most distinguished authors. A discovery of Holt's wife, Frost spent 48 years as a client, one of the longest publisher/author relationships. At his 88th birthday party in 1962, the poet laureate of the United States spoke in plain language about the publishing house that Holt built.

"I have had perfect publisher relations since 1915," he said. "I have never asked anything from them. I have never sent an accountant into the office to see whether they are cheating me, and I have grown richer and richer, and they have grown richer and richer."

As years passed, Holt published more and more textbooks for the kindergarten through postgraduate levels. In 1960 Holt & Co. merged with two other textbook publishers, one founded by John C. Winston in 1884, the other by Stanley Rinehart in 1929. This merging of exceptional educational publishers formed what is today Holt, Rinehart and Winston.

Today HRW is based in Austin, moving from New York in 1988. People often think of publishing as an enterprise dominated by East Coast companies. However,

The company's Austin headquarters.

HRW is part of a major presence in the Texas business community as a subsidiary of Harcourt General and Texas is a leading area for the publication of educational materials. Harcourt General, in addition to HRW, operates The Psychological Corporation in San Antonio and Harcourt Brace College Division in Fort Worth, both leaders in their fields. In addition, the corporation operates a major distribution facility in Dallas and is a partner in Neiman Marcus of Dallas, a world-renowned high-fashion specialty retailer.

"We are fortunate to be a part of the Texas community and to be headquartered in Austin," states Talkington. "The quality of life here is exceptional and we are part of a community and a state that places high value on the education of our children. We have access to the University of Texas, which is an outstanding institution and provides us with a wonderful resource for employees. We also work closely with the state government to ensure that we produce materials that fit the needs of a changing society. There simply is no better place to be a publisher today. The world is changing rapidly and we are at the center of that change."

In April 1983 a report by the National Commission on Excellence in Education concluded the future of the country was threatened by a rising tide of mediocrity in its educational system. The report, "A Nation At Risk," set off a wave of curriculum reform more dramatic than after Sputnik in the early 1960s. At the same time, Texas passed some of the most sweeping educational reforms ever.

"Texas has always prided itself on being the biggest and the best. That philosophy carries through its approach to education and the youth of the state. One aspect of Texas law, in particular, sets it apart from all others. It recognizes that students need access to up-to-date materials and the latest in instructional methodologies. It also recognizes that *all* children should have equal access to the opportunity to learn. Under Texas law every child is guaranteed access to the most current and highest-quality instructional material available. The state funds the purchase of instructional materials to ensure that this happens and has developed a comprehensive adoption process that demands quality. Texas occasionally gets some bad press for its process, but it is the most open process in all of education and it works diligently to ensure that its citizens have a voice in how their children are taught. We like being a part of that process. It works," says Talkington.

The future for instruction is undergoing the same change. The advent of the new communication networks, the affordable access to new technologies, and the explosion of information are changing how students learn and how HRW develops and delivers instructional materials.

"For decades we have been publishers of textbooks," reflects Talkington. "That is changing. We are now learning to work with new technologies to improve the materials and instruction children receive. While I am confident that print will long have a key role in how we teach children, I am equally confident that the new technologies will provide us all with exceptional opportunities to improve instruction and that children will learn in very different ways in the future. Our challenge is to properly understand how the new technologies work and how they can be best used to deliver our products and services to the teacher and the child. It is an exciting and challenging time to be in this business."

In addition to the changes afforded by the new delivery systems, the problems and opportunities of today are changing the very nature of the company. "We are no longer 'just a publisher.' In the past we published the books and sold them to the

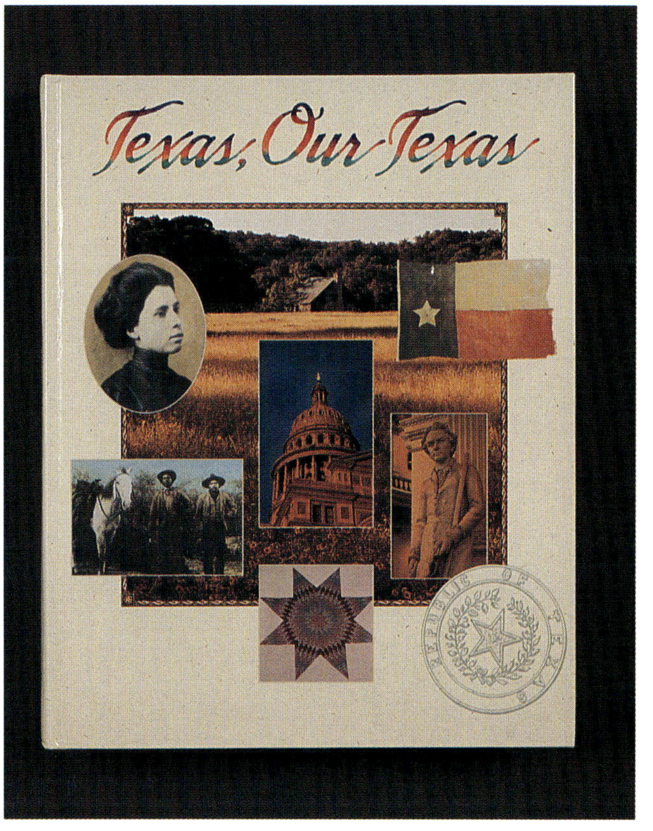

One of HRW's recent publications.

schools. We now view ourselves as a partner with the community in providing instruction to youth. This community includes teachers, administrators, parents, government, and other corporations," says Talkington.

Most of HRW's employees are former teachers who understand what teachers go through on a daily basis. Many participate in HRW's "Adopt a School" program and volunteer personal time as mentors and tutors in the Austin Independent School District. HRW works with the University of Texas College of Education to better understand curriculum changes and innovations in instructional technique. HRW also offers intern programs for college students and summer employment for youth. The company is actively involved in every aspect of the community in which it lives and seeks partnerships with other corporations to improve the quality of life.

The owl that has long watched over Holt now looks over the Austin skyline. It is a company on the move. It wants to be the biggest and the best—just like the state.

Providing Excellence in Education

The seventh-largest university in Texas, SWT has more than 21,000 students on its 422-acre campus. Photo by Don Anders

Right: The Fight of the Stallions, the work of sculptor Anna Hyatt Huntington, has been an SWT landmark since 1951. Photo by Don Anders

SOUTHWEST TEXAS STATE UNIVERSITY

Founded: 1899
President: Dr. Jerome H. Supple

Halfway between San Antonio and Austin, the city of San Marcos can claim some of the most beautiful scenery in Texas. Nestled among rolling green hills surrounding the San Marcos River, it is also home to one of the state's largest institutions of higher learning, Southwest Texas State University.

Though officially designated a university in 1969, SWT opened in 1903 as Southwest Texas State Normal, a college for training teachers. Its first principal, Thomas Green Harris, exemplified the times as a strict disciplinarian and a zealous foe of "demon rum." Harris and his successor Cecil Eugene Evans saw themselves as surrogate parents for the students, who were there to learn, not to have fun. In 1905 Harris issued a list of student regulations specifying everything from study hours to the prohibition of dating.

"Any indications that students are spending their time courting, or in being courted, or in triffling about such matters, will be deemed sufficient for the prompt removal of such students from the Normal," one regulation said.

Mary Brogdon, the dean of women from 1923 to 1949, was ever-vigilant in protecting her girls from harm. She kept a blacklist of men to avoid, and allegedly warned freshman girls not to sit in chairs recently occupied by men until the chairs had a chance to cool. Brogdon's surveillance efforts reportedly included disguising herself as a man as she searched for rule breakers out on the town, according to Ronald C. Brown's book *Beacon on the Hill: Southwest Texas State University, 1903 to 1978*. Her strict supervision of morality prompted a student rebellion in 1925. Students got a chance to air their grievances with the school's president, but change came slowly.

Today Southwest Texas State University has a reputation as a place where students can have fun while pursuing their dreams, and enrollment has increased rapidly. The seventh-largest university in Texas, SWT has more than 21,000 students on its 422-acre campus. In an effort to control growth, the university has raised admissions standards several times over the years, bringing them to among the highest in the state. Students who are admitted enjoy a faculty-to-student ratio of 22 to 1.

SWT offers 130 undergraduate degree programs and more than 40 master's degrees. Its undergraduate program in geography and planning has been repeatedly ranked number one in the nation.

SWT's original commitment to training teachers has never wavered. Today one of every 12 public school teachers in Texas earned either a degree or a certification at SWT.

The university's School of Health Professions is the largest provider of allied health care professionals in the state. Its programs in journalism, music, theater arts, sociology, technology, aquatic biology, and chemistry are earning first-rate reputations. The Graduate School also continues to grow, with master's degrees in accountancy and physical therapy recently added.

Active grant funding has increased dramatically from about $3 million in 1986 to more than $20 million in 1993, fulfilling one of the goals of SWT's eighth president, Dr. Jerome H. Supple, who arrived in 1989.

The university received a $4.8-million federal grant in 1993 to fund a five-year program to teach day-care providers in five states to help children deal with violence in their homes and communities. It's a sad commentary on our society that such a program is needed, but the grant is a compliment to SWT's School of Education, one of only seven institutions to receive funding for the program.

SWT has a long tradition of competitiveness. From the school's founding until the 1930s, one of the most exciting aspects of life at SWT was intercollegiate debate. In the early years, the school yearbook, *The Pedagog*, often devoted an entire page to each SWT debate, far better coverage than it gave athletic teams. Debate attracted many outstanding students to the school, among them a young Lyndon B. Johnson.

SWT's Bobcats today compete in Division I of the NCAA, and are members of the Southland Conference. Then in NCAA Division II, SWT boasted national championship football teams in both 1981 and 1982. The first formal athletic teams were

Above: Historic Old Main, SWT's original landmark building, sits on a hill overlooking a campus that features varied architectural styles. At left here is the Speech-Drama Center while the multi-story J.C. Kellam Building is at right.

Left: The seven-story Albert B. Alkek Library, which opened in 1990, contains library holdings that number around the one-million mark. The library also houses the fascinating Southwestern Writers Collection.

women's basketball. During SWT's first decade women's teams in basketball and tennis outnumbered men's teams.

Today SWT is an integral part of San Marcos. Cooperative efforts of the city, county, and university have aided local business and brought new industry into the region. Residents of nearby Luling will benefit from a rural health care clinic at the local hospital, thanks to a federal grant awarded through SWT. And with the city of San Marcos and Century Telephone of San Marcos, Inc., SWT provides literacy and career advancement training to unskilled laborers.

Aquarena Springs, the historic resort and lake, became part of the SWT campus in 1994. The acquisition will allow the university to protect the fragile habitat of several endangered species and the natural beauty of the area around the springs that form the San Marcos River.

With its first century drawing to a close, Southwest Texas State University appears to be one of the most dynamic and progressive universities in Texas.

Where You Want To Be

STATE NATIONAL BANK

Founded: 1881
Principal: Robert J. Whetten, president and CEO

For State National Bank, banking begins at home. With 113 years of doing business on the U.S.-Mexico border, this financial institution has always understood the importance of investing in the community through lending. Today more than two million people call "The Pass of the North" home. El Paso and Juarez, Chihuahua, Mexico, form the largest metropolitan area on any international border anywhere in the world. This region *is* the gateway for goods and services heading north and south. State National is positioned to help this burgeoning area.

State National Bank is one of a rare breed. It is a strong, independent Texas bank and the largest independently owned bank in El Paso. That independence means decisions are made locally, quickly, and without outside interference. State National provides money for businesses of all sizes, as well as low-income housing loans, home improvement loans, mortgage loans, and personal loans—putting more money into El Paso's needs and dreams than any other local lender.

State National Bank president and chief executive officer Robert J. Whetten says State National is in a unique position for today and tomorrow: "As the North American Free Trade Agreement (NAFTA) brings the barriers down, our location and binational relationships can help businesses on both sides of the border."

Whetten is eminently qualified to run an international bank. He speaks fluent Spanish and banking. After growing up in a Mormon settlement in Chihuahua City, Whetten earned a master's degree in international administration from Brigham Young University in 1969.

After more than 20 years as a banking officer in Mexico and South America, Whetten returned to northern Mexico—to Multibanco Comermex in Juarez, and later, El Paso

This white marble building, opened in 1922, served State National Bank for more than 50 years. Courtesy, State National Archival collection/Gary Bissell

State Bank. El Paso State Bank was later purchased by State National Bank.

"The people of Mexico look at the North American Free Trade Agreement as an opening," explains Whetten. "We offer customers on both sides of the border a comfortable place to do business. We can tailor-make the financial product to best suit our clients' needs." State National works closely with the Texas Department of Commerce to find out who wants to do business with Mexico. "The advantage we offer is our proximity to Mexico. And because we're here, we fully understand business in both countries," says Whetten. "Our credibility is what has built customer confidence, and that's important because banking is a confidence business."

State National has five customer service areas—Agribusiness, including cotton, beef cattle, and dairies; Trust Services and Investments; Community Banking; Specialized Lending; and Corporate and International Banking—to better serve the varying sectors of the regional market. With more than $982 million in assets and $63 million in capital and reserves, State National Bank is a major financial resource in the Southwest.

Robert J. Whetten, president and chief executive officer of State National Bank. Photo by Gary Bissell

State National Bank continues to build on strong relationships and loyalties developed generations ago. The bank's first commitment is to the growth and well-being of El Paso families and businesses. It's the same commitment that dates back to 1881, when State National Bank became the first nationally chartered bank to do business in El Paso.

State National's 22-story tower, completed in 1971, is a prominent part of the downtown skyline. The bronzed aluminum-and-glass skyscraper is the tallest building in El Paso. Anchored in State National Plaza, it looks out over the seven State National bank locations and more than 20 ATM locations. It's been El Paso's bank since frontier days and continues to be an important partner in the financial success of the region.

STATE NATIONAL®
El Paso's Bank Since 1881.
Member FDIC

State National Bank's downtown location is 22 stories of aluminum and glass. Photo by Michael R. Moses

CHAPTER THREE

Urbanization and Industrialization

1900-1940

As Texas entered the twentieth century, its romantic heritage, marked distinctly by such icons as the Alamo and the cattle kingdom, had been stamped indelibly on the American consciousness.

On the immediate horizon, though, another powerful and transforming development was to occur that would gain equal standing with those symbols of the nineteenth century in being a part of the Texas heritage—the discovery of vast quantities of oil.

The impact of the early Pennsylvania oil fields—notwithstanding Standard Oil—paled in comparison to the i*mpact of Texas oil that began with Spindletop in 1901 and continued even beyond the discovery of the fabulous East Texas field in 1930. Spindletop and successive finds in the area spawned the creation of the world's largest oil firms and some of the largest companies of any kind: Gulf, Texaco, Exxon, and Mobil.*

The vast new petroleum resources gave an important boost to the urbanization and industrialization that already was beginning in the American nation and now was poised for takeoff in Texas.

In 1870 nearly 95 percent of Texans had lived in rural areas. By 1900 urban dwellers accounted for 17.1 percent of the population, and by 1940 they had reached 45.4 percent. Houston, Dallas, and San Antonio were the major urban centers, with the upstart cities of Houston and Dallas bypassing older, more historical San Antonio.

Texas cities whose origins lie in their functions as marketing centers for surrounding farmers had begun by 1940 to see themselves in other ways. Cities such as Houston and Dallas became more closely aligned to oil, banking, insurance, and manufacturing than to agriculture.

Frontier Texas, still a vivid recollection and within the experience of many living residents in 1900, had faded from sight by 1940. Most eyes focused sharply on the future.

On this eve of World War II, civic leaders in Houston and Dallas had shown considerable mettle in pushing their cities to the forefront of their regions. In 1900 Houston had been more or less on even footing with older Galveston. By 1940 Houston had surpassed the island city in growth and economic prowess. Dallas similarly was spurred forward through competition with its nearby neighbor to the west, Fort Worth. San Antonio, lacking a significant regional competitor, had lost the lead it had held for several decades in population. By 1940 it trailed both Houston and Dallas.

The fortunes of Galveston and Houston stood in interesting contrast. Galveston's disastrous 1900 hurricane, which killed 6,000 persons, dealt it a blow from which it was difficult to recover. Between 1900 and 1910 its population actually declined. Houston created a well-protected deep-water port 50 miles inland from the coast. It surpassed Galveston in shipping and positioned itself for even more remarkable growth in coming decades.

Dallas' civic leaders were equally creative in improving their own situation over natural obstacles. The troublesome Trinity River, which every few years flooded large parts of the city, found itself in the 1930s strategically confined in an entirely new channel between two lengthy, earthen levees. The old flood plain, disastrously wide, now miraculously had been converted from wasteland into a planned industrial park.

Soon after the turn of the century, cities in Texas as well as in the rest of the nation were beginning to organize themselves in better ways to handle population growth. This included conversion of old-style municipal governments into commission or council-manager plans; the formation of bigger and more efficient electric power companies that brought lighting and power to the cities; the introduction of natural gas via pipelines as a clean and efficient heating and energy source; and the development of streetcar systems that expanded the central cities beyond their "walking" cores. In this latter regard, of course, the automobile began to play an even more prominent role in enlarging the cities' boundaries.

Facing page: Captioned ***Dallas: Brilliant in Achievement,*** this late 1930s photo showcases a city destined for future greatness. Courtesy, Texas/Dallas History and Archive Division, Dallas Public Library

Farming families, traditionally the backbone of the state, prospered for the first couple of decades, but falling prices in the 1920s and 1930s were not kind to them. The Depression of the 1930s caused many of them, especially tenant farmers, to abandon their rural roots and move to the city to find regular wages. The introduction of the tractor and the electrification of some rural areas began to change farm life, too. .

The state's black and Mexican-American residents, while significant in numbers, continued to be overlooked as participants in the self-governing process. Few bothered to protest their secondary status. Women, while having more rights in Texas than in many other states, also continued to be relegated to inferior status in the eyes of the law.

Black residents could not even vote in the state's Democratic primaries, where the ultimate winners always were elected. Because the Republican party had virtually no voice at any level of government, the exclusion of blacks from Democratic primaries effectively eliminated their power at the ballot box.

Yet the Democratic party in Texas was not entirely of one mind. As Governor Oscar B. Colquitt said in 1911, "We have only one political party in Texas, but there are enough . . . fights in that one for half a dozen." Debates over Prohibition, the Ku Klux Klan, "Fergusonism," and the New Deal provided plenty of issues for debate during these decades of Democratic dominance.

In 1936 the state celebrated the 100th anniversary of Sam Houston's victory over Santa Anna and the winning of independence. There was much to celebrate. Texans were pleased at the success of their efforts to turn the eyes of the nation toward the Texas Centennial and Exposition in Dallas and to take note of the state's advancements.

After Spindletop, oil derricks literally covered some areas of the state. Pictured here is the Pierce Junction field, which could be seen all the way from downtown Houston in the 1920s. Courtesy, Houston Metropolitan Research Center, Houston Public Library

On September 30, 1925, hundreds gathered for the opening of Texas Tech. Courtesy, Southwest Collection, Texas Tech University

By the 1920s the streets of Dallas were already so crowded with automobiles that policemen were ticketing illegally parked cars. Courtesy, Texas/Dallas History and Archive Division, Dallas Public Library

The Houston Negro Chamber of Commerce provided black business leaders with an opportunity to promote their businesses and establish ties with one another. Courtesy, Houston Metropolitan Research Center, Houston Public Library

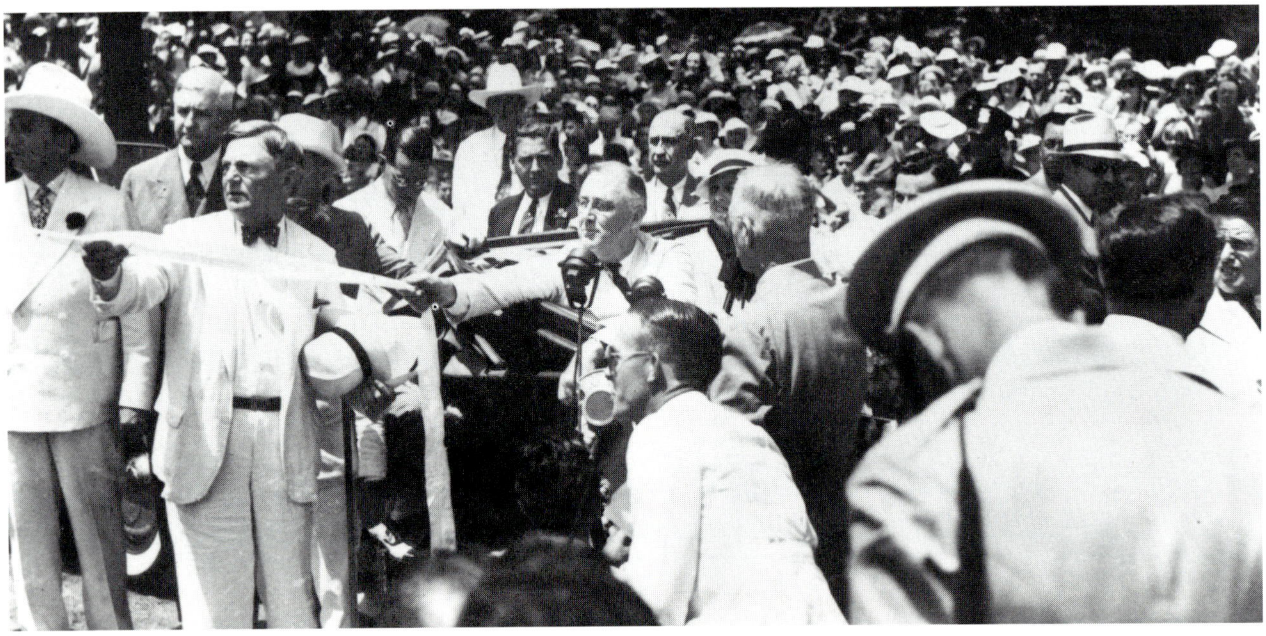

One of the highlights of the Texas Centennial Exposition was FDR's visit to Dallas during the first week of festivities. Courtesy, Texas/Dallas History and Archive Divison, Dallas Public Library

Spindletop Oil Discovery Opens New Era for State

(1901) The huge gusher of oil that burst from the ground and shot into the sky with the sound of a cannon outside Beaumont on January 10 is seen as the harbinger of a new era for the oil industry in Texas and probably for the entire nation. Nothing like it has ever been seen anywhere.

Above: Austrian-born mining engineer Anthony F. Lucas

Top: Beaumont businessman Patillo Higgins

Left: On the morning of January 10, the Lucas Gusher shot more than 100 feet into the sky.

For six days the "black gold" spurted into the air like a geyser. At one point it reached 200 feet into the sky, higher by far than the frame derrick that supported the drill. That drill had descended more than a thousand feet into the ground before it struck oil.

Before the "Lucas gusher" could be "capped" and the unbridled flow halted, a huge reservoir of oil surrounded the site.

On March 3 sparks from a passing locomotive ignited this lake of oil and caused several hundred thousand barrels of the substance to burn in a horrific fire. Luckily, the well itself was not harmed.

The consequences of this enormous oil discovery are acknowledged to be profound, but admittedly difficult to predict with any degree of certainty.

Within days of the discovery speculators crowded into the area ready to take advantage of this petroleum find. Many of the speculators are organizing into companies. [These would include the Gulf Oil Corporation and the Texas Co. (Texaco).]

One particular use of petroleum—for gasoline-powered automobiles—appears to hold great promise. Gasoline, of course, is derived by refining petroleum.

Before this time, the major petroleum fields had been located in Pennsylvania. First notions that petroleum might be found in this part of Texas came from a one-armed, poorly educated Beaumont native named Pattillo Higgins, who believed that oil could be found under a small rise in this coastal plain south of his native city.

On Sunday school outings Higgins would amuse children by sticking his cane into the ground and then setting fire to the escaping gas.

Higgins, however, failed in his first two efforts to locate oil. Needing additional resources, he advertised for help. It came from a mining engineer named Anthony Lucas, whose experiences with salt domes led him to believe that Higgins could be right about the oil.

Lucas assumed control of drilling activities in 1899, and in 1901 his discovery proved to be fewer than 20 feet from where Higgins had predicted it would be found.

The Spindletop well is without a doubt the largest in history. Initial estimates are that 75,000 to 85,000 barrels of oil a day flowed from the well before it was capped.

Fort Worth Raises Money to Bring Packing Firms

(1901) "Fort Worth, the greatest packing house center of the Southwest." That was the cry that rang out from a huge crowd of celebrants who congregated Monday, October 7, at Fort Worth's city hall auditorium to hear the announcement that the city's drive to raise $100,000 to persuade the Armour and Swift packing companies to erect meat-packing facilities there had succeeded.

A substantial percentage of the money—about 16 percent or $15,669—was raised from the crowd at the city hall meeting, a feat that put the drive $600 over the required $100,000.

The meeting was the culmination of a months-long drive to persuade the two major packing companies to select Fort Worth as the site for their Texas operations. Both packers expected the city selected to subsidize construction of the plants.

Fort Worth's leading businessmen worked hard throughout the year to raise the required funds.

When the announcement was made Monday evening that the drive had gone over the top, pandemonium broke out among the crowd. Celebrants threw their hats into the air, waved handkerchiefs, and congratulated one another with backslaps and handshakes.

Swift and Armour have been eager for Texas sites to be closer to the vast Texas cattle ranches that supply so much of the beef for their midwest operations.

The *Fort Worth Register,* in reporting the drive's success, wrote that "Fort Worth made history for herself and Texas last night. Fort Worth will be on the lips of every man, women and child who reads. . . Fort Worth started on her road to greatness last night."

Fort Worth long has been recognized as a cattle center and a railroad terminal for the shipping of cattle out of the state. Meat packing operations in the city, however, have not been nearly of the magnitude of Swift and Armour despite the fact that, overall, the state of Texas ranks meat packing as its sixth-leading industry.

[Swift and Armour built their plants on Fort Worth's North Side and began processing meat in 1902, drawing nearly all of the West's cattle trade to their facilities.]

Impact of Lucas Gusher Still Strong in the Area

(1902) Spindletop, the tremendous oil discovery made last year near Beaumont by Anthony Lucas, continues to exert a major economic effect on the area.

Speculators who rushed to the vicinity have been leasing land as far away as 100 miles. Leasing costs range from as high as one million dollars an acre for nearby land and $1,000 an acre for areas farther away.

In the immediate area of Spindletop, property has been divided and subdivided into tracts as small as 600 feet. Even plots this tiny, so small there is hardly room for a derrick floor, lease for thousands of dollars. The money is well spent because gusher after gusher has erupted.

Besides the lease-hounds and drillers, thousands of tourists have flooded the area. Indeed, Beaumont has begun to resemble a circus. Peddlers of souvenir bottles filled with oil clamor for the attention of tourists. Cafes are packed with customers who line up for entire blocks for a simple meal. Grocery stores are open 24 hours a day. Rooms are in short supply. Two men plopped a mattress down on the sidewalk and slept there. Another man, suddenly rich, was seen flipping through his roll of $100 bills and stopping abruptly when he encountered $10 bills. On these occasions he tore up the $10 bills with the comment, "Small change, what are you doing here?"

Needless to say, bars filled with thirsty men have sprung up as thick as fleas.

On the more serious side, at the close of 1901 production from Spindletop itself was 3.59 million barrels. Current estimates are that it will be nearly six times that amount in 1902.

Judge Roy Bean Dies in His Historic Saloon

(1903) Judge Roy Bean, the legendary "law west of the Pecos," is dead.

Judge Bean, whose age was not known for sure but was estimated to be 78, died in his saloon at Langtry from lung and heart complications aggravated by a recent trip to San Antonio.

Few, if any, westerners have had a more colorful life than the venerable former justice of the peace who once fined the corpse of a Chinaman $40 after finding that amount and a pistol on the body. (Bean found a railroad worker not guilty of the murder because he said he could find nothing in his law books prohibiting the murder of a Chinaman.)

Judge Roy Bean

Bean, a native of Kentucky, never studied law, but in 1882, after a rough-and-tumble frontier life that carried him from Texas to Mexico to California and saw him work as a saloonkeeper, butcher, and freighter and get involved in at least one duel, the Texas Rangers appointed him justice of the peace in the Vinegaroon-Eagle's Nest Springs area. Bean claimed he named the new town that sprang up in the area Langtry after the English actress Lily Langtry.

After his appointment as justice of the peace, Bean won reelection on several occasions. His reputation blossomed as he dispensed justice in his unique and informal but effective manner.

One of his most unusual moments came in 1876 when he staged a heavyweight championship boxing match between Bob Fitzsimmons and Peter Maher on a sandbar on the Mexican side of the Rio Grande. The bout had been forbidden in the United States, and the Texas Rangers who were sent to Langtry to stop the bout were outwitted by Bean.

Bean was born in or about 1825 in Mason County, Kentucky. In 1848 he and his brother organized a trading expedition to Chihuahua. He was later arrested in San Diego for fighting a duel, but escaped from jail. For several years afterward he was the owner-operator of a saloon near Los Angeles. He moved next to New Mexico.

He told a story about being strung up in a tree by an angry rival because of his romantic pursuit of a Mexican girl, only to be cut down and saved by her.

In 1866 Bean married Virginia Chavez. They had four children. Before settling at the present site of Langtry after following the railroad there, he had lived for more than a decade in San Antonio.

Legislature Purchases Historic Landmark, Alamo

(1905, January 25) The sacred building that is one of the most famous structures in the nation and stands as the outstanding icon of Texas' independence will be purchased in whole by the State of Texas and presented to the Daughters of the Republic of Texas to be maintained in perpetuity.

This decision concerning the Alamo's future was made by the Texas Legislature, which passed a resolution directing the governor to purchase the portion of the property now in private hands.

In 1883 the state had purchased most of the site from the Roman Catholic Church. It had placed that portion of the property in the custody of the City of San Antonio for upkeep.

The soon-to-be new

A chapel once part of a Spanish mission, the Alamo gained fame in 1835 as the site of one of the most famous battles to take place in Texas.

owners of the Alamo, the Daughters of the Republic of Texas, belong to an organization whose members are descended from Texas pioneers of the colonial and republican periods. The organization's primary purpose is to perpetuate the memory and spirit of those who achieved and maintained the independence of Texas.

The Alamo's chapel cornerstone was laid in 1744 by Catholics who hoped to Christianize and educate the Indians living in the area. The name *Alamo*, from the Spanish word for cottonwood tree, was said to be derived from a grove of cottonwoods growing near the mission.

Mexican military forces occupied the Alamo from 1821 to 1836 before being surrounded by Texas forces in December 1836. Three months later the Mexican army of some 5,000 men, led by Antonio Lopez de Santa Anna, surrounded a Texan force of approximately 87 men. After a siege of 13 days, the Mexican army overcame the Texas forces and annihilated them.

"Remember the Alamo" became a favorite battle cry of Texans when they overcame Santa Anna's forces at San Jacinto and assured independence for Texas.

Afterward, for some years, the Alamo lay in virtual ruin. Its ownership was uncertain, passing from the Roman Catholic Church to the U.S. government and then to the Texas government.

Insurance Companies Returning to Texas

(1908) The flight of insurance companies from Texas that began in 1906 with passage of the Robertson Insurance Law seems to have subsided. A number of the firms that left because of the act's provisions now are returning. The change in attitude stems from adjustments to the law that have made compliance easier.

The Robertson Insurance Law, passed by the 31st Legislature, required insurance companies operating within the state's boundaries to invest at least 75 percent of their reserves within the state. Securities representing these investments were required to be deposited with the Texas State Treasury or with another approved depository.

Insurance companies fought against the legislation, which was introduced by James Harvey Robertson of Austin, and, when the law was enacted, 21 insurance companies withdrew from the state, citing the law's harshness.

Of the $40-million reserves of these departing companies, less than one million dollars was invested within the state's boundaries.

The insurance industry in Texas had shown unusual growth, and the theory behind the Robertson Law was that the companies properly should reinvest the money within the state rather than elsewhere.

Such investments, it was felt, could only improve the Texas economy. The law also was intended to encourage the formation of new insurance companies within the state.

The rapid industrialization and urbanization of Texas has brought with it a vast increase in the insurance business, and the departure of so many companies in protest of the Robertson Law was viewed by knowledgeable observers as only a temporary phenomenon.

[The law was repealed in 1963 because of changing conditions, but it was widely credited with the birth and growth of a large number of insurance firms within the state.)

Commercial Production of Peanuts Begins

(1910) Just five years after the first commercial crop of peanuts was grown in Lamar County, the peanut industry is thriving.

Three peanut factories have now been established in the area. They were prompted no doubt by last year's huge yield that saw farmers produce 300 carloads from 10,000 acres. This acreage included land in Fannin, Red River, and Jones counties as well as Lamar County.

Typical yields are from 25 to 100 bushels per acre, with each bushel selling at an average of 70 cents. Additionally, farmers sell peanut hay for about $12 a ton. Cost of seed is approximately one dollar per acre.

Not until 1906 did any farmers in the state attempt to grow commercial quantities of the crop, but in that year four or five carloads were grown and sold to a peanut oil, butter, and confectionery factory in Paris, the seat of Lamar County. This was the first such factory in the state.

Since that year crops have multiplied annually, reaching 30 carloads in 1907, 150 carloads in 1908, and 300 carloads in 1909.

Peanuts grow on the same kind of soil as cotton. They require a five-month growing season, moderate rainfall, plenty of sunshine, and sandy soils.

Natural Gas Reaches Dallas and Fort Worth

(1910) The natural gas discovered in 1901 in Petrolia, near Wichita Falls in West Texas, now has reached the urban centers of Dallas and Fort Worth via a long pipeline made tight with couplings.

The fuel provides a clean and—despite the fears expressed by some—safe heating, lighting, and energy source.

Natural gas is considerably less expensive and certainly more satisfactory than the artificial gas being manufactured by some companies. The availability of this new energy source is also expected to stand as competition against electrical companies now providing light and energy sources.

The Petrolia field is a shallow one, a fact that has lowered the cost of drilling and production expenses. There is also oil in the field.

Prison System Reformed by Legislative Act

(1910) The state's controversial prisoner contract lease system in which counties and even private enterprise leased teams of convicts for working on roads and farms has been abolished.

The Prison Reform Act, approved on September 17, 1910, abolishes the practice and creates a three-man prison commission to take complete control of the state penitentiary.

What prompted the change was a series of newspaper articles appearing in 1908 and 1909

Thanks to the newly approved Prison Reform Act, most prisoners will no longer have to wear the traditional black-and-white striped uniforms like those worn by these men hard at work at the Marble Falls Quarry.

revealing widespread abuses of the penitentiary system. These articles, highly sensational in nature, prompted a legislative investigation in 1909.

The legislators' study confirmed the existence of abuses against the prisoners by private contractors, whose chief purpose was in gaining the greatest production from the smallest expenditures. It was determined that convicts had been shot or whipped to death for trivial offenses, that the tasks set for them were unreasonable, and that their food was poor and their sanitation abominable.

The new act not only abolishes the leasing system, but it also authorizes payment of 10 cents a day per prisoner for working. In addition, it abolishes the traditional black-and-white striped uniforms except for the worst class of prisoners.

The new prison commission members are appointed by the governor and paid a salary of $3,600 each.

A number of reforms in the past couple of decades have sought to improve prison life. Perhaps the greatest stimulus came in 1896 when prisoners mutinied in the state prison in Huntsville and attempted to dynamite the facility.

In 1905 and 1906 the state introduced the practice of offering parole as a means of inducing good behavior. In addition, the state separated female convicts from male ones by placing them on a farm near Huntsville.

Citizen of Orange Converts Yellow Pine into Paper

(1911) A major breakthrough has been made in the manufacturing of paper.

Edward H. Mayo of Orange has managed to convert yellow pine into sulfate paper pulp. This seems to indicate the birth of a major new manufacturing industry in Texas—paper manufacturing.

Production of Sulphur Begins in Brazoria County

(1912) What is believed to be a vast deposit of sulphur now is being extracted in large quantities from a large dome at Bryan Mound in Brazoria County.

While the existence of sulphur at this location has been known since 1906, it was not possible to process the material until this year when the Frasch patents expired and became available for commercial use. The Frasch method is a technique in which heated water is forced into sulphur-bearing formations deep in the earth, melting the sulphur and permitting it to be pumped up to the surface.

The Texas Freeport Sulphur Company has been organized to exploit the deposits.

Until now, sulphur has

been extracted largely in the state of Louisiana. It appears in the calcite caprock of some of the salt domes in the Gulf Coastal Plain.

Sulphur is used in the making of matches, paper, and gunpowder.

Sulphur is lifted onto a scale before being loaded onto a box car for transport. The Gulf Coastal Plain contains large quantities of underground sulphur deposits.

Dallas Named Site for Federal Reserve Bank

(1914, April 2) Chances that Dallas would win the distinction of being regional headquarters for one of the 12 new regional Federal Reserve Banks were slim indeed, but the long shot has paid off.

The federal government has named Dallas as the site for the regional bank that will serve all of Texas, two-thirds of Louisiana, half of New Mexico, one-third of Oklahoma, and a section of Arizona.

The selection of the city came after a concentrated drive by civic leaders to claim the honor.

Dallas is the smallest city in the nation to win such a designation.

An advertisement appearing in a local newspaper sums up the local feeling by saying that the selection means the city is:

destined to become one of the most important cities of the United States. It means a great increase in population. It also means a great expansion of our commercial and industrial interests. It means that many new and important enterprises will seek a home in Dallas. In short, Dallas is on the eve of an era of prosperity seldom if ever experienced by another city.

Dr. G.W. Benn of Dallas' Council of Churches reminded citizens to be thankful to God "for his goodness in giving Dallas the national reserve bank." He asked them to give their

The Federal Reserve Bank Building at 1101 Commerce Street, Dallas

special thanks to God on Sunday, April 5, which is "Go to Church Day."

Dallas' civic leaders, in seeking the bank, claimed that Dallas led every city in the Southwest in population, in wholesale business, in the number of wholesale houses, in factory output, in number of factories, in freight business, in postal receipts, and in new building permits. They also pointed out that Dallas now sells a greater volume of goods to Southwestern retailers than does St. Louis, and that 600 of the city's 2,200 traveling salesmen operate outside Texas' borders. Dallas, civic leaders added, has as many residents within a 100-mile radius as do the more widely known cities of St. Louis and Kansas. Moreover, they said, it is growing faster.

Galveston Municipal Plan Gaining Wide Acceptance

(1915) The hurricane that nearly wiped out the city of Galveston in September 1900, killing some 6,000 residents and destroying half the city, indirectly brought with it a change that has proven 15 years later to be a boon to the efficient management of cities across the nation.

This was the introduction of the so-called "commission plan" of municipal government, a plan in which citizens elect five commissioners to head the various departments of municipal government.

The commission plan initially was devised as an efficient ad hoc means of coping with the awful turmoil brought by the floodwaters accompanying the hurricane. It is widely held to permit the introduction of business methods into city government operations. Its success in Galveston was such that other cities took note and began petitioning the Texas legislature for similar charters.

Houston was the second city to adopt the commission plan, choosing it in 1905. At the legislature's next session five other cities also obtained new charters for the plan, including Dallas.

Now, in the year 1915, some 40 commission cities exist in Texas.

The movement has spread nationwide in this era of urban reform. Magazines such as *Harper's Weekly* and *McClure's* have championed the new form of government as a key means of combating the "bosses" that have managed to gain control of so many local governments.

The advantage of the commission plan is the direct involvement of individual commissioners in city administration. Typical plans divide the responsibilities so that one commissioner heads taxes and revenues, another one oversees police and fire operations, another manages water and sanitation, and the fourth commissioner supervises streets and public works. The fifth member is the mayor.

Texas Legislature Approves Highway Department

(1917) Governor Jim Ferguson's recommendation to establish a state highway department has been approved by the 35th Texas Legislature. The act will permit the State of Texas to receive a share of federal appropriations for building a national system of highways.

Under the federal plan, states will build the roads with the assistance of funds obtained from the U.S. Bureau of Public Roads. The Federal-Aid Road Act stipulates that participating states must have a highway department in order to be eligible for the funds.

The idea for a state highway department in Texas actually dates back to the turn of the century when the Texas Good Roads Association first advocated it.

Despite the vast stretches across Texas (the largest of the 48 states), its present road system is widely held to be inadequate. Authority for building roads has been left in the hands of county authorities, and there has been no overall plan for consistent road development.

There are nearly 200,000 vehicles operating in the state in this year of 1917, and that number is growing rapidly each year.

By 1911 the state had approximately 5,125 miles of improved highways out of some 160,000 miles of roads in the state. All these roads were maintained by the county.

Public interest in the automobile as a popular means of transportation had been sparked greatly in 1901 with the Spindletop oil discovery outside of Beaumont.

Governor Jim Ferguson is Impeached

(1917) The Texas Senate, sitting as a High Court of Impeachment, has convicted Governor James E. Ferguson of 10 charges brought against him by the House of Representatives. He has been removed from office.

By a vote of 25 to 3, the senators not only ordered "Farmer Jim" out of office, but also declared him ineligible to hold any office of honor, trust, or profit in the state of Texas.

The most serious charges against him concerned the appropriation of state funds for his own use and irregularities in connection with the deposits of public funds in the Temple State Bank, where he is a stockholder.

Governor Ferguson's troubles seemed to stem in part from his feud with the University of Texas after its board of regents refused to remove certain faculty members he found objectionable. Ferguson promptly vetoed practically the entire state appropriation for the university.

During the campaign of 1916 a number of irregularities were charged against him and his administration, but voters still returned him to office for a second term.

Subsequently, however, a Travis County grand jury indicted Ferguson on nine charges. The governor posted a $13,000 bond and went about his business until the speaker of the House of Representatives called a special legislative session to consider articles of impeachment.

There was no constitutional authority for such an act because the prerogative of calling a special session is reserved for the governor. However, Farmer Jim legitimized the speaker's action by announcing the session himself.

During Ferguson's first term in office several progressive reforms were passed, including state aid to rural schools and a compulsory school attendance law.

Before election to the governor's office, Ferguson was a relatively unknown Temple lawyer-businessman whose charismatic abilities on the speaker's platform quickly brought him political success. He gained wide support from the state's farm constituency by proposing a more equitable distribution of profit for tenant farmers.

War Gives Aviation a Boost in State

(1918-1919) The war effort has brought an unexpected dividend to the state of Texas—a series of Army bases used for training aviators.

San Antonio alone has three air bases. Kelly Field was opened in July 1917 as a training center for pilots and mechanics. Brooks Field trains instructors and aerial observers, and Wise Field is the site of an Army balloon school.

Houston, Fort Worth, Dallas, Waco, and Wichita Falls also are the sites of Army aviation schools.

All these bases are in addition to the regular Army training camps scattered throughout the state.

The primary object of the aviation camps is to prepare pilots for combat duty in Europe. Cadets receive from six to eight weeks of primary training and four weeks of advanced instruction.

By October 1917 Kelly Field, originally known as Camp Kelly, had become the largest flight-training school in the world. It is named for Lieutenant George E.M. Kelly, who was killed in an airplane crash at Fort Sam Houston.

Brooks Field, originally known as Gospert Field, was named for Lieutenant Sidney J. Brooks, a San Antonio native who was killed in an accident at Kelly Field.

Two aviation training facilities exist in Dallas—Camp Dick and Love Field. Fort Worth is home to Taliaferro Field, where aerial gunnery is taught. Rich Field is located in Waco, and Cale Field is at Wichita Falls.

Texas' aviation schools are providing many residents with their first view of aircraft.

The state has been favored by the government

as a site for military installations because of its mild climate and dry weather.

The largest training camp in the state is Camp Travis, located in San Antonio, also the site of three air bases.

Left: Army aviator candidates getting in shape at Camp Dick in Dallas

Bottom left: Employees of Steves Sash and Door Company manufacturing Alamo Airplane Propellers

Texan E.M. House—Key Figure at White House

(1918-1919) Colonel Edward M. House, the man whom President Woodrow Wilson left behind in Versailles to negotiate his 14-point peace plan, is no stranger to his fellow Texans.

He is, unquestionably, also one of the most powerful figures in the entire nation (certainly one of the most powerful figures not to hold a public office).

House has been a behind-the-scenes force in President Wilson's White House, although, by choice, he holds no title.

Colonel House was born in 1858, the son of a wealthy Houston banker. When he was sent to New Haven, Connecticut, to attend Hopkins Grammar School as a youth of 17, he became the close friend of the son of an Indiana senator. Through that connection the youthful House became acquainted with powerful persons in the government.

Upon the death of his father in 1880, House was left a considerable fortune that freed him from the daily rigors of earning a living. Settling in Austin, he rose in state political circles and become campaign manager for James S. Hogg and then became closely associated with the three governors who followed Hogg.

In 1911 House became friends with Woodrow Wilson, whose eyes already were on the presidency. The following year House was instrumental in gaining 40 votes from the Texas delegation for Wilson, an important factor in securing the presidential nomination. He also gained the support of William Jennings Bryan for Wilson.

Thereafter, with Wilson's election, House became the President's

confidante and principal advisor.

House is one of the five American commissioners at the Peace Conference.

Though he is known as a quiet, reserved man, his knowledge of public affairs is immense and his demeanor elicits great confidence.

Woodrow Wilson, pictured here with his cabinet, has chosen Colonel Edward M. House as his most trusted advisor.

Pecan Tree Chosen Texas' Official Tree

(1919) What more worthy state tree could there be than the stately pecan, chosen this year for that honor by the state legislature.

Pecans undoubtedly rank as the oldest crop to be harvested in the state, for they have been found in ancient geological formations. Early explorers commented on the huge pecan trees they found growing along Texas' rivers.

The federal government estimated this year that there were about 1.5 million pecan trees in Texas, but knowledgeable experts believe that figure is grossly understated and that there are from 8 million to 10 million pecan trees in the state.

Today Texas leads the nation in pecan production. Pecans have been exported from the state in commercial proportions at least since 1850, a year in which Galveston alone exported 1,525 bushels. By 1910 Texas pecan production was 5.8 million pounds.

Pecans are grown over a wide area of the state as well. In 1914 all but eight of the state's 254 counties reported the presence of pecan trees.

As those early explorers noted, the trees grow in profusion along streams, especially throughout the east timber belt and along the line of the caprock. They have been introduced into the plains country too.

J.H. Burkett, the Texas State Department of Agriculture's pecan specialist, estimates that this year some 15 million pounds of pecans will be produced, an amount that will fill about 500 railroad cars.

About three-fourths of the crop is exported to northern and eastern markets for use by shellers and candy makers.

One of Texas' first shellers was G.A. Duerler of San Antonio, who bartered with Indians for pecans. The Indians delivered the pecans to him in deerskins. At his shelling plant Duerler used railroad spikes to crush the outer shells and tow sack needles for picking out the "meat."

While pecan trees grow naturally and are not properly classified under agriculture, considerable attention now is being paid to pecan culture. Large orchards of improved trees are now growing in Smith, Dallas, Ellis, and Shelby counties.

Texas Moving Ahead in Mineral Resources

(1924) Figures for the full year of 1924 show that in a single decade the value of the annual production of minerals in Texas has increased by about 700 percent. The dollar value of this 1924 production was $268 million, up from $30 million 10 years earlier.

Texas now ranks sixth among all states in the value of its annual production, a significant increase from the 1914 ranking of 20th. This increase largely has been due to the development of petroleum resources, although by no means entirely.

Excluding petroleum, the U.S. Geological

El Paso's Southwestern Portland Cement Company

Survey estimates that the state has been producing an average of about $60 million annually in minerals for the past several years. These minerals include sulphur, coal and lignite, natural gas, quicksilver, silver, cement materials, brick, tile and pottery clays, granite, marble and a variety of stones, lime, graphite, gypsum, mineral waters, salt, silica, building sands and gravel, and fuller's earth.

The state also has a number of mineral deposits yet to be exploited: tin, borax, mica, asbestos, tungsten, opal, quartz, and molybdenum, to name just a few.

There is much hope that the iron beds of East Texas can be developed into a major industry. This also can be said of the potash beds of West Texas.

As for petroleum, Texas is one of the major producers of the world. It is the third-ranking state, and it produces more oil than any foreign country except Mexico.

"Ma" Ferguson Upholds Campaign Pledge

(1925) Miriam A. "Ma" Ferguson, elected to the governorship after a torrid race in which the Ku Klux Klan was a major issue, has honored the pledge she made during the campaign to prohibit the wearing of masks in public. The legislature agreed with her position, and the new law makes the wearing of a mask in a public place a criminal offense.

During the recent campaign Mrs. Ferguson defeated the Ku Klux Klan candidate, Felix Robertson of Dallas, in the primary run-off after a bitter race. Then, as expected, she beat the Republican contender in the fall general election.

One novel aspect of the race, unrelated to the Klan issue, was Mrs. Ferguson's use of stickers placed on automobile bumpers. "Me for Ma" was one of the slogans appearing. Some drivers added another phrase, "And I Ain't Got a Dern Thing Against Pa."

The campaign was viewed essentially as a referendum on the Ku Klux Klan, an organization whose power in Texas as well as in other Southern states has been immense. The Klan's defeat, however, perhaps signals a waning of the secret organization's influence because many residents have begun to question the wisdom of their vigilante tactics.

Governor Miriam "Ma" Ferguson

Southwest Conference Realigns Once Again

(1925) Once again, the Southwest Conference has realigned, this time leaving the athletic conference with six Texas schools and one from Arkansas.

Oklahoma A&M is the last of three Oklahoma members of the conference to withdraw, having done so in May 1925. In 1921 Phillip's University of Enid, Oklahoma, withdrew, and in 1920 the University of Oklahoma pulled out.

The Conference first was organized on May 6, 1914, at a meeting in Dallas. Original plans called for member schools to be from Texas, Oklahoma, Arkansas, and Louisiana. Louisiana State University was expected to represent that state, but failed to do so. Since the original organization, there has been considerable turnover in membership.

In May 1915 the first conference event, a track and field meet, was held in Austin at the University of Texas. Football competition began in the fall of 1915.

First president of the conference was W.T. Mather of the University of Texas.

Present members include the University of Texas, Texas A&M, Baylor, Rice, Texas Christian University, Southern Methodist University, and the University of Arkansas.

Port of Houston Growing Rapidly

(1925) Recent completion of Houston's 30-foot-deep ship channel linking the city to the Gulf of Mexico is reaping great financial dividends for the city.

The newly deepened channel is designed to accommodate the largest oceangoing vessels.

The volume of business for the fiscal year ending June 30, 1925, includes $273 million in exports and $9.4 million in imports, making the Port of Houston one of the chief shipping outlets in the entire nation. It is second in Texas only to Galveston, which during the same fiscal year shipped out $455 million in exports and brought in $23 million in imports.

As the new deep-water channel gradually was completed, over the past few years the increased volume of business made it evident that the ambitious, expensive, and long-term project would be a fine investment.

The 57-mile channel extends from Houston via Buffalo Bayou to the San Jacinto River and then to Galveston Bay. The depth at low tide is a minimum of 30 feet at all locations; the width of the channel varies from 150 to 250 feet. The turning basin at the end of the channel is 1,000 feet.

Of the $13.5 million spent in the channel-improvement project, some $10.6 million came from the federal government. The remaining amount came from navigation district bond issues.

As work progressed along the channel during the last several years, many large industries began developing along the banks. These included oil refineries, cement works, manufacturers of iron and steel products, flour mills, and other businesses. There are also warehouses and a large wharf frontage.

West Texas at Last Gets Its Own "A&M"

(1925, October 1) First classes are enrolling this fall at the new Texas Technological College, fulfilling a long-time dream of West Texans, who, since the 1890s, have been lobbying for creation of an institution of higher learning closer than the University of Texas or Texas A&M.

The Texas Tech campus is located in Lubbock on the High Plains. The site for the college is west of town on a site of just over 2,000 acres.

The struggle to get Texas Tech has been a long one. It originated in a belief that had arisen by 1915 that the difference in soil temperature and rainfall between West Texas and the more populous eastern portions of the state was sufficient to justify the establishment of an agricultural and mechanical college to serve that area. A formal movement began at Sweetwater in 1916 to establish such a college.

Consequently, the 35th Texas legislature authorized a "West Texas A&M," which was approved by Governor James E. Ferguson. In 1917 Ferguson announced that a locating board of five members had selected Abilene to be the site of the new college. But

Right: More than 20,000 witnessed the cornerstone laying ceremony for the Texas Tech Administration Building in Lubbock on November 11, 1923.

Below: The bill that led to the creation of Texas Tech was signed by Governor Pat Neff on February 10, 1923.

a controversy arose after three of the five committee members signed affidavits swearing that they had not voted for Abilene. In the ensuing dispute and after the impeachment of Governor Ferguson, the law to establish the college was repealed.

But hope for a new institution continued. When the West Texas Chamber of Commerce was created in 1918, one of that organization's top priorities was the establishment of the college. In 1921 the Texas legislature again approved a bill creating the college, but Governor Pat Neff vetoed it on the grounds that the state was not financially able to establish a new institution of higher learning. The initial reaction to his veto was a short-lived movement to declare West Texas a separate state.

The Chamber persevered, however, and the bill once again was passed in 1923. This time Governor Neff signed it into law.

The bill carried an initial appropriation of one million dollars.

When Lubbock was chosen by the new locating committee as the site for Texas Tech, some 10,000 West Texans joined the citizens of Lubbock in celebrating the achievement.

Dr. Paul Whitfield Horn is the college's first president, and some 1,000 students have enrolled in this fall's classes on the campus.

Texas' Exports Second Only to New York State

Men load cotton onto a ship for export.

(1930) Figures released for 1929 confirm what has been thought true now for several years—Texas is second only to New York State in value of its exports.

The total value of exports from the Lone Star State for 1929 amounted to $657 million, a figure considerably lower than the 1928 amount of $817 million.

The most valuable export for Texas (as has been the case for many decades) is cotton, a product greatly in demand for the spindles of Europe. But petroleum, wheat, lumber, rice, corn, cottonseed products, and sulphur also are important export items. In 1929 petroleum exceeded cotton products in total tonnage, 5.3 million to 1.3 million. Still, the value of the cotton products exported was far greater than petroleum.

Highly important in the state's export trade are its principal seaports: Houston, Galveston, Port Arthur, Beaumont, Corpus Christi, Freeport, Texas City, Orange, and Sabine Pass.

Houston now has surpassed Galveston in volume and value of exports and imports. In 1929 Houston exported 4.1 million tons valued at $302.6 million. Galveston exported 2.1 million tons valued at $276.7 million.

A newer port making great headway is that of Corpus Christi, only four years old but ranking next to Houston and Galveston as a cotton-shipping port.

Port Arthur and Beaumont, however, rank third and fourth behind Houston and Galveston in export tonnage.

Ironically, Corpus Christi is having to reclaim the honor of being a seaport of significance. A half century ago the city ranked as a seaport of considerable importance. In 1880, however, railroads were built across the Mexican border to connect with the port of Galveston, which had deepened its waters to accommodate larger vessels. Trade began to bypass Corpus Christi for Galveston.

Corpus Christi's then-neglected port gradually lost its importance. Now it is exporting cotton, crude oil, sulphur, and various manufactures.

Dad Joiner's Discovery Brings New Oil Rush

(1930) Columbus Marion "Dad" Joiner's predictions have come true, and the gusher that he brought in with his Daisy Bradford No. 3 well in Rusk County opens up a tremendous new oil field that will overshadow even the famed Spindletop.

Joiner, a veteran wildcatter working out of Dallas, defied the greatest oil exports with his insistence that a huge reservoir of oil lay beneath the Texas grounds. Then, after two "dry holes," he struck pay dirt with his third well on land leased from the widow Daisy Bradford.

His success has attracted scores of lease-hounds who have created the biggest leasing campaign in the history of the oil industry.

While cotton remains "king" in Texas because of so many people employed in its cultivation and processing, the annual value of petroleum in Texas surpassed cotton in 1929.

Dad Joiner's new well and all those around him promise to extend that figure by a significant amount.

Federation of Women's Clubs Urges Number of Reforms

(1930) The Federation of Women's Clubs, an organization composed of women's clubs from throughout the state, is recommending a broad program of social reform.

The women took aim, during their 1930 convention, at problems in the correctional and eleemosynary systems, urging modernization of the state prison system and the creation of an institution for the care, treatment, and safekeeping of the criminally insane.

Members also urged the state legislature to enact a more comprehensive compulsory attendance law for schoolchildren, a retirement system for teachers, and lump sum appropriations for state colleges.

When the Federation targets problems for correction or improvement, its record for success is noteworthy. Some of the laws that have come about, at least partly, as a result of the work of the organization include pensions for mothers, compulsory school attendance, child labor regulations, improved conditions for women in the work force, a system of state parks, county libraries, city zoning regulations, and women's suffrage.

Such serious concerns have been the business of the organization since the federation assumed its present form in Waco in 1897. In 1894 a number of the independent organizations had come together at the State Fair in Dallas as the Women's Congress. By 1901 some 135 clubs with a combined membership of 3,500 belonged to the federation.

In 1912 the federation urged the passage of laws giving women the freedom to enter into contracts. That same year discussion concerning women's suffrage was held, and in 1915 it was endorsed.

In addition to the resolutions of the 1930 annual meeting mentioned earlier, the Federation went on record as favoring a Texas centennial celebration, the naming of a poet laureate for Texas, a Texas State Museum, a driver's license law, and the exclusion from courtrooms of persons under 16 years of age who might hear testimony detrimental to their welfare.

Texas Leads Nation in Agriculture

(1931) Once again, as it has done for the past 11 years, Texas leads the entire nation in the total value of its agricultural crops.

Figures for 1930 show a total crop value of $434 million. Producing this amount were 496,007 farms with land totaling 31 million acres.

Declining prices place the 1930 value of Texas crops far below the $687 million average over the past decade.

Cotton, of course, is the state's leading crop. It represented 53 percent of 1930's total crop value. New crops, however, have been introduced in recent years. Especially noted here is the rapid growth of the citrus fruit industry in the lower Rio Grande Valley

and the truck crop industry in other South Texas regions.

Wheat now is being grown on a large scale in the Panhandle, and cotton has been extended to the South Plains area around Lubbock as well as the coastal region near Corpus Christi.

(In the South Plains area the spread of cotton in recent years has been remarkable. In 1916 the South Plains counties of Lubbock, Dawson, Lynn, Crosby, and adjacent ones were producing 2,000 to 3,000 bales each. In 1930 production in these counties was ranging from 40,000 to 50,000 bales.)

Even though Texas already leads the nation in agriculture, it still has more soil resources for expansion than any other state. The percentage of land in cultivation is just 18.4 percent of the state's 167.9 million acres.

While much of that unused acreage is unsuitable for cultivation, the presently cultivated area undoubtedly could be doubled and possibly even tripled.

Cotton's importance in the state can hardly be overstated. It is produced in 223 of the state's 254 counties, yet about one half of that annual production comes from just 35 to 40 counties.

The leading producing county in 1930 was Nueces.

Above: Hundreds of laborers picked cotton in the El Paso Valley during the 1930s.

Left: Sig Frucht, a leader in the Texas citrus industry known as the "Grapefruit Kid of Houston," poses amid his produce.

Williamson and Ellis counties are also known for producing prodigious quantities, and the record production for any county was made in 1920 in Williamson County with 168,509 bales.

A conservative guess by the *Texas Almanac* of 1931 states that 70 percent of Texas' population is dependent primarily upon cotton for a living.

In 1930 the Port of Houston led the entire nation in cotton exports, and the city's firm of Anderson, Clayton and Company was one of the largest cotton brokerage firms in the world.

Dallas Selected as Site for Texas Centennial

(1934, September 9) Dallas, an upstart city that had not even been founded when Texas gained its independence in 1836, has been chosen to be the host for the state's centennial observance in 1936.

The centennial committee, chaired by Cullen F. Thomas, announced its decision in Austin.

Dallas won the honor over the historic towns of San Antonio, site of the famous Alamo, and Houston, early capital of the Republic of Texas and namesake of Sam Houston.

On the first ballot Dallas received 13 votes to Houston's 8 and San Antonio's 6. On the third ballot Dallas won the unanimous vote of the committee.

Dallas' energetic bid to host the observance, which will amount to a world's fair, was led by a triumvirate of bankers: Robert L. Thornton of Mercantile National Bank, Fred Florence of Republic National Bank, and Nathan Adams of First National Bank.

In addition to offering the use of its state fairgrounds in East Dallas as the site for the exposition, Dallas submitted a monetary bid of $7.8 million dollars. This topped Houston's offer of $6.5 million and San Antonio's $3.8 million.

"We accept this honor in a spirit of humility and thankfulness," Robert L. Thornton said in his acceptance speech. "It is a heavy obligation. It will require all we have of strength, of cash and of credit to portray faithfully and adequately the century of achievement in this great empire of Texas."

In arguing on behalf of Dallas, Thornton had cited its central location, its abundant surrounding population, its experience in putting on huge state fairs, its excellent transportation facilities, its financial resources, the unification of its citizens in seeking the centennial, and its ample hotel accommodations.

Thornton said that a traffic check of U.S. Highway 80, which passes through Dallas in an east-west direction, revealed that 730,000 cars containing out-of-state guests already passed through Dallas every year.

As to the city's lack of history, Thornton said that the history of Texas should be viewed through economic progress made possible through the patriotic sacrifice of the state's founders."

Fred Florence of Republic National Bank was among the Dallas bankers responsible for securing the Texas Centennial Exposition for that city.

Centennial Closes Doors After Successful Run

(1936, November 29) Texas' and Dallas' special days in the nation's spotlight have ended with the closing of the Texas Centennial, but during its run of more than five months better than 6.3 million visitors attended the event.

Never before had the nation's news media paid so much attention to Texas or to Dallas.

The value of the event from a public relations standpoint, say city leaders, is incalculable.

An additional important effect of the Centennial, insofar as Dallas was concerned, was the fact that it defied the worst months of the Depression. In midsummer of 1936, as the Centennial opened after a burst of construction in Fair Park, City Manager Hal Moseley reported that the previous 12 months had seen "probably the most spirited building growth" in the city's recent history.

A consensus of businessmen interviewed by a *Dallas Morning News* reporter declared that the city generally had made more progress in the six months of the exposition than in all its previous existence.

Early estimates were that hotel business was up 35 percent; restaurant sales increased by 50 percent; wholesale sales ranged upwards from 22 to 40 percent; and local bank deposits soared.

One month after the Centennial opened, bank deposits in Dallas increased more than $30 million.

With all the favorable publicity coming from the nation's press, it seems that Dallas will never again view itself as a small town hoping to become something. Dallas has arrived.

From the wording on this pamphlet cover, it looks like Dallas is trying to attract out-of-state visitors to the Centennial Exposition.

A Total Quality Approach

PROGRESSIVE INSURANCE COMPANIES

Founders: Joseph M. Lewis and Jack H. Green
Founded: 1937 in Cleveland, Ohio
Principal: Peter Lewis, chairman of the board, president, and CEO

Most people rank dealing with insurance companies along with getting their teeth pulled. But the Progressive Insurance Companies are bringing something new to the scene: a consumer-driven view of how the automobile insurance industry should work.

"When you can get a pizza in 30 minutes and eyeglasses in an hour, we don't think you should have to wait two or three days when something serious like a car accident happens," says William Graves, president of the south-central division of Progressive.

Progressive sells automobile insurance, primarily coverage for people considered high risks by other companies. With corporate headquarters in Cleveland, Ohio, Progressive's south-central division is based in Austin, managing operations for Texas, Oklahoma, Arkansas, and Louisiana.

Half a continent away in 1988, California voters lashed out at the insurance industry with Proposition 103, setting profitability standards for insurers and calling for a rollback of insurance rates. While most companies vainly fought the reform effort in court, Progressive decided to change the way it does business.

"The typical process for handling auto insurance claims is that if you have an accident, you might call your agent, or you might call your company, and they'll put you in line," Graves explains. "And after a couple of days—or with some companies, weeks—they'll get back to you. To us, that's unacceptable customer service."

Viewing Proposition 103 as a wake-up call, Progressive responded with Immediate Response^{SM} claims service, 24 hours a day, every day.

"We're much more into the total-quality approach to business, which says you must exceed the customer's expectations all the time," Graves says. "We measure our response time in hours now. Our goal is to respond immediately."

Right and facing page: Progressive Insurance's Immediate Response^{SM} claims service is available 24 hours a day, every day.

Progressive also decided to take the nightmare out of shopping for auto insurance with its Express Quotes^{SM} rating service. Customers can get a quick comparison of rates by calling a toll-free number and giving an interviewer details that affect their rates, such as their age and driving record. The answers

are fed into a computer and the risks rated. Progressive then mails a list of auto insurance rates from the largest insurers in the area, tailored for the customer. California got the service first, with Texas and Florida set to have it soon.

"Progressive's auto insurance rating service is intended to answer the buyer's question: How can I find the cheapest insurance premium?" said consumer advocate Ralph Nader in an op-ed piece for the *New York Times*.

Nader himself may have had some influence on Progressive's growing preoccuption with pleasing consumers. One of his classmates from Princeton was Peter Lewis, who went on to become president and chief executive officer of Progressive.

The son of Joseph M. Lewis, who founded the company with Jack H. Green in 1937, Peter Lewis bought the company from Green in 1965 after his father's death. He is no typical insurance executive. A committed Democrat with a fondness for black Stetson hats and contemporary art, Lewis has dared to do business with customers deemed too risky by other companies. But since 1980 Progressive has consistently made money, proving that even people with blemished driving records can be insured profitably.

The company that Lewis' father co-founded with a $1,000 investment in 1937 is now the nation's 38th-largest property and casualty insurer, with $1.3 billion in revenues and 6,000 employees nationwide.

Progressive's Austin office opened in 1980 as a customer service branch. It became south-central division headquarters in 1986, and now has about 230 employees.

Graves, who has been division president since 1990, likes to foster an open and supportive environment in the workplace. Dress is casual, and communication is encouraged.

Progressive has empowered its employees to help solve problems once only solved by managers. The division's "Your Ideas Database" allows them to send electronic mail comments and suggestions to any of the top managers, who reply into the system for all to see.

Living up to its name, Progressive is moving forward. In 1990 it started selling standard and preferred auto coverage, a segment that represents about 80 percent of the auto insurance market. State Farm, Allstate, and other "household name" companies long have dominated this segment of the market. Now, Progressive is gearing up to go head-to-head with the big guys.

"With services like ours, we can compete with any company in the business," Graves says. "There's no reason why we won't become a much larger company very rapidly."

A Leader in Environmental Technology

SIMPSON PASADENA PAPER COMPANY

Founded: 1937 near Pasadena, Texas

From its beginning in 1890 as a tiny timber company in Washington, Simpson has grown into an international firm employing 7,500 people.

In 1937, 100 years after Texas won independence at the Battle of San Jacinto, a pulp mill started production on the Houston Ship Channel. Located at the edge of Pasadena and a few miles west of the San Jacinto battleground, the 154 acres is the site of the capture of Santa Anna, president of Mexico. Santa Anna was captured as he tried to flee General Sam Houston's victorious Texas Army. Markers tell of the capture as well as the burning of Vince Bayou bridge by "Deaf" Smith to delay the retreating enemy.

Purchased by Simpson Paper Company in January 1987, the mill was built by Champion International Corporation. Simpson changed the name to San Jacinto Mill to commemorate its historic location. The San Jacinto Mill manufactures more than 250,000 tons of bleached kraft pulp each year and close to 300,000 tons of fine coated and uncoated papers. Most of this paper is finished into rolls and about 80,000 tons a year into sheets. The papers are used in corporate communications, advertising materials, packaging, and other graphic arts applications.

Just three years after start-up, in 1940, a new machine was on-line and producing coated paper for *Life* magazine. Converting to uncoated grades in 1977, the machine is still producing 250 tons a day. A second paper machine began operation in the 1950s and contributes 160 tons a day of uncoated paper. Another, truly Texas-size, machine started up in 1965. It is 20 feet wide and 866 feet long. Running at 2,500 feet of paper per minute, it produces 400 tons of coated paper each day.

An integrated mill, San Jacinto starts with wood chips and produces 750 tons of bleached kraft pulp every day. The process includes cooking the wood, washing out the chemicals and residues, and bleaching the resulting pulp. Because there is more pulp than needed on the paper machines, the mill is able to market 250 metric tons of pulp produced daily. Water is removed from this excess pulp and the dried sheets are baled for shipment.

Historically, the mill has been an important presence in the state. When the mill's 300 employees started producing pulp on February 14, 1937, it was the first mill in the United States to use southern pine in the manufacture of paper. In more than 50 years of operation thousands have relied on the mill, with jobs provided not only locally, but throughout East Texas. More than half the state's 23 million acres of timberland are located in East Texas. More than a million tons of wood chips used by the San Jacinto Mill each year are supplied by the lumber and plywood operations and whole log chipping mills located in that part of the state.

The mill manufactures more than 250,000 tons of bleached kraft pulp and nearly 300,000 tons of fine coated and uncoated paper each year.

More than 1,000 employees make the San Jacinto Mill special. That special quality is also reflected in the many contributions they make to the community. The company regularly contributes to worthwhile nonprofit groups.

When a project to restore the San Jacinto Battle flag was proposed to the state legislature, Simpson felt it was appropriate to provide funding. Along with painstaking restoration of the original flag, four replicas were made as part of the project. To preserve the original flag, which hangs in the state capitol, one replica hangs in the capitol when the legislature is not in session. The other three replicas hang in the San Jacinto Museum of History at the battleground, the Pasadena City Hall, and at the San Jacinto Mill.

A leader in environmental technology, the San Jacinto Mill has invested in advanced facilities for chemical recycling and waste treatment. Simpson's environmental group in Pasadena is dedicated to protecting our environment. Also, an on-site research laboratory provides product development support and technical assistance.

When Simpson decided to expand to the Sunbelt, the firm was new to Texas but not to the industry. In 1890 Canadian logger Sol Simpson founded a company in Matlock, Washington, which has spread across the country. From its beginning as a tiny timber company with "50 men and 12 horses," Simpson has grown into an international company employing some 7,500 people in forest management, building products, pulp, paper, and plastic pipe operations in nine states.

Today Simpson operates three subsidiaries under a holding company, Simpson Investment Company of Seattle, Washington. The largest of the operating companies, Simpson Paper Company (SPCo), is headquartered in San Francisco, California. SPCo employs more than 4,000 people in the production of high-quality printing and writing papers, specialty papers, bleached and unbleached kraft wood pulp, and linerboard.

Simpson provided funding for the restoration of the San Jacinto Battle flag.

A Delicious Family Tradition

Right: Ninnie L. Baird began the company that still bears her name in 1908.

MRS BAIRD'S BAKERIES

Founder: Ninnie L. Baird
Founded: 1908 in Fort Worth

The equipment in Mrs Baird's Bakeries today is certainly more modern than when Ninnie L. Baird began baking bread in her wood-fired kitchen stove back in 1908, but the bread that carries her name is still baked with the same care.

Family pride spanning five generations has made Mrs Baird's Bakeries the largest family-owned and -operated bakery in the nation.

"There's a tremendous amount of heritage in this company," explains Allen Baird, board chairman of the Fort Worth-based bakery and Mrs. Baird's grandson. "Our family is as closely involved in the business today as when Grandmother started it."

In fact, the Baird family was inducted into the Texas Business Hall of Fame in 1992, the first time an entire family was recognized. Baird family members lead company management today, ranging from Mrs. Baird's grandsons to a great-great-grandson.

It has always been that way at Mrs Baird's Bakeries. Mrs. Baird first baked just for her large family. That changed in 1908, when her husband became ill. Widowed at age 39, she began baking to support her eight children.

"All she knew was that she had to take care of her family," says her grandson. "That was her driving force. Heading a major bakery was never in her mind."

Mrs. Baird's children helped from the start. Her oldest son helped bake and his three brothers delivered their mother's bread after school—on foot at first, then by bicycle, and later in the family buggy as the business grew.

She started baking in her wood-fired kitchen stove, but soon bought a second-hand commercial oven capable of baking 40 loaves at once. Baking was centered in a small building behind her home until 1919, when she moved the growing company into a 30-foot by 72-foot plant. In 1928 Mrs. Baird opened a bakery in Dallas, her first outside Fort Worth.

The company currently has nine bread bakeries throughout Texas (located in Fort Worth, Dallas, Lubbock, Abilene, Waco, Austin, Houston, San Antonio, and Victoria) plus a cake bakery in Fort Worth and a pie bakery in Abilene. Altogether, Mrs Baird's Bakeries makes 150 varieties of breads and cakes.

Most of the bakeries have deep community roots. "People feel we are their local bakery in each market we serve," says Allen Baird. "Often, their grandparents were raised on Mrs Baird's bread and so were they and their own children. They have a relationship with us and we take that trust very seriously."

He is especially proud of the company's newest bakery in Fort Worth, the nation's most modern, which opened in 1992. "There's technology in that bakery not in any other bakery in the country," he says. "The process is totally computer controlled to produce the perfect loaf of bread, from the moment the ingredients are placed in the mixer to the end when the loaf of bread comes off the bagging

The company's fleet of delivery trucks, circa 1938.

Mrs. Baird's sons delivered their mother's bread after school in the family buggy.

machine. The only place a human hand ever touches the bread is hand-twisting."

That deft hand twisting of two pieces of dough into one is one of the secrets of Mrs Baird's home-baked taste. Baird explains that twisting the dough elongates its cell structure, improving the bread's texture and keeping qualities. "It's that gentle motion of the hands of a skilled twister that gives our bread that extra Mrs Baird's quality," he continues.

Mrs Baird's also bakes with other time-honored techniques often foregone today, techniques that ensure a silky texture, better flavor, and wonderful aroma. Many bakeries dump all ingredients into their mixers in a single step and skip the initial rising stage, for example. At Mrs Baird's Bakeries, flour, water, yeast, and yeast food are mixed to make a "sponge" that is allowed to rise naturally, then the sponge is mixed with the remaining ingredients to make dough. After the dough is cut into half-loaf pieces, it is flattened—much as Mrs. Baird used to do with her rolling pin—then formed into long rolls, two of which are hand twisted to become a single loaf that then rises fully.

Although each Mrs Baird's bakery turns out 75,000 loaves of bread daily, it takes a full eight hours to make each loaf. "We don't want to rush the process," Baird explains. "We take our time making the bread and do our rushing in delivery so that what we baked last night is on the shelf this morning." Each Mrs Baird's bakery serves communities no farther than three hours away to make certain that products arrive fresh.

Mrs. Baird watched as the bakery she began in her kitchen grew into a Texas institution, dying in 1961 at age 92. Even after turning over day-to-day operations to her grown sons, she actively guided the company's growth. Later she made sure her grandchildren, one after the other, worked in the bakery

Mrs. Baird began baking to support her eight children and her business grew steadily.

during school breaks to "learn what it meant to get that loaf in the bag," recalls Baird.

With three generations now active in company management, the warm aroma of freshly baked bread and cakes will continue wafting through the kitchens of countless Texas homes. "The family name is on our products," Baird says. "All of us are doing our utmost to continue the family tradition of baking the best-tasting products possible."

An Industry Leader

CONTINENTAL AIRLINES, INC.

Founder: Walter Varney
Founded: 1934

Continental Airlines has called Houston home for more than a decade, with both its corporate headquarters and a substantial hub in the bayou city on the Gulf Coast. During these turbulent times for the airline business as a whole, Continental has emerged as a recognized leader in the industry, ranking among the top competitors both domestically and internationally.

Continental Airlines officially became a Texas corporation in a merger with Texas International Airlines in 1982. Yet this company is a "native son" in the truest sense, with roots that stretch back to the very first flight of what was to become the Continental Airlines known today.

On July 15, 1934, a tiny Lockheed Vega took off from El Paso, Texas, bound for Pueblo, Colorado. This was the inaugural flight of Varney Speed Lines, a company that existed mainly to carry mail under a contract from the U.S. Postal Service. Nonetheless, founder Walter Varney promoted passenger service on the little Vega, which could seat five people. That first flight carried only 100 letters, but marked the beginning of the company that would evolve into Continental Airlines.

In 1937, with the purchase of three heavily mortgaged Lockheed twin-engine planes, the company officially became Continental Airlines, based in Denver. In the years until—and throughout—the war, Continental continued a pattern of slow and steady expansion. In the fiscal year that ended June 30, 1944, the amount of mail carried had more than quadrupled in the previous four years. More important, Continental had carried 51,800 passengers, compared to only 11,400 four years before, and passenger revenue was greater than revenue from mail contracts for the first time.

In the prosperous postwar years Continental added more planes, the first jets, and expanded into international service. This pattern of steady, continuous growth quickly promoted Continental from a regional airline into the top ranks of passenger airlines in the United States.

Perhaps nothing so changed the industry as the Airline Deregulation Act of 1978, which created the atmosphere for a tumultuous decade to follow. Gone were the complicated procedures for route allocations, and in the ensuing free-for-all Continental faced serious market erosion. The airline was approached for takeover by Texas Air Corporation, parent company of Texas International Airlines, and stockholders

The El Paso postmaster swears in Varney Speed Lines' first pilot, Jesse Hart, on July 15, 1934.

officially approved the merger on July 13, 1982, retaining the Continental name.

Texas International Airlines had carved its place in the Texas market and was perhaps best known for "Peanuts fares," deeply discounted rates that competing airlines were forced to match. The merger brought synergy on some fronts, but finances were such that in September 1983 the airline filed to reorganize itself under Chapter 11 bankruptcy laws. It was a desperate measure, but without it the airline, which had such a proud and distinguished history, might have ceased to exist.

The startling financial step notwithstanding, Continental Airlines battled back in the 1980s, coming out of reorganization in 1986. The decade also brought mergers with PeoplExpress, Frontier, and New York Air. The Gulf War and ensuing fuel price inflation forced the airline into another reorganization—and out again—in 1993. Few companies are capable of surviving such dramatic changes in an industry, coupled with the blending of a number of disparate corporate cultures into one whole. The strength of Continental today speaks volumes for its employees, their determination, and public support.

Out of that experience has come Continental's corporate vision: to be recognized as the best airline in the industry by customers, employees, and shareholders. That vision is built on key corporate values of safety, integrity, commitment, caring, and quality. Continental has recognized that critical factors for success include a customer-driven culture with higher-quality service than the competition. With that comes the recognition that employee treatment determines customer treatment and that employees require appropriate support and the commitment of resources.

This vision has fueled exciting new services that are bringing fundamental change to Continental and having repercussions industry-wide. Foremost among them is a new short-route program introduced in October 1993 and internally code-named CALite.

Since deregulation, airlines have operated around the hub system in a major city. Planes fly into the hub and wait there as passengers from other flights arrive, and then connect to travel to other cities. The CALite program represents a fundamental change in the way the system works and gives passengers more point-to-point service at lower, sim-

Above: After Continental and Texas International merged operations in 1982, the new airline retained the Continental name and set up its headquarters in Houston.

Top left: A Continental jet takes off over Houston's distinctive skyline. Continental's hub at Houston Intercontinental has 342 daily departures.

Left: In 1993 Continental placed orders for $4 billion worth of new Boeing aircraft as part of its fleet revitalization program.

Continental is one of Houston's largest employers, with nearly 8,000 employees. Worldwide, Continental employs more than 40,000 people, including 4,000 pilots, 6,000 flight attendants, and 5,000 mechanics.

plified fares.

CALite provides service between cities within two hours' distance or less. This point-to-point service enables planes to turn around much faster at their destinations. Whereas the old system might call for a plane to wait at a gate for almost an hour, Continental's goal with CALite is to trim 30 minutes or more from that figure. Turning planes around in 20 minutes or less generates a tremendous boost in productivity. From the airline's standpoint, that productivity provides the airline with more options and more flexibility.

That turnaround also means more flexibility for the customer as the number of flights in the market increases. In some cities, which might have had one or two flights per day, CALite has increased that number to six or seven.

Coupled with better and faster service are cheaper fares, which Continental has called Peanuts Fares. An average of 50 to 80 percent lower than usual market fares, Peanuts Fares are the result of more efficient operations.

These advantages fuel the program as they generate more business. The attractive fare structure means that those people who might stay home and phone, or plan a trip by car, can now fly instead. In its first month of operation in its first 15 cities, CALite boarded 350,000 passengers. Continental Airlines

Continental maintains the highest training standards in the aviation industry. This high-tech 737 flight simulator is located at Houston Intercontinental Airport.

plans to continue expansion of this service and has taken a giant leap over its competitors in recognizing that the time for operational changes had come.

Just as CALite is changing the look of the short trip, another innovative, customer-oriented service, BusinessFirst, is changing longer flights.

Continental first looked at the transoceanic market and discovered that first-class service was under-utilized while business class was in demand, if not completely satisfactory. BusinessFirst is the merger of these two classes into one, a distinctive program that combines the quality of first-class service with the competitive pricing of business class. Today BusinessFirst is available on both transoceanic and some transcontinental flights.

In a major commitment to service and quality, Continental Airlines has reconfigured the front cabins of its aircraft. Gone is the middle seat, which provides a 55-inch seat pitch (well above the industry average of 40 inches) and more comfort and privacy. In its place, aircraft have been refitted with electronic sleeper seats. The seats have adjustable headrests, electronic leg rests, and lumbar support. Each comes fitted with a personal entertainment system offering a variety of choices on an individual screen, and each arm rest contains a digital control unit for music or news. The executive meal option allows flexibility in dining before or after regular meal service.

BusinessFirst has been a tremendous success in every route introduced and has been ranked first in international business flights by both *Traveler* and *Entrepreneur* magazines.

Continental Airlines now serves well over 100 airports in the United States and internationally. It has expanded service within the immediate region to include all the nations of Central America, and is poised to take the lead in growing markets. Continental Airlines and its subsidiaries have a commitment to the more than 40,000 people employed around the world. The corporate headquarters and operations in Houston make the organization one of the city's largest employers.

Continental Airlines stands poised for the challenges of the next century. In a tumultuous industry that has been turned upside down in recent years, Continental has emerged not only as a tough competitor but a leader in service, both personal and visionary, knowing what the customer wants and being able to deliver it.

Left: The introduction of Peanuts Fares in October 1993 signaled a new era of leadership for Continental Airlines. The Continental Peanuts system expanded in 1994, while major competitors were still planning similar programs.

Below: Luxurious new BusinessFirst service, launched in 1992, represents another way Continental is leading the aviation industry into the 1990s and beyond.

The Emergence of Modern Texas

1940 - 1963

These momentous years, 1940 to 1963, began on the eve of American entry into World War II. They ended with the tragic assassination of an idealistic young President on the streets of Dallas, the impact of which was felt the world over. Surely no similar period in history brought more change to the world. Texas was no exception. It quickly shed its historically agrarian roots and became unmistakably urban and industrial.

At the beginning of the period more than half of all Texans, 55 percent of them, lived in rural areas. Just two decades later that figure had dropped to 25 percent, with three out of four Texans living in urban areas. A gradual transition toward urbanization had been underway since the *turn of the century, as had been true for the nation, but in no comparable period in Texas had the changes come so rapidly and dramatically. They represented far more than farmers merely moving to the city, although that was a part of it.*

Between 1940 and 1960 the state's population increased by almost 50 percent. The additional 3.1 million residents in Texas were positioning themselves where the jobs were—in the cities.

The number of farms in Texas between 1945 and 1960 dropped sharply, more than 40 percent, down from 385,000 in number to 227,000. Those farms remaining were bigger in acreage.

Familiar rural communities centered around little white schoolhouses withered away entirely. The one-room schools, once centers for community life, consolidated with larger school districts. Towns, which on Saturdays had attracted crowds of shirt-sleeved farmers who socialized on the streets and shopped for supplies, dwindled too. Farmers started going to big cities such as Dallas, or Houston, or Waco.

Despite laments for an era gone forever, the overall picture for modern Texas agriculture was a bright one. In size and variety of agricultural output, Texas was second only to California. Agricultural revenue was divided about equally between crops and livestock and their products. Texas' cotton crop remained unequaled anywhere. It continued to account for 10 to 20 percent of the world's total production.

Texas not only had the largest livestock production of any state, it was also the most diversified. It led all others in number of cattle, beef cattle, goats, sheep, and horses. It led all others, too, in wool and mohair production.

All this seemed diminished, though, with the rise of industry and manufacturing, whose origins were in serving agriculture with cotton gins, cottonseed oil mills, meat packing plants, farm implements and transportation equipment. Then had come a second industrial stage ushered in by oil. Now arose still another industrial era, that of "brain-powered industries"—petrochemical plants and aerospace and electronics industries. In 1962 Dallas became the first metropolitan area in the southern half of the nation, aside from Los Angeles, to employ more than 100,000 persons in manufacturing. Texas industry and manufacturing were vital parts of the nation's economic well-being.

The state's love affair with aviation had paid off. Airports, especially at Dallas and Houston, were busy each day with direct flights to cities all over the nation. By 1963 Texas was fourth in the nation in the number of enplaned air passengers. Dallas alone enplaned more passengers than any of 36 states in the calendar year of 1961, a typical year.

Beyond aviation was space exploration. "Space City, U.S.A." was none other than Houston, where the National Aeronautics and Space Administration built a huge complex to guide the nation's expensive probes into the next frontier. By mid-1963 NASA was pouring one million dollars a month into the Houston area economy.

In the nation's capital, Texans spoke with powerful voices. Lyndon B. Johnson, who as a young Congressman had been one of Franklin D. Roosevelt's favorites, now sat in the oval office of the White House as President of the nation. Sam Rayburn of Bonham was in the midst of a long reign as Speaker of the House.

Yet, the absolute dominance that Democrats had wielded in the state for so long seemed destined to end. When Johnson left his Senate seat to become John F. Kennedy's Vice President, a special election was held for his seat. The winner was a Republican, John Tower, a political science professor at Midwestern University in Wichita Falls, whose conservatism reflected a growing tendency in state politics.

This era also saw an end to another age—that period in which the state's minorities quietly accepted their status as second-class citizens. The war fought to safeguard the American democratic way of life had caused many of them to question the artificial boundaries that denied them equal participation in enjoying the benefits of their own country. Before the war ended many of them had begun to press for change through the courts, and two of the most important Supreme Court decisions advancing their cause originated in Texas.

First came the struggle to gain the vote. The 1944 Texas case Smith v. Allwright, *saw the U.S. Supreme Court outlaw the Democratic Party of Texas' all-white primary. As a result, Negroes could participate in the all-important primary elections.*

This was followed by another Texas case decided by the U.S. Supreme Court, Sweatt v. Painter, *1950, in which the segregated law school at the University of Texas was ordered to admit a black postal worker. This case clearly paved the way to the 1954 decision,* Brown v. Topeka, *which introduced a new era into American life by declaring that separate but equal facilities were inherently inferior and unconstitutional.*

President John F. Kennedy's administration, a time marked by growing fermentation in the matter of civil rights with profound implications for the nation and the world, tragically ended in Dallas on November 22, 1963.

Facing page: Ground was broken for the Harris County Domed Stadium (known also as the Houston Astrodome) on January 3, 1962. It was the first of the indoor stadiums. Courtesy, Houston Metropolitan Research Center, Houston Public Library

B-24 bombers undergo construction in Fort Worth during the World War II years. Courtesy, Lockheed Fort Worth Company

During the Second World War women working in defense plants comprised a large portion of the work force. These "Rosie the Riveters" are constructing B-24s in Fort Worth. Courtesy, Lockheed Fort Worth Company

Women played a major role in the war effort as is evident in this view taken inside a Fort Worth B-24 plant. Courtesy, Lockheed Fort Worth Company

The U.S. Navy ran a Flight Preparatory School at the University of Texas for naval aviation cadets. Courtesy, The Center for American History, The University of Texas at Austin, Prints & Photographs Collection

A confetti-covered Dallas street makes a fitting setting for soldiers, sailors, and female residents celebrating VJ-Day in 1945. Courtesy, Texas/Dallas History and Archive Division, Dallas Public Library

Above: Braniff International serviced the Houston area in the 1950s from Houston International Airport. Courtesy, Houston Metropolitan Research Center, Houston Public Library

Right: Mack H. Hannah, Jr., the first black to own and operate a savings and loan association in Texas, was also active at Texas Southern University. Courtesy, Institute of Texan Cultures

Top right: KLVL was the first Spanish-language radio station to serve the Mexican-American community of Houston. These KLVL luminaries are celebrating the station's sixth anniversary in 1962. Courtesy, Houston Metropolitan Research Center, Houston Public Library

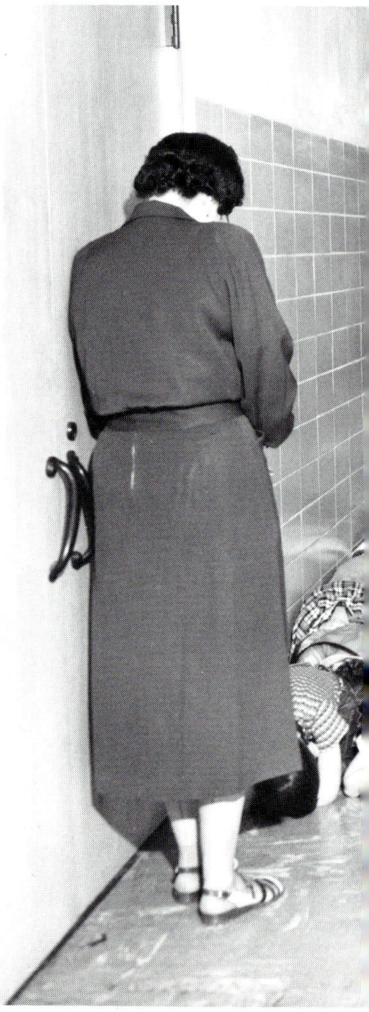

In the 1950s, living in fear of an atomic bomb attack, schoolchildren were made to "duck and cover" in the school hallway in an effort to "protect" themselves from deadly radiation. Courtesy, Texas/Dallas History and Archive Division, Dallas Public Library

HAPPY BIRTHDAY
SIXTH Anniversary
HAPPY BIRTHDAY
KLVL
1480KC
MORALES
KLVL
1480KC
MORALES

Texas' Future Bright Despite Grim Depression

(1940) Depression decade or not, the new 1940 census population figures show a bright, expanding future for the Lone Star State.

Texas' 1940 population has been established at 6.4 million, a 10.1 percent increase over the 1930 figure.

The density of the population, 24.4 per square mile, is only a little more than half the density of the population of the United States, leaving considerable room for expansion. The prevalence of fertile soils, minerals, plant and animal life, and favorable weather conditions seem to assure a great future.

The state has the natural resources to support a great industrial movement in the years ahead, and the growing tendency to withdraw essential industries from the Atlantic and Pacific seaboards suggests even more promise. Indeed, the state's central location within the continent and its numerous warm-water ports augur well.

Even though the state's population grew 10.1 percent in the 1930s, a rate greater than the nation's 7.2 percent, this was the state's smallest 10-year growth rate in history. Moreover, in rank, Texas dropped from fifth to sixth among the 48 states, trailing New York, Pennsylvania, Illinois, Ohio, and California.

Still, because of the many advantages cited, the future of Texas is bright indeed.

Number of Farmers in State Declining

(1940) Texas long has been recognized as a state where farmers have dominated the economy and the culture—and the population, as well. But that situation appears to be changing.

The 1940 census reflects the fact that the state is becoming more and more urban.

The new figures reveal that rural dwellers constitute 54.6 percent of the population and urban dwellers 45.4 percent. Ten years ago the rural population represented 59 percent of the population; 30 years ago the figure was 75.9 percent.

Seen in another way, the overall rural population grew during the decade by just 2 percent while the urban population jumped at a 21.8 percent rate.

Many farmers, especially tenant farmers, migrated to the cities during the 1930s in search of higher-paying jobs.

The growing urban nature of the state is reflected also by the fact that four Texas cities now are ranked in the top 50 cities of the nation in population—Houston is 21st; Dallas, 31st; San Antonio, 36th; and Fort Worth, 46th.

36th Infantry Division Serving as Occupation Force

(1945) Texas' own 36th Infantry Division, so accustomed to answering Uncle Sam's call in times of crisis, now has taken on another new assignment with the end of hostilities. Its new role: to stay in Europe and serve as an occupation force over conquered Germany.

The 36th, part of Texas' National Guard, compiled an outstanding record of achievement following its mobilization at Camp Bowie into the U.S. Army on November 25, 1940.

After training in Texas, Louisiana, and Florida, the 36th became the first American division to set foot in Europe, landing at Salerno, Italy, on September 9, 1943. The division then worked its way up through intense combat into France and into Germany. Enormous casualties were suffered.

A widely circulated photograph showed a group of 36th infantryman in Italy "hitch-hiking" behind a sign that read, "5,872 miles to Austin, Texas."

At the end of the war the troops found themselves not in Austin but in Austria.

During its 19 months of combat, the division suffered 27,343 casualties—3,974 dead, 19,052 wounded, and 4,317 missing in action. This amounted to the third-highest casualty list of any American division in the entire war.

Famous war correspondent Ernie Pyle, later to die himself from a sniper's bullet, traveled with the 36th Division and wrote probably his most famous column about a Texan, Captain Henry Waskow of Belton, who was killed on Mount Sammucro in December 1943.

World War II was not the first time that the Texas division had distinguished itself in combat. Its service in the First World War was widely praised for heroism. The division, organized in 1917 from various Texas National Guard units, arrived in France in 1918. During only 23 days of combat, it suffered 2,601 casualties, an indication of the fierceness in which the soldiers found themselves suddenly thrust.

Among the cited accomplishments in the First World War for the 36th was the freeing of Rheims.

Texans Distinguish Themselves in War

(1945) Texans throughout the years have been fierce partisans for whatever cause in which they have believed, and World War II has proven to be no exception.

A number of individual Texans have distinguished themselves with their valor during this worldwide conflict, ranging from a black sailor to a small-town infantryman to the chief of naval operations.

The young black sailor, Doris Miller of Waco, was awarded the Navy Cross in 1942 because of his heroic actions aboard the U.S.S. *West Virginia*. Miller, whose target practice as a youth had consisted of shooting squirrels in the Brazos River bottoms, was beneath the deck when Japanese dive bombers attacked the U.S.S. *West Virginia*.

Miller hurried to the deck and relieved a wounded machine-gunner. Before the battle was over, he had brought down four Japanese bombers. Later, Miller was killed.

Appreciative Waco citizens named their YMCA center in his honor.

The small-town infantryman, Audie Murphy, became the most decorated American of any war. Murphy, a slight lad from Farmersville in northeast Texas, had tried to enlist in the Marines and the paratroopers at age 16. He carried barely 100 pounds on his five-foot-seven-inch frame, and he was rejected.

At the age of 18, though, he was accepted by the U.S. Army. He served in nine major campaigns. Besides his numerous American medals, Murphy was decorated by the French, British, and Belgian governments. He won every American combat citation except the Asiatic-Pacific service ribbon.

Still another distinguished Texan came from the officer ranks. Admiral Chester W. Nimitz of Fredericksburg, who graduated from Annapolis in 1905, was commander of the Pacific Fleet. Admiral Nimitz, from a pioneer central Texas family of German descent, was aboard the U.S.S. *Missouri* when the Japanese surrendered.

And one mustn't forget that Dwight David Eisenhower, commander of the D-Day forces, was born in Denison, Texas.

Admiral Chester Nimitz

Texas Leads Nation in Military Training

(1945) The end of the war provides an opportunity to reflect on the great role played by the state of Texas in winning the peace through military might.

No state in the union was home to a wider range of activity in the training of men for combat.

An estimated 1,250,000 servicemen in all branches of the military trained in Texas, including more than 20 combat Army divisions.

Fifteen posts and camps were in operation for this purpose at the height of activity.

Beyond that, the military also operated 21 prisoner of war camps in Texas.

Year-round climatic conditions and accessibility to a wide range of terrain made the state ideal for training operations.

The favorable climate and vast expanses of flat terrain were especially conducive to the training of pilots, navigators, and bombardiers.

Figures available from January 1, 1942, to May 1, 1944, reveal that Texas installations trained 44,958 pilots, 12,534 bombardiers, and 12,706 navigators. At the peak of operations there were more than 40 airfields and air stations in the state.

Navy installations

Under simulated combat conditions, men install airplane engines at Amarillo Army Air Force Base.

Above: Men and women are hard at work in the Bergstrom Army Air Field machine shop.

Right: Lubbock Army Air Field

included the world's largest naval air training facility at Corpus Christi, a complex that covered 20,000 acres.

While many of the Texas trainees were from other states in the union, an estimated 750,000 Texans served in the war. Most of these, 542,000, donned the khaki of the U.S. Army. An estimated 185,000 served in the Navy, Marine Corps, and Coast Guard.

Not to be overlooked are the 12,000 Texas women who served in the military.

A preliminary survey shows that more than 30 Texans in the Army won the Congressional Medal of Honor.

Six Texans received the Navy's highest award, the Medal of Honor.

Either born in Texas or having lived in the state for some time were 155 Army generals, including Dwight D. Eisenhower.

Texas soldiers suffered 15,764 fatalities, or 4.72 percent of the Army's war dead.

Texas casualties in the Navy totaled 7,258.

Texas Raises First U.S. Crop of Silk

(1945) Silk-raising for centuries has been the domain of the Orient. Eighty-five percent of the world's supply comes from Japan and China. That may be changing, however, if an ambitious group of Texans from Mineral Wells has its way.

In September it produced the first big commercial crop of silk ever raised in the United States.

A group of Mineral Wells businessmen joined together to launch the enterprise and, to make the endeavor profitable, they used a new machine invented by an American that automatically unreels raw silk from cocoons.

Silk, as most schoolchildren know, is produced by silkworm moths that dine on mulberry leaves.

The Texas silkworm moths produce enough cocoons so that a new crop of silk may be gathered every 45 days.

The eggs (about one ounce of them, or 30,000 in number) that become worms that become moths will eat about 1,500 pounds of mulberry leaves by the time they reach worm maturity. That takes a lot of mulberry leaves: 1,500 pounds.

To produce this amount of leaves, the Mineral Wells businessmen have 130,000 mulberry trees. They expect to produce 40,000 pounds of silk next season.

A hosiery plant is beginning operations in Mineral Wells to use the silk.

U.S. Judge Orders Admission of Negro to U.T.

(1946, November) A U.S. district judge has ordered that the University of Texas law school admit its first Negro. He is Heman (yes, Heman, *not* Herman) Sweatt, a 34-year-old letter carrier who lives in Houston. However, the University of Texas has been given six months to create a separate but equal law school for Negroes.

Judge Roy C. Archer suspended his ruling for that period of time.

Thurgood Marshall of the National Association for the Advancement of Colored People argued that Sweatt should be admitted right away to the university, and he promised to appeal the six-month suspension of the ruling.

Marshall said it would be impossible for the state to create a separate law school for Negroes equal to the U.T. school. "It would have to have 65,000 law books and it could not get them by Feb. 1," he said. "It would have to have ten full professors and four associate professors to have a school equivalent to the University of Texas law school."

Heman Marion Sweatt was finally allowed to register for classes at the University of Texas

When Sweatt applied to the law school a year ago U.T. President T.S. Painter referred the matter to the state attorney for a ruling. Attorney General Grover Sellers denied Sweatt's right to be enrolled, observing that segregation is widely established in the state. He said that Sweatt "will never darken the door of the University of Texas."

Supporters of Sweatt have been holding rallies to support his cause. Well-known English professor J. Frank Dobie and Dr. Frederick Eby of the education department are among those supporting Sweatt's admission.

Steel Industry to Return; State Booming Everywhere

(1947, April) The industrial revolution that is changing the very nature of the Lone Star State soon will include, for the first time in peace, the steel industry.

A consortium of state entrepreneurs, led by John W. Carpenter, has put together $8.5 million to purchase Lone Star Steel's blast furnace and plant, built by the federal government during the war but closed down with the end of hostilities.

Officials in Washington, D.C., are expected to approve the deal in early April. If so, Carpenter predicts that the first steel will be shipped from the Daingerfield plant in a matter of weeks.

The new enterprise is just another in a growing number of developments that are transforming Texas from being a cattle, cotton, and oil state into one that is a leader among the industrial states.

The state's industrial revolution may be said to have begun in 1934 when American Cyanamid Company built a $7-million alkali plant in Corpus Christi. Others, attracted by the region's raw materials—lime, sulfur, salt, sea water, gypsum, etc.—soon followed American Cyanamid's move to the Texas Gulf Coast.

The war brought expansion into the synthetic rubber industry, and the war's end did not signal a decline in this endeavor.

In the next few years some $300 million is expected to be spent on chemical and industrial investments, which will add up to some $1.5 billion invested in the state since 1940.

DuPont spent some $60 million on new plants; Dow, over $35 million; Monsanto, $11 million; and Celanese, $7 million.

Concomitant with this phenomenon is the awakening of once-slumbering towns into thriving centers of industry. Borger, a small town in the Panhandle, has become the nation's number one producer of carbon black. Taylor in Central Texas has developed one of the nation's largest bedding factories. Orange, a small town near Beaumont, has a new $52-million DuPont nylon salts plant.

Signs of the new age are nowhere more evident than in the state's largest city, Houston. Already the center of oil fields and refineries before the war, the Houston area now boasts some 20 percent of the nation's synthetic-rubber plants and 145 major chemical plants. New installations continued unabated after the war, and the skyline is being dramatically altered with new skyscrapers.

Television Makes Debut in Southwest

(1948) Fort Worth's WBAP-TV became the Southwest's first television station when it began broadcasting Monday, September 27.

Its introduction came through a televised speech by President Harry S Truman, whose visit to Fort Worth persuaded the station to begin broadcasting two days earlier than previously scheduled.

The first picture televised over the airwaves showed a crowd of spectators just west of the speaker's platform at the T&P Terminal Building in the south part of downtown.

The broadcast lasted just 49 minutes.

Two days later WBAP-TV began its regular broadcasts. Station founder Amon G. Carter and station director Harold Hough were the first speakers. That evening's program concluded with a local news show, "The Texas News," under the guidance of news director James A. Byron.

Early programming is scheduled to be about 15 hours a week, but that figure is expected to increase soon.

While Fort Worth's station is the first in the Southwest, other stations already are planned for Dallas, Houston, and San Antonio.

WBAP-TV is owned and operated by Carter Publications, Inc., publisher of the *Fort Worth Star-Telegram.*

Broadcasts from the station will cover Dallas as well as Fort Worth.

Texas Senate Candidate Goes to Air for Campaign

(1948) Politics in Texas always is surprising, but the current senate runoff campaign between Democrats Lyndon Baines Johnson and Coke R. Stevenson has introduced a new element in campaigning.

Reaching voters across the vast expanse that is Texas always has been difficult, but campaigner Johnson, a 39-year-old New Dealer who has moved his political views toward the right, has begun traversing the state in a helicopter.

It is believed to be the first time a political campaigner anywhere has used the helicopter.

The uniqueness of the helicopter landings has brought out large, excited crowds, eager to see the 'copter, many of them no doubt seeing one for the first time.

They hear Johnson's message of "peace, preparedness and progress," a message that places him to the left of the ultraconservative Stevenson, a former governor.

Johnson is still the underdog in the run-off primary election, but his youth and his ability to draw crowds is boosting his chances.

The winner of this Democratic run-off is expected to win the fall general election against a Republican opponent.

Johnson, who was elected to Congress as an ardent supporter of Franklin D. Roosevelt in the 1930s, also made good use of the helicopter in the primary. He made 375 landings.

Starting from far behind the popular Stevenson, Johnson managed to gain his run-off spot even though he trailed Stevenson by 457,000 to 293,000 votes. The presence of other candidates prevented Stevenson from gaining a majority of the votes cast.

Lyndon B. Johnson and wife Claudia Alta Taylor Johnson ("Lady Bird") prepare to take off for their Texas ranch.

Eisenhower Carries State Over Democrats

(1951, November) For the second time in history, a Republican rather than a Democratic presidential candidate has carried the state.

GOP candidate Dwight David Eisenhower, supported by a large number of conservative Democrats who bolted the party rather than vote for Adlai Stevenson, won in Texas by a vote of 1,102,878 to 970,128. He will be inaugurated as President of the United States in January 1952.

Eisenhower, himself a native Texan who was born in Denison but soon moved out of the state, won popularity in the state especially because of his belief that Texas' tidelands should be owned by the state rather than by the federal government. The issue was an important one to Texans because of the oil riches located in the offshore area.

The federal government has contended that Texas can legally claim only the first three miles from the shoreline; Texas claims 10 miles. Stevenson supported the federal government's claim.

Eisenhower also profited from the anti-New Deal sentiment many conservative Democrats have held since Franklin D. Roosevelt's presidency.

Texas Governor Allan Shivers led the state's

Above: Dallas Mayor Wallace Savage presents Dwight D. Eisenhower with a certificate naming him an "Honorary Texas Democrat" during a 1951 campaign stop in Dallas.

conservative Democrats in bolting the party.

The only other time a Republican presidential candidate carried the state was in 1928 when Herbert Hoover defeated Democratic nominee Al Smith, the New York governor who was a Catholic.

Some speculate that Eisenhower's win in Texas may foreshadow a transformation into a two-party state. That, however, will depend on whether the conservative Democrats have left the party on a permanent basis, a dubious proposition.

Greater Houston Makes It to One Million Mark

(1954, July 3) Today, July 3, is "M" Day for Greater Houston, which is to say, Harris County.

The one millionth person will take up residence there, making Greater Houston the first metropolitan area in Texas, the South, and the Southwest to reach that population mark.

Growth has been phenomenal. In 1900 Harris County's population was 63,000. Then, in 1901, came Spindletop. By 1940 the population had reached 528,000. On the first day of January 1954, it was estimated to be 973,000.

The city was founded in late 1836 near the San Jacinto battlefield where General Sam Houston had won Texas' independence from Mexico.

Just how it is known that July 3rd is "M" Day for Houston and for Harris County was figured out by the Greater Houston Chamber of Commerce, which planned something special for the millionth resident.

But who would be designated as the millionth resident?

Several suggestions that emerged but were rejected were these: (1) set up a road block at the county line and pick the millionth person from those crossing it; (2) have Houstonians vote on the lucky person; and (3) have individuals make applications for the honor.

Finally, the chamber decided to pick a person who was head of a household and who was moving into Greater Houston for the first time. His name would be chosen from among the applicants for utility services.

Cotton, Cattle Make Geographical Swap

(1955) A quiet but dramatic revolution has taken place in Texas' twin enterprises that have brought it so much attention throughout its history—cattle and cotton. It involves a surprising but little-noticed geographical switch.

The cotton kingdom has moved to the western part of the state and the cattle empire is now prospering in the eastern half.

It was in the 1930s that cotton growers learned that the grazing lands of West Texas, when irrigated, would produce prodigious quantities of high-grade, long-staple cotton. Now, about 80 percent of the state's entire cotton crop is grown in West Texas. Around Lubbock alone 18 counties produce about 10 percent of the cotton grown in the United States.

Meanwhile, cattlemen made a similar discovery. The lusher lands of East Texas made for better grazing grounds for the new breeds of cattle they were preferring over the old longhorn. The East Texas pastures required fewer acres, too, for feeding the same number of cattle. Now more than half of Texas' cattle herds are found in the eastern part of the state.

Together, these two ranch and farm enterprises are prospering. Income from crops and livestock for 1955 are expected to reach $1.9 billion, about four times what it was in 1939.

There are about 8.5 million head of cattle in the state, making Texas by far the nation's leading cattle-raising state.

This year's cotton crop is expected to yield about 4 million bales, worth about $689 million.

Cows graze the land near Houston

Oil, Gas Industry Still Strong

(1956) Twenty-six years after Dad Joiner in East Texas brought in the world's most prolific oil field, oil and its frequent partner, natural gas, still provide much of the state's wealth.

In 1955 Texas produced just over one billion barrels of oil, 43 percent of the nation's entire total. Its proven reserves amounted to 14.9 billion barrels, half of the nation's total.

The oil and gas industry together contributed $188 million to the state treasury. This was 30.3 percent of all the state taxes levied.

Oil and gas are found in every part of the state—from East Texas to the Panhandle, even under the water just off the Gulf Coast.

Nowadays the Permian Basin in West Texas, where about 1,250 separate fields

Above: Oil exploration has moved from the land to the waters of the Texas Gulf.

Top: El Paso's Standard Oil Refinery, an important part of the city's economy and a contributor to the state's post-World War II refining industry

are found, is the center of oil activities. Production in 1955 in the Permian Basin was more than 480 million barrels.

The thriving towns of Midland and Odessa are the Permian Basin's capital. From a 1940 population of 9,352, Midland now is near 50,000. More than 450 oil companies and affiliates have offices in the town's air-conditioned buildings, while many of the workers live in Odessa.

Texas Gets Rave Review in National Magazine

(1956, November) "Texas . . . is shaping up as the new powerhouse of the United States . . . Oil fields are booming. Big, new industries are springing up. Quiet towns are being transformed, almost violently, into large cities with towering skylines."

In such glowing terms the current November 23 issue of *U.S. News & World Report* describes the state.

The magazine has a special 21-page section on Texas and its economy. The key word seen throughout the report is "transformation," something said to be impacting cattle raising and farming, industry (particularly the oil industry), and cities.

Moving into the state to help run these new enterprises are lots of Easterners and Westerners. They're flocking into the oil refineries, chemical plants, and aircraft factories.

The petrochemical industry, born out of the oil industry, now threatens to outgrow its parent. Eighty percent of the nation's petrochemical output comes from Texas.

The state has half the oil in America and most of the known sulphur in the world. It continues to grow more cotton than any other state. It leads the nation in oil refining. It has the biggest ranches and the most cattle. Its rice crop equals about one-fourth of the entire nation's. Its coastline of 370 miles has 13 deep-water ports, and unlikely Houston, half a hundred miles from the Gulf of Mexico, is the second biggest port in the United States.

While Texas now ranks sixth in population with 8.6 million residents, it is projected to reach 12.1 million by 1975.

The growth of the state's cities has been remarkable. Twelve Texas cities have populations of more than 100,000. Sixteen years ago only seven Texas cities had more than 60,000 people. Today one out of every three Texans lives in Houston, Dallas, San Antonio, or Fort Worth. The state has 10 of the 35 fastest-growing cities in the nation.

Now, for the first time, more Texans live in urban areas than rural.

Satellite Beep Signals Opening of TI Facility

(1958, July) The emerging new giant in the electronics field, Texas Instruments, Inc., opened its new plant 11 miles from downtown Dallas in a way that was entirely fitting with its Space Age identification.

A radio beep from the *Explorer* satellite far above the earth set off the ribbon-cutting ceremony for the new $5-million, 7.5-acre plant.

It was fitting in another way, too, for TI had produced the transistors that gave the *Explorer* its voice.

Texas Instruments, so named in 1951 from the original Geophysical Services Inc., soon began to downplay its seismic work for the oil industry and latch onto new space-age technology—the transistor in particular. With this new emphasis beginning in 1952, sales that year hit $20 million; this year TI is expected to gross $85 million.

The new facility will permit the company to produce 2.5 million transistors and related electronic parts each month.

At dedication ceremonies for the new plant, an executive with Bell Telephone Laboratories predicted that by 1968 the company's transistor sales would reach $500 million.

TI President Patrick E Haggerty explained that what TI is doing is "making new technologies commercial."

Pro Football War Centers in Dallas

(1960, Fall) The football battle between the National Football League and the upstart American Football League has centered on Dallas, where two new professional teams are vying for public approval.

The Dallas Cowboys, owned principally by Clint Murchison and coached by Tom Landry, represent the NFL's expansion team.

The Dallas Texans are owned by Lamar Hunt, son of the noted oilman H.L. Hunt, who often is cited as the richest man in the world.

Lamar Hunt, who had sought the NFL expansion franchise for Dallas but who was thwarted in his bid, not only decided to found his own football team but also to establish the league for it to play in. Thus the American Football League came into being.

As far as winning football is concerned, undoubtedly the Cowboys have the toughest struggle, for while their roster is made up of beginners and cast-offs, they are competing with seasoned NFL teams.

The Texans, on the other hand, are competing against other teams that also are new and composed of beginning players.

How long both teams will be able to survive in this city is an interesting question, but it is highly unlikely that both teams can remain indefinitely.

Houston Wins Coveted Honor as Space Exploration Headquarters

(1961, September) Houston—national headquarters for space exploration.

That is the import of the September 1961 announcement made by James E. Webb of the National Aeronautics and Space Administration to build a $60-million facility southeast of Houston on a 1,000-acre tract of land donated by Rice University.

Reasons cited for the coveted designation have included location—the area is equidistant from the two coasts; weather—mild year-round climate; labor—a bountiful supply; scientific support—research facilities and excellent universities close at hand.

There are still other reasons, of course. One is Vice President Lyndon B. Johnson, a Texan through and through. Johnson, designated head of the nation's space program by President John F. Kennedy, favored his native Texas as space headquarters.

Yet another is the person of Rep. Albert Thomas,

This area will become Site 1 of the Manned Spacecraft Center.

One day soon this area near Houston will be transformed into NASA's Manned Spacecraft Center.

a Texan who, as chairman of the House appropriations subcommittee, controlled NASA's funds. Thomas insisted on Houston as the site.

NASA's goal, set forth by President Kennedy, is to land a man on the moon and to return him safely to earth before the end of the decade.

NASA's new complex south of Houston is expected to bring countless high-level jobs to the area and to infuse the economy with money. Supporting industries are expected to locate nearby.

Mexican-Americans Emerging as Powerful Political Faction

(1963) The old image of Mexican-Americans has been jolted in Crystal City, Texas, where a slate of Mexican-American municipal candidates captured the mayor's office and every city council seat. Thus ended the long-time domination of local politics by Anglos.

For years Mexican-Americans, although outnumbering Anglos by a 4-1 margin, had only watched as the Anglos ruled over this city of 9,500 persons, a city noted as "The Spinach Capital of the World." But, encouraged by John F. Kennedy's vigorous campaigning through "Viva Kennedy" clubs, the Mexican-Americans in Crystal City decided to do something to make their voices heard.

After sweeping the city offices, the new council and mayor appointed a Spanish-speaking city manager.

News of the Mexican-American political awakening in Crystal City sent shock waves throughout the state, garnering the attention even of the *New York Times.*

Supporting the victorious slate was a national organization called PASO (Political Association of Spanish-Speaking Organizations), which has 20,000 members in Texas alone.

Albert Peña, chairman of the organization, said: "Crystal City has opened the eyes of the sleeping giant. We are not on a slow freight anymore. We are on the American express, and we are going to ride first-class."

Also crucial to the victory by mayor Juan Cornejo and his slate was the help of the Teamsters Union, which sent money and organizers to assist in getting a heavy Mexican-American voter turnout.

It has been reported that the alliance between PASO and the Teamsters will be seen in future races throughout the state.

Peña summed up the new mood: "We are going to put an end to Jim Crow in a sombrero hat."

Four Days of Tragedy Rack Dallas, Texas, and Nation

(1963, November 24) Texas and the nation, still in deep grief after Friday's assassination on a downtown Dallas street of their President, John F. Kennedy, experienced further shock on Sunday when the suspected assassin was slain in the basement of the city's police station.

The fatal shooting of the suspect, Lee Harvey Oswald, 24, occurred in the midst of a crowd of newsmen and police officers as he was led from the city jail into an adjoining basement parking garage to be transferred to the Dallas County Jail.

Nightclub owner Jack Ruby, 52, fired the fatal shot into Oswald's stomach with a pistol, an act that was televised live over the entire nation to a population already numbed by the death of President Kennedy.

President Kennedy, passing through the streets of Dallas in an open-topped convertible en route to a speaking engagement, was shot just after 12:30 p.m. Friday by a marksman alleged to have been Oswald.

Police arrested Oswald, a former U.S. Marine who once defected to the Soviet Union, in a movie theater shortly after he allegedly shot and killed a Dallas police officer who had attempted to stop him for questioning as he walked down a street in a residential neighborhood of the Oak Cliff section of Dallas.

Oswald was an order-filler at the Texas School Book Depository, from where the presidential ambush allegedly occurred. He fled the building after the shooting.

Police have linked Oswald to the rifle found on the sixth floor of the building, from where they say three shots were fired at the President.

Texas Governor John Connally himself, riding with his wife in the presidential limousine with President Kennedy and his wife Jacqueline, was wounded seriously with a bullet in his chest.

The sequence of tragic events in Dallas has caused a cascade of long-distance telephone calls to pour into city hall and the police station from irate citizens who have expressed shock and dismay at the assassination and then at the killing of the number one suspect while in police custody.

President Kennedy's Vice President, Lyndon Baines Johnson, himself a Texan and also in the motorcade, was sworn in as President by U.S. District Judge Sarah T. Hughes of Dallas aboard Air Force One.

Just how Ruby gained access to the police basement is uncertain, but it is believed that he slipped past a police guard at an automobile entrance.

Oswald was taken to the same hospital where President Kennedy had been declared dead. He died there without uttering a word.

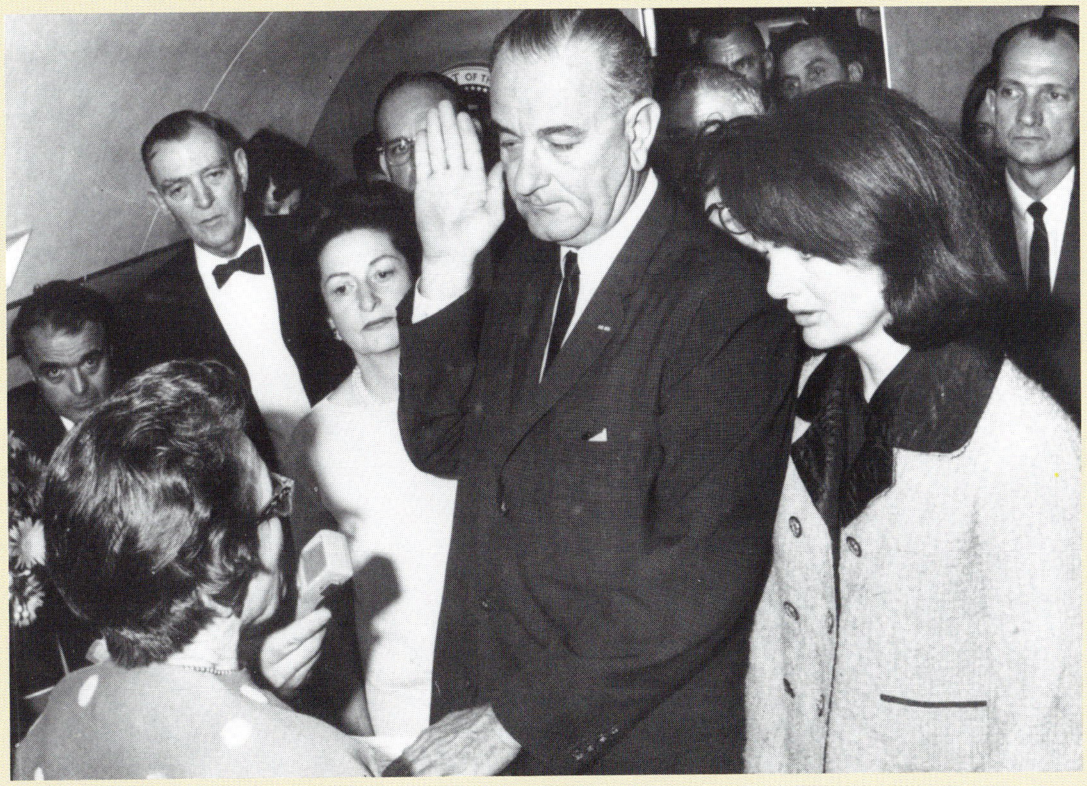

A shocked and grief-stricken Jacqueline Kennedy and somber-faced Lady Bird Johnson look on as Lyndon B. Johnson is sworn in as President of the United States aboard Air Force One in Dallas following the assassination of President John F. Kennedy.

A Leader in Flow Control Applications

Since 1985 Keystone Chairman and Chief Executive Officer R.A. LeBlanc has been responsible for expanding Keystone product offerings through strategic mergers with key process control suppliers.

Right: A wide range of flow control valves and automation packages is manufactured, sold, and serviced by Keystone International, Inc.

KEYSTONE INTERNATIONAL, INC.

Founder: C.K. Stillwagon
Founded: 1947
Principal: R.A. LeBlanc, chairman and chief executive officer

Long before "global marketplace" became the buzzwords they are today, Keystone International, Inc., was expanding around the world as a recognized leader in flow control applications. In essence, the flow control industry is the manufacture, sales, and service of valves, as well as the actuators that automate these valves for such operations as chemical, refining, brewing, and pulp and paper plants.

Keystone's international scope strengthens company capabilities in each global region, as well as providing a measure of flexibility for all of its subsidiaries. Its worldwide operations—in Europe, the Americas, and Asia—employ more than 4,100 people at 24 manufacturing facilities located in 13 countries and in virtually every major trade market worldwide.

This global capability enables Keystone to seize opportunities, such as in the Pacific Rim, where Keystone's operations in Singapore, Korea, Australia, China, and Japan provide a solid foundation for continued growth in the markets of the Far East.

Keystone views the ability to provide quality products and services to customers around the world as a critical component of success in today's global market. To that end, Keystone has embraced ISO 9001 certification as a key element of its Total Quality Process. This certification, under the International Standardization Organization, entails an extensive assessment of company procedures and policies requiring thorough documentation of these practices.

All of Keystone's operations have either achieved the ISO 9001 standard of excellence or are in the painstaking process of certification. Not only is this commitment to quality a source of pride throughout Keystone, it is also a strong marketing tool that gains increasing value as the company seeks to penetrate new world markets.

Following a series of acquisitions—begun in 1986 with the objective of broadening its product range and continuing its position as a global leader in the flow control industry—Keystone restructured its organization into six strategic business units (SBU).

The Industrial Valve SBU, which is comprised of **Keystone Valve** and **Keystone Richards Ball Valve**, manufactures industrial valves and products that include butterfly and high-performance rotary valves, along with plug and hygienic valves, and ball, check, and knife gate valves.

The Safety and Environmental SBU, which is comprised of **Keystone Anderson Greenwood**, manufactures safety relief and needle valves, instrument valves and manifolds, instrument enclosures, safety selector valves, and rupture discs.

The Keystone Controls SBU, including **Keystone Controls**, **Keystone Biffi**, and **Keystone Morin**, manufactures automation equipment. This SBU also produces electric and pneumatic actuators, hydraulic and subsea actuators, and distributed control systems, as well as specialty actuator and control accessories.

The Specialty Products SBU, comprised of **Keystone Yarway**, manufactures products that include steam control and pump protection valves, steam traps and expansion joints, and boiler trim valves and boiler instrumentation.

The Keystone Vanessa and Keystone Valvtron SBUs produce critical service rotary valves, with **Keystone Vanessa**

manufacturing "zero-leakage" butterfly valves and **Keystone Valvtron** producing high-pressure ball valves for severe service applications.

A wide range of markets utilize these flow control products. In fact, today the valve has become a ubiquitous piece of industrial equipment. As a result, Keystone valves can be found throughout industries ranging from petrochemical and pharmaceutical plants, food and beverage processing and power generation, to refining and municipal water and wastewater plants.

Keystone's roots are traced to January 24, 1947, when C.K. Stillwagon founded Keystone Tool Corporation, naming the company after his native state of Pennsylvania, the Keystone State. Keystone began commercial operations in Houston in the spring of the following year, selling oil field equipment and tools for general industry.

Company fortunes continued to improve when Stillwagon used his remarkable skills to develop and patent improvements to the butterfly valve that revolutionized the application of the product. Stillwagon's butterfly valve proved to be lighter and more economical than the butterfly valves previously being used in the oil fields. Keystone's technology and production processes continue to maximize the inherent cost and application advantages of rotary valves.

Production of the improved butterfly valve began in 1951, launching Keystone to prominence. This "better butterfly" extended the capabilities of the common valve beyond the oil industry and into literally any process control application requiring positive flow control. The new butterfly design was judged to be superior to the competition, and, as a result, propelled Keystone into the global marketplace. During the ensuing years Keystone's product line expanded to include a variety of sizes and applications.

Today Keystone International registers more than $500 million in annual sales. Not content to rest on past accomplishments, the company expects to continue to grow and prosper by focusing on development and acquisition of flow control products and providing a superior level of customer service in key global markets.

Above: Keystone products provide critical control, transport, safety, and environmental functions in virtually every country around the world.

Top: Keystone's international headquarters, based in Houston, oversees operations at 24 manufacturing facilities in 13 countries and sales offices in over 50 countries. The company employs 4,100 people.

Ensuring Customer Success in a Global Marketplace

EDS

Founded: 1962
Principal: Les Alberthal, Jr., CEO

In Spain, Telefonica de España is relying on new billing and collection systems as it expands throughout the European Community. In Germany, a tire manufacturer is using a sophisticated computer-aided design system to design products that will help it become the leader in its industry. In Australia, a communications company is winning its share of business in a competitive cellular market. And in California, one of the United States' largest health maintenance organizations is improving its operational efficiency and reducing the cost of delivering care to its members.

Adding value. Increasing profitability. Ensuring customer success in a rapidly changing global marketplace. These accomplishments are possible with EDS, a Dallas-based company that applies information technology to benefit businesses, governments, and individuals worldwide. Founded in 1962, EDS has a track record of helping customers achieve their business objectives through the innovative and creative application of technology.

Les Alberthal, Jr., of EDS was one of the top 10 CEOs of companies over one billion dollars named by the *Gallagher Report*.

COMMITTED TO CUSTOMER SUCCESS

Throughout its 32-year history, EDS' goal has been to help customers succeed by helping them better serve *their* customers profitably. In the early days, EDS helped customers by enhancing their efficiency and boosting processing power. Today, smart technology plays a fundamental role in ensuring business success. It enables businesses to advance into the future—and to compete along the way. With economic, political, and social change happening more quickly than ever before, that ability to anticipate change and adapt quickly in order to maintain a competitive edge is critical.

EDS offers its customers a variety of flexible services: systems development, systems integration, systems management, process management, and consulting. The company's consulting division stands ready to help customers yield real, tangible results for their businesses by taking a no-nonsense approach to long-range planning and strategy. Customers in industries ranging from manufacturing to entertainment are able to compete globally with applications of information technology that assure successful results. The EDS teams that support these customers capitalize on the skills and talents of people from all over the world to respond immediately to customers' needs—and to help them bridge the "impact gap," the difference between the power of technology and the ability to use that technology for competitive advantage.

EDGING OUT THE COMPETITION

Having a competitive advantage helped Prince Manufacturing win its game. Using sophisticated Unigraphics® computer-aided design and manufacturing technology from EDS, Prince created Vortex, the most advanced tennis racquet on the market today. Six months after its introduction, it became Prince's top-selling racquet. This new technology has helped Prince shorten its design time and get new and better products to market sooner.

With the same technology, Melitta, a Germany-based household products company, cut its product development time by 50 percent. And because product design ultimately determines the success of Melitta's products, the speed and flexibility of EDS' system allows Melitta designers to quickly design, modify, and improve products.

With technology from EDS, Prince Manufacturing has created the most advanced tennis racquet on the market today.

BENEFITING FROM EDS RESOURCES

With revenues of $8.2 billion in 1992, EDS has a solid financial foundation its customers can rely on. But the most important assets of EDS are the skills, imagination, and dedication of its people. More than 70,000 employees help ensure the success of EDS customers in more than 30 countries around the world. To better serve customers, EDS spends more than $150 million each year to train its technical and professional employees. Customers also can draw from the talents of companies associated with EDS through joint ventures or acquisitions.

ENSURING A FUTURE OF SUCCESS

Contributing to customer success also means contributing to the community and its future. Since the 1990 opening of the Smithsonian Institution's Information Age exhibit in Washington, D.C., EDS, a founding sponsor of the exhibit, has helped more than three million visitors understand and appreciate the contributions of technology. EDS is also an active supporter of education, providing financial and technical resources for the JASON™ Project, which encourages hundreds of thousands of North American schoolchildren to become more involved in science. EDS has sponsored the project, which allows students to join with scientists in exploring ocean depths, since 1989. By helping stimulate students' interest in science—an area in which American students need a boost—EDS helps ensure its future success and that of its customers.

MAKING INFORMATION TECHNOLOGY PAY

Delivering the kind of results that help our customers serve their customers more profitably is what EDS is all about. For governments, individuals, and companies large and small around the world, EDS—in case after case—has demonstrated how information technology can contribute to success in dozens of measurable ways.

Managing The Process Better

FISHER-ROSEMOUNT

Officers: Charles F. Knight, chairman and CEO, Emerson Electric Co.; J.J. Adorjan, president, Emerson Electric Co., and CEO, Fisher-Rosemount; John Berra, president, Fisher-Rosemount Systems, Inc.; L.W. Solley, chairman and CEO, Fisher Controls International, Inc.; and Robert Bateman, CEO, Rosemount Inc.

Charles F. Knight (seated, right), chairman and chief executive officer of Emerson Electric Co., and J. J. Adorjan (standing, left), president of Emerson Electric and chief executive officer of Fisher-Rosemount, are at the helm of the world's leading process management company.

Neither the paint on your walls nor the paper in this book were manufactured by the Texas firm of Fisher-Rosemount. But it's likely that the firm's process controls helped make the paint the right color and the paper the right thickness.

All around the world, Fisher-Rosemount's control valves, regulators, transmitters, analyzers, and process management systems help control and measure processes in chemical plants, pulp and paper mills, food-processing plants, refineries—any manufacturing environment where liquids and gases flow through pipes.

THE WORLD LEADER IN PROCESS CONTROL

The Fisher-Rosemount family of companies is the world's number-one process management supplier, as well as the industry's undisputed leader in customer service.

Fisher-Rosemount reached the top in October 1992. That's when St. Louis-based Emerson Electric Co.—parent company of Rosemount Inc., the world leader in measurement and analytical devices—acquired Fisher Controls International, Inc., the foremost control valve supplier. The marriage of Fisher and Rosemount not only created an enterprise that eclipsed the competition, but also one that could provide everything manufacturers needed to manage their processes more effectively. To better serve these customers, Emerson also merged the systems businesses of Fisher and Rosemount to create a new company, Fisher-Rosemount Systems, Inc.

TEXAS CONNECTIONS, GLOBAL NETWORKS

Fisher-Rosemount's history is very much a Texas story. All told, some 18 Texas-based Fisher-Rosemount facilities, including manufacturing sites, service centers, and sales offices, provide jobs for more than 1,500 people—from engineers to programmers to sales representatives.

Fisher-Rosemount Systems, for example, maintains its world headquarters in Austin, Texas, in addition to manufacturing and technology centers in Minnesota, California, Canada, England, and Singapore. The company's line of microprocessor-based systems—the "brains" that automate and control today's plants and mills—includes the PROVOX™, RS3™, and RMV9000™ process management systems. Today more than 600 employees focus on PROVOX manufacturing and marketing at Fisher-Rosemount Systems' 32-acre Austin campus.

While Fisher-Rosemount Systems' headquarters may be in Texas, the Austin site's roots are in Marshalltown, Iowa—Fisher Controls' hometown and control valve headquarters. Originally called the Fisher Governor Company, Fisher Controls was founded in 1880 by inventor William Fisher. The company's flagship product was a pump control device, or governor, that maintained constant liquid or gas pressure in pipes. As years passed, Fisher developed control valves and regulators, becoming a leader in the process control industry. In 1981, a year after introducing the PROVOX system, Fisher moved its growing process instrumentation division to Austin.

Elsewhere in Texas, Fisher Controls operates two Dallas-area plants. Fisher's McKinney plant, which employs about 400, manufactures gas regulators for plant air regulation and gas storage and transport, including residential service. The nearby Sherman plant, with some 275 employees, makes rotary valves and actuators for tough process control applications.

Fisher Service Companies, which provide field and factory diagnostic and repair services for both Fisher and third-party control valves and instruments, are located in Longview, Beaumont, and Pasadena.

Fisher-Rosemount markets its products, systems, and services—locally and globally—through a worldwide network of direct sales offices and independent representative organizations. This responsive network puts Fisher-Rosemount experts at the doorsteps of customers. For instance, Texas-based Representatives (which primarily sell Fisher's final control equipment and Fisher-Rosemount process management systems) include Vinson Supply Company, with sales offices in Dallas, Carrollton, Amarillo, and Odessa; Puffer-Sweiven, Inc., in Houston, San Antonio, Corpus Christi, Freeport, and La Porte; and Scallon Controls, Inc., in Beaumont.

Rosemount Inc. also maintains direct sales offices in Houston and Dallas to market its measurement and analytical products. Xomox Corporation—another member of the Fisher-Rosemount family and a world-leading supplier of process valves, actuators, and flow control products—has a sales and service center in Houston.

NEXT-GENERATION DIGITAL SOLUTIONS

Fisher-Rosemount introduced its real-time process management solutions in the fall of 1992. These digitally based solutions extend process management capabilities by combining systems, services, and products—including "smart" transmitters, valves, analyzers, and other field devices—from across the Fisher-Rosemount family of companies.

Fisher-Rosemount became a founding member of the Austin-based InterOperable Systems Project (ISP) in 1992. ISP's goal is to develop a single international, interoperable fieldbus standard and deliver ISP-based products, enabling digital communications between process management systems, valves, transmitters, and other field devices. Once established, this fieldbus standard will give process manufacturers the freedom to mix and match the best field devices and systems for their needs—without sacrificing functionality or integration.

COMMITTED TO A CLEANER WORLD

Meeting the stringent requirements of today's environmental, health, and safety regulations and adhering to strict international quality standards are also crucial goals for Fisher-Rosemount. A case in point: In 1993 Fisher's McKinney plant won recognition in the Texas Governor's Awards for Environmental Excellence program. Fisher-McKinney has reduced solid waste generation by 95 percent, eliminated use of ozone-depleting chemicals and toxic air emissions, and reduced hazardous waste by more than 90 percent. Fisher-Rosemount's commitment to environmental stewardship extends not only to reducing pollution within its operations, but also to helping customers meet their own environmental challenges.

Fisher-Rosemount's Texas facilities are also justifiably proud of having achieved ISO 9001 certification. By meeting the international quality standards established by the International Standardization Organization, these company sites have demonstrated their continuing commitment to total quality. And since ISO compliance is a basic requirement to conduct business in Europe and elsewhere around the world, Fisher-Rosemount has secured its rightful place as a global supplier of world-class process management solutions.

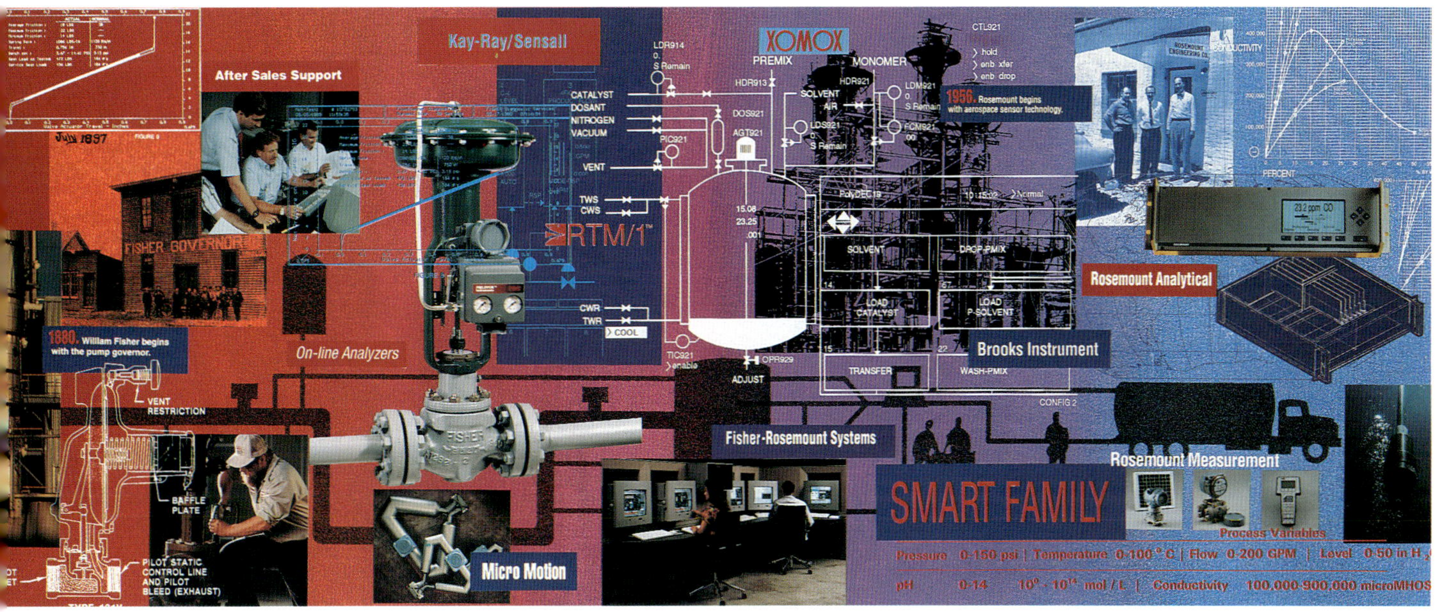

From analytical and measurement devices to control valves to process management systems, the Fisher-Rosemount family of companies offers the process industries' broadest range of products, services, and solutions.

Serving the Aviation Industry Worldwide

BF GOODRICH AEROSPACE COMPONENT OVERHAUL & REPAIR INC.

Founder: Don Castleberry
Founded: 1958 in Corpus Christi

The next time you marvel at how big airliners manage to stay aloft, thank an Austin company for helping to make it possible.

BFGoodrich Aerospace Component Overhaul & Repair Inc. serves the air transport, regional airline, and general aviation industries worldwide—helicopters as well as airplanes. AerCOR specializes in overhauling, repairing, and certifying aircraft instruments, avionics, autopilots, and controls.

Today the company has offices in Austin, Fort Lauderdale, Toronto, and the Netherlands, but it all began in a one-room shop with three employees and $3,000.

Don Castleberry had learned about instrumentation and electronics working for the U.S. Navy Civil Service in the 1950s. In 1958 Castleberry and two partners scraped up a $3,000 initial investment to establish Aircraft Instrument Service Inc. at a former naval air base in Corpus Christi. Their objective: to repair air-driven and vacuum instruments, mostly military surplus equipment common to aircraft of the day.

Castleberry bought his partners out approximately 6 months after opening, and the firm became more of a family enterprise as Castleberry's wife and three children chipped in to fill important roles. By 1968 the business had grown to 50 employees.

In August 1970 Hurricane Celia roared into the Texas coast, destroying much of the company's equipment and leaving it without electricity and telephones for weeks. AIS managed to rebuild, but transportation through Corpus Christi became more difficult as the company grew.

Don Castleberry (right) talks to a technician about the company's IRIS 2000, which is extremely high-tech automated test equipment.

Two days after closing shop in Corpus Christi in May 1975, the firm opened for business in Austin. More of a hub than Corpus Christi, Austin allowed AIS to expand the range of its sales and service market. Castleberry merged Aircraft Instrument Service Inc. with a holding company he had previously established, forming Castleberry Instruments and Avionics Inc.

With a new name came a new way of serving customers, a practice that would revolutionize the aircraft instrument repair industry.

Castleberry set up an exchange system. When a customer needed an instrument repaired, the firm traded a rebuilt instrument for the faulty one, which would be repaired and resold. The result was satisfied customers who could get back into the air more quickly.

Don Castleberry's reputation for fairness and quality attracted the attention of BFGoodrich Aerospace, which bought the business in 1986.

BFGoodrich had entered the aerospace industry in 1909 with the product for which it is perhaps best known: a tire, used on an airplane called the Glenn Curtiss pusher. Since then, the firm has developed gear ranging from evacuation systems to ice protection.

BFGoodrich expanded Castleberry's operation, adding capabilities to service the air transport and regional airline markets. In 1991 BFGoodrich merged Castleberry with Simmonds Precision Product Support Operations. Later, with the purchase of automatic test equipment from the Eastern Airlines estate, BFGoodrich Aerospace Component Overhaul & Repair Inc. was born.

Today AerCOR has more than 250 employees and $15 million in inventory. A sophisticated information and telecommunication system manages about 6,500 accounts.

Don Castleberry retired in 1992. But thanks to him, the skies are a little safer.

Continuous Country

KVET/KASE

Chairman: Roy Butler
President: Ron Rogers

Ron Rogers, president and general manager of KVET/KASE since 1975.

"Country music has been cool for the past five years," says Ron Rogers, president and general manager of Austin's KVET and KASE radio. "Of course, we've been liking it since **before** it was cool."

Indeed, it's hard to imagine Texas without country music, and Austin radio without KVET/KASE. Through the years the sister stations have maintained a loyal following with their distinctive blends of music, news, and occasional wackiness.

KASE-FM has dominated the radio market since the mid-1980s, ranking number one in Arbitron ratings, often with twice the audience of its nearest rival. Since taking the reins at KVET/KASE in 1975, Rogers has presided over not only radio stations, but a rich part of Austin's history.

KVET Radio first went on the air on Tuesday, October 1, 1946, founded by a group of young World War II veterans. KVET founders included J.J. Pickle, who went on to represent Austin in Congress, and former Texas Governor John Connally. In fact, Connally was the station's first disc jockey.

KVET's early programming reflected radio's Golden Age. Live and recorded music, dramas, soap operas, game shows, news, and variety shows provided the prime time entertainment of the day.

Television threatened to steal its audience in the 1950s, but KVET held a loyal following of listeners and advertisers, drawn by a combination of positive community involvement, sports coverage, and programs targeted at African American and Hispanic listeners.

Austin businessman Roy Butler purchased KVET in 1965. Butler beefed up the station with more broadcast power and more prominent on-air personalities, and by 1969 turned KVET into "The Country Giant." That same year Butler debuted KASE-FM, 100,000 watts of "Beautiful Music," on FM 100.7.

The two stations did well during the 1970s. KVET became known for outrageous contests and on-air shenanigans, which have been enjoyed ever since by a large and loyal audience.

On September 15, 1981, KASE-FM dropped its Beautiful Music format, and began playing "Continuous Country." Supported by truck and automobile give-aways and other imaginative promotions to attract country listeners, KASE soared to number one in the Austin radio market.

As with other AM stations, KVET saw its audience decline during the 1980s as listeners switched to FM frequencies. Yet it remained a player in the Austin market with a community-oriented emphasis on news, sports, and personalities, as well as on country music.

In September 1990 KVET became one of the first AM stations in the country to lease the option to simulcast its AM programming on an FM frequency. In a deal with the owner of Austin's 98.1-FM, the station became KVET AM-FM.

Since 1990 KASE has continued to dominate the Austin radio market with its focus on Continuous Country. KVET continues to feature news and sports, along with Paul Harvey and other personalities, as well as country music.

KASE has been named Station of the Year by the Country Music Association four times, more than any other station in the nation. Ron Rogers was named Broadcaster of the Year in 1991, the highest honor bestowed by the Texas Association of Broadcasters, and acquired the first General Manager of the Year Award by the Country Music Association in 1987. KVET and KASE have also collected awards for Disc Jockey of the Year and Program Director of the Year.

Both stations are honored annually by groups such as Keep Austin Beautiful and the Veterans of Foreign Wars for public service performed both on the air and off. Not content to just run public service announcements, KVET-KASE employees are active in their community. In 1983 the National Association of Broadcasters awarded KASE its Crystal Radio Award for excellence in public service.

Legendary Texas football coach Darrell Royal (right) with KVET's Jim Dodd during the station's early 1970s "Tenna Topper" promotion.

Working Toward the Future

1821-1861

J. Frank Dobie's death in 1964 marked a symbolic passage of a storied era for Texas and its frontier background. The books of Dobie and contemporaries Walter Prescott Webb and Roy Bedichek shared common themes by describing intimate relationships of Texans with their land and heritage. The outspoken, white-haired Dobie was famous for his tales of explorers, settlers, cowboys, Indians, and lost gold mines. Webb, who died one year before Dobie in 1963, gained worldwide attention for his learned theories about the frontier and his insights as to how the emergence of settlers from the woodlands of the East to the plains of the West peculiarly shaped the area's history, culture, and institutions. Bedichek, who died in 1959, wrote of natural history and Indians. *These three pals sometimes shared a campfire at Dobie's hill country ranch to mull over the Texas experience. It was conversation pretty much devoid, one can feel certain, of some of the main elements of the new Texas experience of petrochemicals, manufacturing, the aerospace industry, computers, and urban complexities. The literary treatment of these new themes awaited the arrival of another generation of writers who perhaps could find the same romance and intrigue in them that others had found in the earlier frontier.*

Another threesome—these not campfire buddies—provided a different kind of window for seeing the changes that had occurred as the state progressed from ranching to oil to computers. These bigger-than-life figures transcended even the ample Texas stage for national and international platforms.

Lyndon Baines Johnson, a Central Texas native with deep family roots in the rural hill country, was comfortable wearing boots and Stetsons, lived on a ranch, and left deep and lasting tracks on American society during his activist years in the White House's oval office.

A second Texan who served his nation as President was George Bush, a child of the privileged East who came to the state after World War II and enjoyed a successful career as an oil wildcatter before moving into politics and holding a series of high-profile offices, including eight years in the vice presidency, then a term as President.

Completing the transition to the future was H. Ross Perot, who became one of the world's richest men by being at the front edge of the new computer age, something that was about as far removed from cattle, cotton, and oil as one could ever imagine. Perot came close to being President himself in 1992 by running as an independent with plenty of money and easy access to the nation's receptive media, and it appeared that his role as one of the nation's most influential individuals was far from over.

Despite the rapid transition from the past to the high-technology age of the present, the influence of the past was not totally forgotten. Farms and ranches continued to be important economically as well as symbolically. While by the 1990s just about 2 percent of the state's population depended on farms and ranches for their incomes, agricultural production, in terms of its monetary value, went up five-fold between 1958 and 1987. The two most valuable products were not unfamiliar: cattle and cotton. Texas continued to be a leading state in its agriculture, including both cattle and farming.

Even Larry McMurtry, the rising new star who assayed to replace Dobie, Webb, and Bedichek, all of whom he had criticized for their avoidance of urban themes, experienced the power of the state's colorful heritage. McMurtry, in his passage away from the old Texas he seemed to dislike, left his small hometown and moved on to Houston and then to Washington, D.C. Finally, though, after a series of books that explored the urban themes he touted, he returned to a traditional setting that turned out to be his greatest work, Lonesome Dove, *which won widespread acclaim and a Pulitzer Prize.*

Still, there was no way to deny contemporary urban dominance in Texas and its overpowering presence. The state's image, as much as by anything else, now was marked by glittering, big-city skylines. Dallas' and Houston's towering skyscrapers seemed more a part of Manhattan than the Lone Star State. Three Texas cities—Houston, Dallas, and San Antonio—ranked among the nation's top 10 in population. No other state could make such a claim.

The more than 17 million residents (twice as many as in 1940) gave Texas the third-largest population in the nation. And here was something significant: one-third of these people had been born outside the state. While these newcomers may have appreciated their adopted land's colorful history, they had no special ties to it nor any reason to try to preserve its tradition. Two-thirds of the newcomers hailed from places other than the Old South, from where so many new residents in the past had come.

Persons who spoke Spanish or had Spanish surnames constituted 25.5 percent, by far the largest percentage of minorities, and they were the fastest-growing ethnic group, too. With African-Americans constituting 12 percent of the population and also growing at a rapid rate, and with still other minorities in the population, it was clear that in the not-too-distant future these minorities would become a majority.

One could see the various new dimensions of modern Texas in many tangible ways. An important one was the emergence after so many years of a two-party political system. Republican presidential candidates now had as good a chance as Democrats in presidential elections. Nixon, Reagan, and Bush carried the state—and Republicans even held the governor's seat on two occasions (both times by the same man, William P. Clements).

The poll tax, which had limited the participation of minorities at the ballot box, was gone. A sales tax, which was previously seen by most as detrimental to the state's best interest, was enacted in the early 1960s and by the 1990s was accepted without question.

Women in this "he-man" state were being elected mayors of the biggest cities, including Houston and Dallas, as well as to other political offices. Minorities had assumed important

Facing page: The future of the Texas economy lies in its ability to adapt to new technology. In that respect, the future looks promising. Biotechnology and medical research are making great inroads in the state. Photo by Matthew Borkoski/The Stockhouse, Inc., Houston

roles in government, education, and business. Civil rights activities by African-Americans and Hispanics had become commonplace.

Education was increasingly important to Texans. The "no pass-no play" rule enacted by the state legislature in 1984 prohibited high school athletes from playing unless they were passing all their courses. The same law introduced competency testing for pupils, teachers, and administrators, and teacher pay was increased.

In higher education the University of Texas at Austin, Texas A&M University, and Rice University especially were recognized over the world for their graduate programs. State-supported medical schools were among the nation's elite, and the Houston medical community became a world leader in cancer and heart treatment and research.

While the state had taken gigantic strides in the 1970s and early 1980s in both population and economic growth, the collapse of oil prices in the early 1980s introduced a period of uncertainty the likes of which Texas had never experienced. The petroleum industry suffered great losses—in both profits and prestige. Banks accordingly diverted a much larger percentage of their lending money toward the booming real-estate development business where huge profits were being made, seemingly overnight. When real estate prices plummeted, the result was disastrous. The state's lending institutions stumbled and fell with a loud thud. Before the 1980s had ended, the state's biggest banks, once so independent and so proud of their roles in financing the state's economic development, had collapsed. Out-of-state banking empires now held the reins, and the Texas economy was looking for recovery.

It was undeniably the world of high technology—electronics, aerospace components, NASA, medical research, and computers—that had captured the state's spotlight and seemed to be the key to the future. One could see that the new challenges amounted to a return to an old theme—the frontier! Here were new boundaries waiting for strong individuals to probe their limits. The state was poised to plunge into this enterprise with all the old energy of the cowboys driving their herds to Kansas, with all the old determination of the homesteader creating his farm in a hostile environment, and with all the old nerve of the wildcatter searching the depths of the earth for oil.

The historic Texas would never be forgotten, but a new Texas had arrived.

Left: **Colorfully costumed dancers perform a traditional Mexican dance during a festival in Houston. More than one of every four Texans is of Hispanic (primarily Mexican) background. Photo by Chad McNair/The Stockhouse, Inc., Houston**

Lyndon Baines Johnson, the 36th President of the United States (1963-1969), was born on this ranch near Stonewall, Texas, on August 27, 1908. Photo by Rust & Rust/The Stockhouse, Inc., Houston

Cotton, which ranks second to beef cattle in Texas' agricultural sector, is grown in three main areas of the state: the South Plains of the Panhandle (centering in Lubbock), the West Gulf Coastal Plain near Corpus Christi, and the Lower Rio Grande Valley. Photo by Henry A. Kokojan/The Stockhouse, Inc., Houston

Above left: San Antonio, the seat of Bexar County in south central Texas, is more than a living museum to Texas' heritage, it is also a mixture of Spanish, Mexican, and American culture. Photo by Richard Stockton/The Stockhouse, Inc., Houston

Left: The state's second-largest city, Dallas boasts a distinctive skyline that includes the futuristic looking Reunion Tower. The city, located on the Trinity River in northeastern Texas, is the seat of Dallas County. Photo by Richard Stockton/The Stockhouse, Inc., Houston

Above: Houston, the seat of Harris County and Texas' largest city, has developed into an important financial and petrochemical center. Photo by Scott Berner/The Stockhouse, Inc., Houston

Left: The seat of Nueces County in southern Texas, Corpus Christi is a port of entry on Corpus Christi Bay. The city is known as a major shipping point and center for petroleum and natural gas processing. Photo by Scott Berner/The Stockhouse, Inc., Houston

The largest campus in the state-controlled University of Texas System, the Austin campus offers colleges of liberal arts, architecture, business administration, communication education, engineering, fine arts, natural sciences, pharmacy, social work; a graduate school; schools of law, library and information sciences, nursing, and public affairs. The university was established in 1876, but its first classes were not held in Austin until 1883. Photo by Scott Berner/The Stockhouse, Inc., Houston

Above: Texas A&M University at College Station in Brazos County was originally established as the Agricultural and Mechanical College of Texas in the early 1870s. This state-controlled and state-supported university comprises colleges of agriculture, engineering, veterinary medicine, geosciences, liberal arts, science, architecture and environmental design, education, and business administration. In addition, there is a graduate college. Photo by Scott Berner/ The Stockhouse, Inc., Houston

Left: Houston's Rice University grants degrees in architecture, engineering, humanities, music, natural sciences, and social sciences. The school originally opened in 1912 as the William M. Rice Institute for the Advancement of Literature, Science and Art. Photo by James A. Ellenburg/The Stockhouse, Inc., Houston

Above: **Texas, especially Houston, has long been a center of medical research. Photo by Pete Saloutos/The Stockhouse, Inc., Houston**

Left: Texas City, located on Galveston Bay about 30 miles southeast of Houston, ships tin, petroleum products, and chemicals from its port. The city was founded in 1821 by Jim Campbell, a former lieutenant of pirate Jean Laffitte. Photo by Bill Pogue/The Stockhouse, Inc., Houston

Above: The Houston Ship Channel, completed in 1914, served as a catalyst for major industrial growth for the city of Houston. The channel, which allows oceangoing vessels to travel within two miles of downtown Houston, contributes tremendously to the city's ability to export petroleum, petrochemical products, sulphur, cattle, and agricultural products. Photo by Scott Berner/The Stockhouse, Inc., Houston

Texans Now Conserving Wildlife Resources

(1964) The first settlers of Texas killed the abundant wildlife with abandon. It seemed necessary as an important food source, as it had been for the Indians, and it also was a step taken to make the new land more suitable for their livestock, sheep, and poultry.

Now a new era has arrived. The overriding message is to conserve.

Today in 1964 wildlife is an important factor in the state's economic life as well as a source for recreation. The 1960 U.S. census reported that 2.4 million Texans spent $383 on hunting and fishing.

Even though early Texans paid little attention to any need to conserve their wildlife resources, they did pay *some* attention to it through the years.

As early as 1861 Galveston Island declared a two-year closed season on quail.

Additional game laws were enacted by the state in 1881. In 1895 the Fish and Oyster Commission was established, and in 1909 the state passed the first legislation requiring hunting licenses.

Today the Texas Parks and Wildlife Department oversees regulation of Texas' native animals and birds.

Above: Armadillo

Top: Wild turkey

Mule deer, Guadalupe Mountains National Park

The state's most important game animals, by far, are deer. During the 1964 hunting season hunters killed 202,777 deer. This was a decrease from 1963's 220,649.

There are an estimated one million white-tailed deer in the state. Other species are less numerous.

Other native mammals that still live in Texas include the armadillo, badger, bats, bear, beaver, bighorn sheep, various cats such as the jaguar, cougar, and ocelot, chipmunk, ferret, fox, gopher, squirrel, javelina, mink, mole, muskrat, opossum, otter, porcupine, prairie dog, rabbit, raccoon, shrew, skunk, weasel, and wolf.

Another favorite target for Texan sportsmen are wild turkey, whose numbers in the state are larger than those of any other state. In fact, nearly half of all wild turkey in the United States are found in Texas. The wild turkey kill for 1964 was 14,345, up from 13, 680 in 1963.

More than 540 species of birds have been identified in the state. Of special interest among them is an almost extinct species, the whooping crane, a small flock of which winters each year in the Aransas Wildlife Sanctuary. In 1964, 42 whooping cranes wintered there.

Texas is in the migratory path of practically all species of wild duck, some of which spend the winter on the Gulf Coast. Many geese also either winter in the state or pass over it in their migratory flights.

Forest Resources Winning New Appreciation

(1965) For many years East Texas' bountiful forests were being reduced to planks at a rate that by 1930 saw them facing exhaustion. But gradually that trend has been resisted, and now it is reversed. These days the growth of timber in the East Texas Piney Woods is greater than the annual harvest of trees.

The annual growth in Texas forests of softwoods during 1963, according to the U.S. Forest Service, was 1.2 billion board feet. The amount removed from the forest was just 1.1 billion board feet. Figures for hardwood show the same. A total of 443 million board feet were grown as opposed to 306 million board feet removed.

The East Texas Piney Woods area covers all or parts of 43 counties that produce nearly all the commercial timber in Texas. That timber, in 1965, is worth $775 million. Last year (1964) the state produced 995 million board feet with a value of $101 million.

Most of the state's approximately 200 sawmills are in the Piney Woods. About one-fourth of the pine lumber produced in Texas is shipped out of state, and nearly half of the hardwood lumber leaves the state.

The forested areas of Texas total an estimated 26 million acres.

Conservation measures that have made such an impact on preserving the state's forests include tree planting by landowners, timber-cutting practices that encourage natural reforestation, and intensive control of forest fires.

Many agencies have been participating in the work, including federal bureaus, state agencies, district and county governments, timber producers, processors, and wood products manufacturers.

Not since 1956 has more than a billion board feet been produced in the state. The highest years of production were between 1899 and 1929, with the peak year being in 1907 when 2.19 billion board feet were produced.

Above: The Big Thicket Wilderness area of East Texas

Top: A truck carries logs away from a Texas forest. East Texas is the most important area of the state for commercial timber production.

White House Moves to Pedernales

Above: After taking Agriculture Secretary Orville Freeman on a tour of the ranch in November 1964, LBJ rests on the porch of the house in which he was born.

Below: President Johnson and Vice President Elect Hubert Humphrey enjoy barbecued spareribs at a presidential victory celebration at the LBJ Ranch on November 4, 1964.

(1965) These days the eyes of the world focus very frequently not on Washington, DC., nor on New York City, London, or Paris, but, rather, on the Pedernales River near Johnson City, Texas, in the hill country. That's where the leader of the most powerful nation in the world spends his holidays and more and more of his working days. It's also where Lyndon Baines Johnson, the first "real" Texan to serve as President, was born and reared. (Dwight Eisenhower was born in Denison, but he left the state as a child.)

This is the part of Texas where President Johnson was schooled, where he won his first race for Congress in 1937 as an ardent admirer of Franklin D. Roosevelt and his New Deal, and where he returns with increasing frequency as the burdens of office weigh on him.

Johnson says that he has learned that he is far more productive on his ranch than in the fishbowl atmosphere of the White House. In the White House he is constantly surrounded by tourists on all sides; airplanes from nearby National Airport disturb his sleep; and conferences with government officials are a daily routine.

"I feel like I'm in the middle of an air raid," Johnson once said of his Washington, D.C., office. "At 8 a.m., when I'm trying to read a report, all the tourists are going by right under my bed. And in the afternoon, when I'm trying to take a nap, Lady Bird is in the next room with Lawrence Rockefeller and eighty leaders talking about daffodils on Pennsylvania Avenue."

The President says that at his LBJ Ranch in Texas he can accomplish in a few hours what would keep him busy into the late hours of the night at the White House.

In Texas Johnson wears khaki or tan twill instead of a blue business suit. In Texas he does his walking by strolling over 438 acres of his ranch instead of on the manicured lawns of the White House. In Texas he swims in his outdoor pool instead of in the dark tank located in the basement of the White House.

In Texas he does his paperwork and makes his famous and incessant telephone calls from a massive mahogany desk in a large, pine-paneled office on a wing of his ranch house.

So LBJ stays abreast of

LBJ demonstrates how to "cut" a cow from the herd at a press barbecue at his ranch on November 4, 1964.

worldwide developments, a courier plane bearing newspapers, intelligence data, and stacks of reports lands each morning on the strip behind his ranch. Arriving by teletype are regular reports from the State Department and the Central Intelligence Agency. A short-wave radio is also available.

Top cabinet officials and advisers come frequently to the White House on the Pedernales. Important visitors to the ranch inscribe their names on concrete blocks that have been put together as a "Friendship Walk."

Texas, and certainly the hill country, has never seen anything quite like the goings-on on the Pedernales these days.

Texas Instruments Reports Largest Earnings Ever

(1966) Texas Instruments' road to the top of the high-tech electronics industry has been spectacular as indicated by gross sales for 1966 reported at $590 million with profits of $33.3 million. But, if Chairman of the Board Patrick E. Haggerty is right, that's just the tip of a growing iceberg. He is shooting for sales of $3 billion in 1976.

Whatever the future holds, according to *Dun's Review,* TI's recent progress makes it "one of the most spectacular growth companies of the post-World War II period."

Financial observers believe that TI's sales for 1967 could reach $755 million.

TI's progress may be charted through a series of new products that has been instrumental in revolutionizing the electronics industry.

In the early 1950s the company developed the low-cost, high-frequency germanium transistor that made possible the pocket-sized transistor radio. In 1954 the company produced the first commercially available silicon transistor, which in turn enabled the company in 1958 to produce the first semiconductor integrated circuits.

These devices, formed in a tiny silicon slice, are able to perform the same functions as far-larger assemblies of numerous transistors, resistors, and capacitors.

TI's integrated circuits today may be found in Zenith hearing aids, in Polaroid Land Cameras, in Minutemen II ICBMs, and in a large number of other products. Even so, only 50 percent of TI's revenues comes from electrical and electronic components.

In 1963 the company revolutionized the seismic exploration business by becoming the first company to apply statistical communications theory to the analysis of and processing of seismic data.

The company operates under a decentralized management plan, having 51 product-customer centers that operate with great autonomy in creating products, making them, and marketing them.

The company has managed to avoid creating status symbols for its management. There are common dining room facilities, equal parking privileges, and tenure-related identification badges. Office furnishings are strictly functional.

Since 1964 the company has added 15,000 new employees.

Artificial Heart Placed in Human

(1969) Texas' famed heart surgeon, Denton Cooley of Houston, has placed an artificial heart in one of his patients. It is the world's first transplant of an artificial heart by anyone, and it is a further indication of why Houston's medical community has become world-famous.

The patient, a 47-year-old-man from Skokie, Illinois, received his artificial heart during a three-hour operation at St. Luke's Episcopal Hospital.

Cooley, the surgeon, has performed 18 heart transplants, more than any other doctor in the world. Thirty heart transplants have been done in Houston.

Cooley and his older Houston colleague and former tutor, Dr. Michael E. DeBakey, have placed Houston on the world medical map with their innovative and successful heart transplants and open heart surgery. DeBakey made the first use of the heart bypass operation in 1966, and he has received much credit for devising the artificial heart.

DeBakey had expected to be the first surgeon to use the artificial heart, and insiders say he is greatly disappointed that his former protégé with whom a considerable rivalry has developed, gained the distinction that DeBakey felt should belong to him.

The artificial heart itself cost $5,000, and the electronic power device for it cost another $20,000. The device contains all four of the usual blood chambers in a heart.

Cooley, 49 years of age, is the son of a Houston dentist who became a basketball star at the University of Texas at Austin. He studied medicine at Johns Hopkins.

DeBakey, 61, is president of Baylor College of Medicine and chairman of its Department of Surgery. He also is chief of the Cardiovascular Research and Training Center.

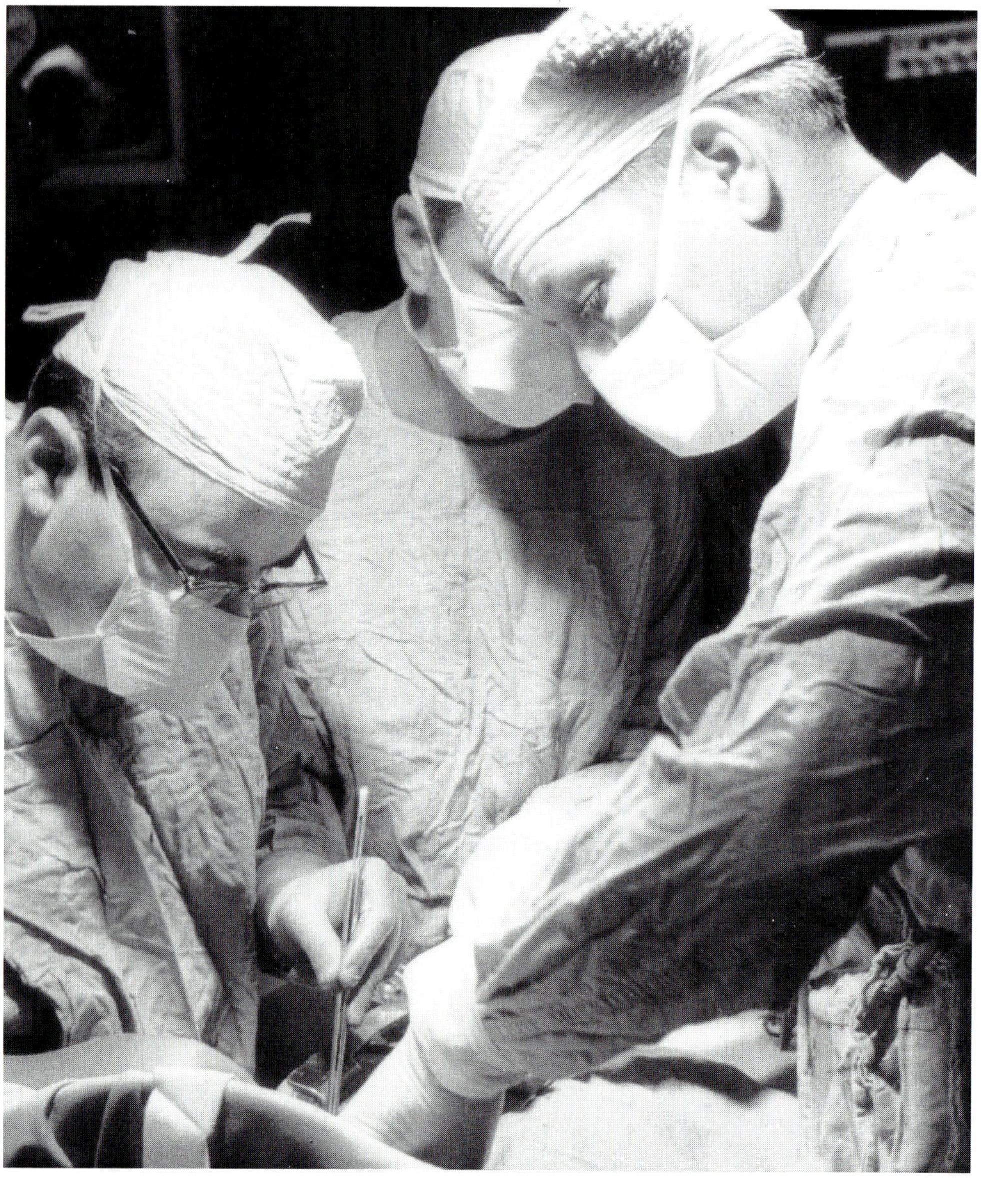

On April 5, 1969, in Houston, the surgical team of Dr. Denton A. Cooley (right), Dr. Domingo Liotta (left), and Dr. Robert D. Bloodwell implant a mechanical device known as an Orthotopic Cardiac Prosthesis (the first total replacement for a human heart) into the chest of Haskell Karp of Skokie, Illinois.

Manufacturing Showing Great Gains in State

(1969) Texas' manufacturing industries are showing rapid expansion, and one of the fastest-growing segments is that of space-age electronic goods.

In a three-year period, from 1960 to 1969, the value of manufactured goods jumped by 30 percent, rising from $9.7 billion in 1966 to $12.6 billion in 1969.

The state's "electric machinery" payrolls, which include not only space-age electronics, but household appliances as well, listed over 51,000 workers by the end of 1968. Some two dozen new plants were constructed during 1968. The heaviest concentration in electronics is in the making of components and systems for aerospace communications and navigation and for industrial and scientific controls.

Despite the state's rapid growth in manufacturing, Texas is seventh in the nation, following New York, California, Ohio, Illinois, Pennsylvania, and Michigan.

Nearly 709,000 Texans were at work in manufacturing factories by the end of 1968. During that year 321 new plants were announced for construction and 545 expansion projects were announced. The chemical industry accounted for most of the plant expansions.

In all, there were 11,661 industrial plants in the state.

Greater Dallas-Fort Worth Airport Opens as World's Largest

(1974) Texas-size is the new Greater Dallas-Fort Worth International Airport. Which is to say, it's the largest airport facility in the world.

Built at a cost of $750 million, it covers 17,500 acres or about 27 square miles. This is bigger than the entire island of Manhattan, six times as big as Los Angeles International Airport, and three times the site of Kennedy Airport.

Plans for the airport (dedicated in 1973 but with operations beginning this year) had their genesis in 1965 when Dallas and Fort Worth ended several decades of dispute over the building of an airport midway between the two cities.

D-FW is located almost exactly between the two cities on the Tarrant-Dallas County boundary.

D-FW has a unique design that permits passengers easy access by automobile to each terminal. Instead of having a huge, single terminal with extending fingers, it has a series of half-circle terminals spread along both sides of a wide thoroughfare. A passenger rail system connects the terminals.

J. Erik Jonsson, chairman of the airport, former mayor of Dallas, and a key figure in getting the airport built, said: "We were determined to build the best airport that anybody had built up to that timepoint; to think it through as far ahead as we could see . . . to have enough land to expand and add runways, widen and lengthen them, for safe accommodations of larger and heavier planes without difficulty."

J. Erik Jonsson, the first chairman of the board of the Greater Dallas-Fort Worth Airport, had served as mayor of Dallas from 1964 to 1971.

Construction of the airport reaffirms Texas' leading role in the aviation industry in both commercial and military flight. The state ranks among the nation's leaders in most categories.

Texas Monthly Success Story Continues in New Quarters

(1976) *Texas Monthly,* the Austin-based magazine that has proven that there is a national audience for a slick publication that concentrates on Texas as its subject, has moved into plush new quarters that are a far cry from its first location next door to a false-teeth factory.

The magazine's staff of 50 now is working out of the posh 16th floor of an Austin bank building.

Many people scoffed in 1970 when Michael R. Levy, a 1969 University of Texas law school graduate, began touring the state in search of a proper editor for his ambitious project. They scoffed for good reason, for many efforts in the past to launch and sustain a successful Texas magazine had failed.

But Levy, a former United Press International reporter and advertising salesman with *Philadelphia* magazine, hired as his editor Bill Broyles, an assistant to the Houston school superintendent without magazine experience. In 1973 Levy, Broyles, and a small staff put out their first issue. It contained only six pages of advertising and had a circulation of 20,000.

Now, only three years later, circulation is nearly 200,000. The October 1976 issue will have 111 pages of advertising. The magazine is available on newsstands throughout the nation.

The National Magazine Award for specialized journalism was presented to *Texas Monthly* after its first year of publication, the first time ever that the honor had been bestowed so soon after start-up.

This year the magazine's editorial budget is $700,000, or some 17.5 percent of anticipated revenues. Other leading U.S. monthlies have editorial budgets averaging something under 11 percent.

Bill Clements Elected First GOP Governor in Modern Times

(1978) A Republican oilman-businessman and former Department of Defense assistant secretary, William P. Clements, has become the state's first Republican governor since Reconstruction.

Clements, a plain-spoken newcomer to the electoral process, spent more than $7 million in the primary and general elections to defeat Democratic candidate John Hill, former attorney general. In the primary Hill had upset incumbent Democrat Dolph Briscoe, who had been in office for two terms.

Democrats continue to hold huge majorities in the Texas House and Senate. Republicans have 23 members in the House and four in the Senate.

Clements appealed in his race to the increasingly conservative mood of Texas voters. He stressed especially a need to reduce state expenditures by cutting the cost of government and eliminating state workers.

Dallas' Apparel Mart Attracts 70,000 Buyers

(1978) In days gone by, retail buyers from throughout the nation had to travel to New York City to examine and purchase the garments that their stores soon would be offering their customers. These trips to Manhattan were very long and very expensive, but now that situation has changed.

In 1964 Dallas' Trammell Crow, in conjunction with brothers John and Storey Stemmons, took a gamble by building a huge Apparel Mart in Dallas that they felt would attract hundreds, perhaps thousands, of buyers who would be happy to shift the expense and trouble of their trips to New York.

Crow and his partners (who sold out to Crow in the early 1970s) were right. This year some 70,000 retail buyers from 50 states and 30 countries will come to the Apparel Mart to see samples from manufacturers who also hail from throughout the country as well as New York City. This year's buyers are expected to spend some $1.75 billion.

Above: Trammell Crow, developer of the huge Dallas Apparel Mart, poses inside the seven-story World Trade Center.

Left: The Apparel Mart

This new development represents a fundamental change in the way Americans buy and sell clothing at the wholesale level. Regional marts such as the one in Dallas now flourish not only in Dallas, but also in Los Angeles, Chicago, and Atlanta.

Manufacturers who offer their clothing to the buyers at these regional markets recognize that there are fashion ideas and wants that do not necessarily follow those of New Yorkers.

Dallas' Apparel Mart has 1,500 showrooms that Crow rents for an average of $9.50 per square foot per year. Since the building opened in 1964 it has been expanded twice. An additional two stories now are being built.

American Airlines Comes Home to Texas

(1979) American Airlines' much ballyhooed decision to move its corporate headquarters from New York City to a site adjacent to Greater Dallas-Fort Worth International Airport represents a return to the company's roots, for its origins may be traced to 1927 with the establishment of a pioneer carrier called Texas Air Transport.

Texas Air Transport was founded by Fort Worth businessman Temple Bowen, whose success at operating a bus line there prompted his interest in aviation. A year after the airline was founded, it began air-mail service on two routes, one to Houston and Galveston, and the other to Waco, Austin, and San Antonio.

Still another year later, after having been purchased by A.P. Barrett, Texas Air Transport initiated the first passenger service in the state.

Barrett merged his new airline with another new one, Gulf Coast Airways, and the new airline took the name of Southern Air Transport. Then in 1930, in combination with several other carriers, American Airlines came into being.

Fort Worth's leading citizen, Amon Carter, was a major shareholder in the airlines from 1928, when he helped Barrett acquire it from Bowen, until his death in 1955.

The new corporate headquarters are being constructed on a wooded site just south of several other major American facilities. In the immediate area already are American's flight-attendant and pilot-training complexes, built in 1957 and 1971 respectively. In 1975 American built its headquarters for the SABRE computer system in the same area.

All these facilities are not much more than a stone's throw from the Greater Dallas-Fort Worth International Airport, which opened in 1973 as the world's largest airport. American Airlines is expected to augment its already heavy schedule from D-FW.

Perot Sells EDS to General Motors

(1984) H. Ross Perot has sold the computer company that he began singlehandedly in 1962 to General Motors in a deal that is expected to bring him some $2.5 billion for his 50 percent interest in the company. He also gets a seat on the GM board of directors.

GM is expected to use EDS' expertise in computers to streamline its operation and even to help in designing automobiles.

Perot, a Texarkana, Texas, native who graduated from the U.S. Naval Academy and then served in the Navy, began work in Dallas in 1958 as an IBM computer salesman.

One colleague, Robert Fulghum, said: "He came to work earlier, stayed later, worked harder and smarter than anybody else." Fulghum also said he had a "long view" of the future impact of computer technology on business

Billionaire entrepreneur H. Ross Perot sits at his desk in his Dallas office. The founder of the hugely successful Electronic Data Systems, Inc., Perot built his business empire virtually from scratch.

and the American way of life.

It was with that view that he incorporated EDS on June 27, 1962, with the notion of introducing and handling computer work for companies.

Oil Production Down for 12th Consecutive Year

(1984) 1984 marked the 12th consecutive year that production of crude oil in Texas declined; even so, the state is not even close to yielding its traditional ranking as first in the nation.

Crude oil production for 1984 was 875 million barrels, a drop from the historic peak year in 1972 of 1.3 billion barrels. Each year since 1972 has seen consecutive declines.

The current decline in the price of oil also has reduced drilling activity. In 1982 there were 1,404 rigs in operation; in 1984 the average is about 850.

The value of 1984 crude oil production was over $25 billion. This, combined with $13 billion in the related field of natural gas production, yielded royalty payments of $378 million to the state's permanent school fund and $155 million to the permanent university fund.

According to the Texas Mid-Continent Oil & Gas Association, the petroleum industry is the state's largest taxpayer to state and local governments, totaling more than $4.3 billion in 1983.

The oil and gas industry in Texas account for about one-third to one-fourth of the nation's entire production each year. Texas has led the nation in oil production since the turn of the century. The riches it has brought have been the major cause of the state's rapid growth and economic progress in the twentieth century. A decline in prices, such as that experienced beginning in 1982, sends major economic shock waves throughout the state as well as nation. Estimates of the oil and gas industry's impact on the overall state economy range from 20 to 50 percent even though oil and gas extraction account for only 4.3 percent of the state's jobs.

Most experts believe that the outlook for the industry in the immediate future continues to be grim. If they are correct, it is bad news for the state's economy.

Oil rig in the Gulf of Mexico, 1983

Texans Diversifying as "Good Old Days" Depart

(1985) With the economic decline precipitated by the fall in oil prices, Texans are seeking more than ever to diversify their economy to regain the competitive edge that the energy and petrochemical industries provided throughout this century.

Last year Texas produced some $209 billion in goods and services, or about 7.5 percent of the gross national product. About 22 percent of that came from energy and petrochemicals.

The future for Texas appears to be headed toward high technology.

H. Ross Perot of Dallas became a billionaire through his Electronic Data Systems, a computer service firm, and others are aiming in the same direction.

Austin, in particular, has taken off as a research and development center through such companies as Microelectronics of Computer Technology Corp. (MCC), a firm whose goal is to develop advanced computers. Dozens of cities throughout the nation had competed to be headquarters for MCC in 1983, but Austin won the honor, and that decision alone prompted a rush to the area of other high-tech businesses.

Houston is busy developing its already famous medical complexes into the next step—medical technology companies.

Dallas and Fort Worth business leaders put up $5 million for a robotics center at the University of Texas at Arlington in hopes that it would encourage more high-tech endeavors.

Dallas is already the headquarters for a pioneer in the high-tech field, Texas Instruments, whose work in the 1950s helped introduce the computer age.

Oilman-rancher Clayton Williams of Midland is an example of a "traditional" Texan who has been diversifying. Williams has been selling some of his ranches and a million acres of his oil leases as he enters a new business—telecommunications. Williams specializes in high-speed digital connections for computers and telephones serving banks and oil companies. Through his firm, ClayDesta Communications, he is building a $40-million network of microwave towers to connect such cities as El Paso, Amarillo, and Abilene.

Above: Circuit boards on a burn rack in one of Texas' electronics manufacturing companies.

Below: Biotech laboratory technicians direct their attention to their work.

Women Mayors Ruling in Texas

(1988) Texas, the Lone Star State, the land of cattle and oil, the place where rugged men long have held dominion, is making a new reputation these days. A plethora of women mayors run cities, including the state's two largest.

In Houston Kathy Whitmire, 41, is the top executive in a city of 1.8 million residents. In Dallas the mayor is Annette Strauss, 63. Betty Turner reigns in Corpus Christi, and Jan Coggeshall does the same in Galveston.

These women have taken office during a shake-up period in which dramatic changes are occurring in the way city officials are elected. Massive redistricting has occurred as the U.S. Justice Department has sought to ensure that all minorities are given a fair shake at the ballot box. City after city has abandoned the old methods of citywide at-large elections for city council members. Two-party politics has emerged. Hundreds of thousands of workers have moved to Texas from other parts of the nation.

Whitmire took advantage of these changes in Houston by winning the support of a combination of women, blacks, Hispanics, and homosexuals. One of her first moves was to

Kathy Whitmire, Houston's first female mayor

hire a black police chief, Lee P. Brown. Since taking office in 1981 she has reduced the city payroll by 10 percent, a total of 2,235 workers.

Strauss was elected mayor in Dallas, a highly conservative city, by defeating a Republican businessman. She, as was Whitmire, was backed by minorities, women, and other groups normally out of the mainstream. Strauss had been an active civic worker for many years in Dallas.

Coggeshall is a native of New York. She won her race in Galveston even though she was branded an outsider. A local newspaper tagged the race, "Outsider vs. Native."

Turner, a resident of Corpus Christi since 1955, defeated a lawyer and former president of the League of United Latin American Citizens.

Some observers believe that the state's next governor well may be a woman. State Treasurer Ann Richards won her race in the last election by gaining more votes than any other statewide candidate, including the governor.

Bank Failures Greater Than in Depression

(1989) The Texas economy continues to struggle. First came the collapse of oil prices, then the busting of the real estate boom. Now, inevitably, the woes have hit the banks. The bank failure rate now is higher than it was in the depths of the Depression.

Even the state's largest and the nation's 12th largest bank, InterFirst Corp of Dallas, a recent combination of Dallas' FirstRepublic and InterFirst, failed in 1988. It was the most expensive bank failure in the nation's history, costing taxpayers $3.6 billion. The bank's assets were seized by the federal government and sold to an out-of-state bank in North Carolina, NCNB.

In 1987 the banking industry in Texas lost nearly $2 billion; 59 banks shut their doors. Another $1.7 billion was lost in the first quarter of 1988, and 113 banks went under during the year.

Now, in 1989, some 1,700 Texas banks are believed to be on the endangered list.

Of the 10 largest banking companies existing in the mid-1980s in the state, all but one had been forced to merge with stronger out-of-state banks or had been rescued by the federal government. Independent banking in Texas has virtually ended.

Preceding the bank failures were those of a large number of savings and loans firms, many of which did so in sensational circumstances.

A number of criminal cases have been filed by the federal government.

The immediate precipitating reason for so many failures was an over-extension in speculative real estate development.

Though bank failures in Texas were worse in 1989 than during the Great Depression, several of the state's banks continued business as usual.

Texas' Female Governor Setting Fast Pace

Texas Governor Ann W. Richards

(1991, March) Silver-haired Ann Richards, Texas' first female governor since Miriam "Ma" Ferguson in the 1920s, has been in office just three months but already is sending strong signals that she will be a distinctly activist occupant of the governor's mansion.

Richards, a Democrat who defeated favored Republican candidate Clayton Williams in November and who took office in January, instituted a hiring freeze of state employees within days of taking office. She has proposed a tough ethics reform bill to scrutinize and regulate legislators' links with lobbyists and campaign contributors, and she has forced a two-year moratorium on the development of new hazardous waste sites.

Living up to campaign promises, nearly one-half of the 384 appointments she had made to boards, commissions, and agencies have been women and minorities.

Richards won the governor's office after one of the most sensational gubernatorial campaigns in years. Her opponent, oilman/cattleman/businessman Clayton Williams, had been heavily favored until the last weeks of the campaign. He spent more than $20 million in the race, some $7.9 million of it his own. But his campaign faltered after he pointedly refused to shake Richards' hand and called her a liar in a joint campaign appearance in Dallas. He also made a number of gaffes that troubled him, including comments that were deemed sexist and racist.

Richards called Williams a "polluter" among other things. Former Governor John Connally said the mud-slinging that occurred in the race was "almost tragic" and unfair to voters.

Richards served as state treasurer for eight years before winning her first race for the governor's office. She earlier served as a county commissioner in Travis County. She rose to national prominence after making a well-received keynote speech at the 1988 Democratic National Convention.

Richards, who grew up in Waco, defeated Attorney General Jim Mattox and Former Governor Marc White to gain the Democratic nomination.

She succeeded Republican Governor William P. Clements, who declined to run for reelection.

Ross Perot Ready to Run for President

(1992) H. Ross Perot for President? Maybe so.

The Texas tycoon, the richest man in Texas, and one of the richest men anywhere, acknowledged on February 20 to Larry King on his CNN interview show that he would run for the top office as an independent if voters would register him in all 50 states.

Already speculators are observing that with his billions of dollars Perot could purchase sufficient advertising and commercial time to make himself a very viable candidate.

Perot's penchant for making headlines includes his 1969 venture to provide relief for American prisoners of war held by North Vietnam by leasing two jets, loading them with food and gifts, assembling a group of journalists, and attempting to land in Hanoi. While the effort failed, it received worldwide attention and supposedly prompted North Vietnam to provide better treatment for American prisoners.

In 1979 he engineered the sensational rescue of two of his Electronic Data Systems employees from an Iranian prison.

Then, in 1984, he sold EDS to General Motors for some $2.5 billion, and as the company's biggest individual shareholder, he earned a seat on GM's board of directors. After his attempts to shake up the company failed, he resigned from the board.

NAFTA Promises Special Economic Prizes for Texas

(1993, November) Texas' wealthiest resident, H. Ross Perot, opposed it with all his might, but all but six of the state's 30-member delegation to Congress voted for the North American Free Trade Agreement on November 17, and it was approved by the House by a 234-200 margin.

Governor Ann Richards joined most other Texans in being ecstatic over the economic riches the agreement is expected to bring to the state. She lobbied strongly for NAFTA's passage.

"This is going to be the front door of the United States now," she exclaimed. "The commerce is going to be simply staggering coming through that border."

While NAFTA involves Canada as well as Mexico in a free-trade agreement with the United States, between Canada and Mexico, the latter nation has by far the greater potential for development. Mexico has a population of some 90 million residents compared to Canada's 27 million.

Texas' border with Mexico is by far the longest of any state, and the area is expected to flourish with economic development and new factories.

Texas' thriving industry and computer industries especially are well-matched for trade with Mexico.

The president of the Greater Houston Partnership, Jim Kollaer, said that by the year 2000 the treaty will have created 15,000 jobs in Houston alone and an annual economic impact of $2.1 billion.

Another Houston businessman, Eduardo Pellon of Zoilo's Furniture Store, said that his company conducted a survey showing that 80 percent of the young people in Monterrey, Mexico, had never slept on a mattress. "It could be an incredible market," he said.

Perot, the Texas computer billionaire, had gained wide publicity in campaigning against NAFTA. He predicted that the loss of American jobs to Mexico would create a "giant sucking sound."

The trio of the United States, Canada, and Mexico will be the world's largest and richest trading bloc.

Tariffs will be removed over the next several years through a gradual process.

Passage of NAFTA represented the culmination of a seven-year debate introduced during the Republican presidency of Ronald Reagan. Democratic President Bill Clinton took up the pro-NAFTA arguments following the Reagan-Bush presidencies and lobbied hard for its victory.

Texas Ready to Surpass New York in Population

(1994) Sometime in March 1994 Texas bypassed New York state as the nation's second most populous state.

Texas, according to state demographer Steve Murdock, is growing at a rate of 29,000 persons a month compared to New York's rate of 7,300 a month.

The state, as indicated by U.S. Census Bureau figures, grew by 2 percent during the one-year period ending July 1, 1993, a higher rate than California or New York, both of whom trailed the national average of 1.1 percent with rates of 1 percent and 0.5 percent.

These figures indicate that Texas is growing four times as fast as New York and twice as fast as California.

The state's rapid climb in population has seen it jump from sixth in 1960 to third in 1990. In 1980 its population was 14.2 million, and by the 1990s it had climbed beyond 17 million.

Murdock said Texas' growth is the most balanced of all the four largest states, having a healthy percentage of migration from other parts of the country and 25 percent from foreign migration. Of California's growth in the past year, 95 percent was accounted for by foreign migration.

The 2 percent growth rate for Texas represents the highest rate since the early 1980s, when a 3.9 percent rate was reached in 1981-1982. This fell to .3 percent in 1987-1988.

The fastest-growing state in the nation in 1992-1993 was Nevada with a 3.9 percent rate, followed by Idaho, 3.1 percent.

The Future

Texas. From earliest frontier times, even before the terrain was part of the United States, the very word was magical. It conjured up the delectable aroma of hope, of escape from the accumulated wrongs of the past, of passage to a bright future, of endless possibilities.

As the year 2000 approaches, the word "Texas" brings to mind a similar picture, different only in degree and with much of the mystery now removed. The state, planted firmly and strategically as an anchor at the bottom center of the nation, continues to exert a powerful pull. If the great expectations of its magical promise have diminished slightly, its actual impact upon the rest of the nation has only grown stronger.

Its location has become even more strategic in an international sense with the passage of the North American Free Trade Agreement, for trade with Mexico promises to bustle in the future. No state stands to benefit more than Texas.

Sometime in the first half of 1994, Texas became the second most populous state in the nation, passing New York. Is it only a matter of time until it becomes first among all the states? Its growth rate is almost twice that of the leader, California. By the year 2000 Texas' population is projected to be 19.5 million; by the year 2030, 27 million.

Not only is Texas gaining population faster than the rest of the nation, its people are more diverse. Already nearly half the population is minority. By 2015 minorities will become the majority. The fastest-growing population group by far is the Hispanics. By 1990 they already constituted more than one-fourth of the population.

There were economic troubles in the 1980s—a devastating drop in the price of oil, a crisis in banks and thrifts that saw record numbers of failures, massive vacancies in the downtown centers of the largest cities. Those blows were taken and they were dealt with. While the growth rate momentarily paused, it soon accelerated once more, and easily began outpacing that of the nation's.

The super-conducting super collider, located just south of Dallas and touted as the nation's next great adventure in science with a budget to match, encountered an obstinate and budget-minded Congress in 1993 that dramatically axed the project. This too, the state shook off, although regretfully.

Texas' personality is marked by an emphasis on human resources rather than natural resources, by the maturing of new high-tech industries, by the arrival of increasing numbers of tourists and tourist dollars, by headline-making explorations of new frontiers in medical science, and by new glamour enterprises such as movie making, which has brought a steady stream of famous film personalities.

Some things will be constant for many years to come. For example, cattle raising, cotton growing, and their related activities have led the nation in most categories and will almost certainly continue to do so. Nor are the important and long-time endeavors in oil and gas, petrochemicals, and aerospace technology expected to wither away.

While one sees the future only with uncertainty, it is hard to imagine an end to the magical quality of the word "Texas." And the facts of the 1990s seemed to justify it. Texas' days of greatest influence and authority lie ahead.

Clockwise from above: Primroses and bluebonnets paint the landscape of Brenham, Texas. Photo by Scott Berner/The Stockhouse, Inc., Houston

Whooping cranes, Aransas National Wildlife Refuge. Photo by James A. Ellenburg/The Stockhouse, Inc., Houston

Palo Duro Canyon is the picture of natural beauty. Palo Duro Canyon State Park, with 16,400 acres, is the largest state park in Texas. Photo by Richard Stockton/The Stockhouse, Inc., Houston

Above: Two cowboys strike an archetypal pose in a West Texas field. Photo by Skeeter Hagler/TexaStock

Left: While more than 4,000 species of wild flowers grow in the Lone Star State, it is the yellow rose of Texas that will forever be linked to the state thanks to the song of that name. Photo by Kennedy/TexaStock

Facing page: Five Franciscan missions are among the many points of historical interest in San Antonio. Pictured here is the Mission Nuestra Señora de la Purisima Concepción, founded in 1731. Photo by James Blank

Left: Some of Dallas' many skyscrapers are visible in this view taken from Municipal Plaza Park. Photo by James Blank

Right: The granite Texas State Capitol in Austin, the largest state capitol in the United States, was constructed in 1888. The Goddess Liberty stands atop the dome holding a five-pointed star, the symbol of Texas. Photo by Scott Berner/The Stockhouse, Inc., Houston

Above: Every October State Fair Park, Dallas' largest park, is the site of the biggest state fair in the nation. One of the many buildings that make up the State Fair complex is the Hall of State. Photo by James Blank

Above: The 1980s saw a revival of Fort Worth's downtown area with many of its older buildings restored. Photo by James Blank

Right: Fort Worth's skyline rises above the city's unique Water Garden, designed by architects Philip Johnson and John Burgee. Photo by James Blank

CNB

Above: One of San Antonio's major tourist attractions is the Paseo del Rio. Here a tour boat navigates the San Antonio River as it meanders through the downtown district of the city. Photo by James Blank

Right: San Antonio's colorful Sunken Gardens are a feast for the eyes. Photo by Scott Berner/The Stockhouse, Inc., Houston

Above: The striking Wortham Fountains stand in Houston's Tranquility Park. Photo by James Blank

Left: Dallas' State Fair Park is home to that city's Museum of Natural History. Photo by James Blank

Facing page: Houston's Gus Wortham Theater Center is part of the city's Civic Center complex, located in the central business district. Also situated in the complex are the George R. Brown Convention Center and the Jesse H. Jones Hall for the Performing Arts. Photo by James Blank

Left: The Houston Astrodome, the world's first enclosed sports stadium, is home to the Oilers and the Astros. Photo by Scott Berner/The Stockhouse, Inc., Houston

Left: It's "Batter up!" for the Houston Astros. Photo by Jo. L. Keener/The Stockhouse, Inc., Houston

Top: Football is more than a game in Texas; it is in the heart and soul of almost every Texan. Pictured here are the Dallas Cowboys. Photo by Steve Pelluer/The Stockhouse, Inc., Houston

Above: In this 1987 game the Rockets battled the Chicago Bulls. Photo by Jo. L. Keener/The Stockhouse, Inc., Houston

Big Bend National Park, in the southwestern part of Texas, measures more than 1,250 square miles. Deep canyons, desert plateaus, and the Chisos Mountains are all contained within the park's borders. Photo by Scott Berner/The Stockhouse, Inc., Houston

Above: Six Flags Over Texas is just one of many of Dallas' recreational attractions enjoyed by residents and visitors. Photo by James Blank

Right: The Lyndon B. Johnson Space Center, the 1,600-acre complex that houses mission control headquarters for manned U.S. space flights, opened this new visitor center in 1992. Photo by Bill Pogue/The Stockhouse, Inc., Houston

Overleaf: Mexican folk dancers entertain during the Diez y Seis Festival at the capitol in Austin. Photo by Larry Kolvoord/ TexaStock

Making Work Easier for Researchers and Engineers

NATIONAL INSTRUMENTS

Founders: Dr. James Truchard, William Nowlin, and Jeffrey Kodosky
Founded: 1976 in Austin

Before National Instruments went to work, a researcher wanting to use his or her computer to monitor an experiment would have had a problem.

Until the mid-1970s it was difficult for most people to use a voltmeter, or oscilloscope, or any other instruments with most computers. Machines that measured things couldn't easily talk to machines that analyzed things.

Three University of Texas researchers set out to change that in 1976 when they founded National Instruments in Austin. Dr. James Truchard, William Nowlin, and Jeffrey Kodosky created the company with the mission of making it easy to create computer-based instrumentation systems for test and measurement, data acquisition, process monitoring, and control applications.

Within a year they released their first product, a plug-in instrumentation interface board for a computer made by Digital Equipment Corporation. National Instruments went on to create a myriad of hardware and software products to make work easier for researchers and engineers. It has also become a major force in establishing industry standards for electronic interfaces between computers and instruments.

In 1983 National Instruments released its first interface board for the IBM PC, a move that spurred the use of affordable computers for instrumentation applications. That same year IBM selected the firm as supplier of this GPIB interface for its IBM PC-based instrument controller.

"Of course, a vital part of all this is the software," says Dudley Baker, vice president of marketing for NI. "A board plugged into a computer doesn't do anything unless you have software that's well designed, well thought out, and easy to use."

In 1986 the company introduced LabVIEW® for Macintosh computers, the first instrumentation software system to use graphical programming techniques. LabVIEW redefined the way engineers and scientists performed and analyzed tasks—instead of writing text-based programs, users could create virtual instruments with icons. In 1987 NI introduced its DOS-based LabWindows® software, with automatic code generation capabilities for programmers who prefer using a text-based solution. Both products now run on Windows PCs and UNIX-based SPARCstations, as well.

LabVIEW is the dominant graphical instrumentation software product. It has earned two *MacUser* magazine Editors' Choice Awards, a WIN 100 Award from *Windows Magazine*, an R&D 100 Award from *Research & Development* magazine, and Test Product of the Year from *Test & Measurement World* magazine.

LabWindows is the premier text-based instrument software product, winning awards from *Test & Measurement World, Electronics Test, BasicPro*, and *Scientific Computing and Automation* magazines.

Dr. James Truchard, co-founder, president, and chairman of the board, received the Texas High Technology Entrepreneur Award in 1987 for nurturing NI into a rapidly growing, successful company. In 1991 Truchard was awarded the Master Entrepreneur of the Year Award.

Today, with more than 700 employees worldwide, National Instruments has plans to expand its headquarters to a 65-acre site in north Austin. Long-term plans include building a corporate campus on the property.

"This property will give us the growing room we need to house the employees and equipment necessary to realize our long-range business plan," Truchard explains.

Right: Dr. Vida Vogel investigates the structure and function of membrane mimetic interfaces using LabVIEW software on a Macintosh IIci, an epifluorescent microscope, a Langmuir trough, and a high-power laser system. Here Dr. Vogel examines the block diagram and front panel of a LabVIEW program used to control the motion of barriers in an experimental trough and monitor the barrier position and surface pressure. Courtesy, the University of Washington and National Instruments

Below: Fiber engineers at DuPont's Camden, South Carolina, plant use LabWindows and a high-speed data acquisition system based on the AT-MIO-16F-5 to study—and eliminate—instantaneous upsets responsible for process breaks on fiber spinning machines. The system monitors and analyzes pressure, temperature, and rate-of-flow of air and molten polymer via 64 sensors connected to a fiber spinning machine. Courtesy, DuPont and National Instruments

Committed to Quality

MINCO TECHNOLOGY LABS INC.

Founders: Liz Coker, owner and chief executive officer; Don Potter, president and general manager; Mary Mooney, international sales manager; and Rebecca Shackelford, chief financial officer

Liz Coker, owner and chief executive officer of Minco Technology.

Right: ECL A.C. testing station. Photo by Michael Rafferty

"If you saw it in Desert Storm, we have parts in it," says Don Potter, president of Minco Technology Labs Inc. "It's that simple."

Minco tests and sells unencapsulated semiconductor devices to hybrid circuit manufacturers, components that have found their way into machines ranging from missiles and war planes to super-secret military satellites.

About 80 percent of the market for Minco's tiny transistors and integrated circuits is military. But military spending isn't what it used to be. Some of Minco's competitors have gone down in flames in the fight for marketshare. Minco has survived, and even thrived, through the power of a simple concept: Quality.

Minco Technology Labs is the brainchild of native Texans Liz Coker, Don Potter, Rebecca Shackelford, and Mary Mooney. Founded in Los Angeles in 1981, Minco moved to Austin the following year, soon after breaking its first million dollars in sales.

Other milestones would follow:

In 1985 sales tripled from $3 million the year before to $9 million. In 1988 the company spun off a separate subsidiary, Austin Semiconductor Inc., which does custom packaging for high-performance chips.

The firm established a beachhead in the European market in 1992 when it achieved ISO 9002 registration from the French government. This earned Minco credibility that has attracted other European customers, explains Coker, owner and chief executive officer.

Minco has been lauded for excellence by customers including Teledyne and Raytheon. Customers polled in Minco's annual survey gave the company a 99.5 percent quality rating in 1992. During 19 supplier audits, not one discrepancy was found. Its "No Questions Asked" return policy shows Minco's confidence in its work.

The company that began with four people now has about 130 in its north Austin building with annual sales of about $11 million. One reason for Minco's vitality may be Coker's respect for her co-workers, whom she views as equals. "You'll never hear me use the word 'employee.' It's

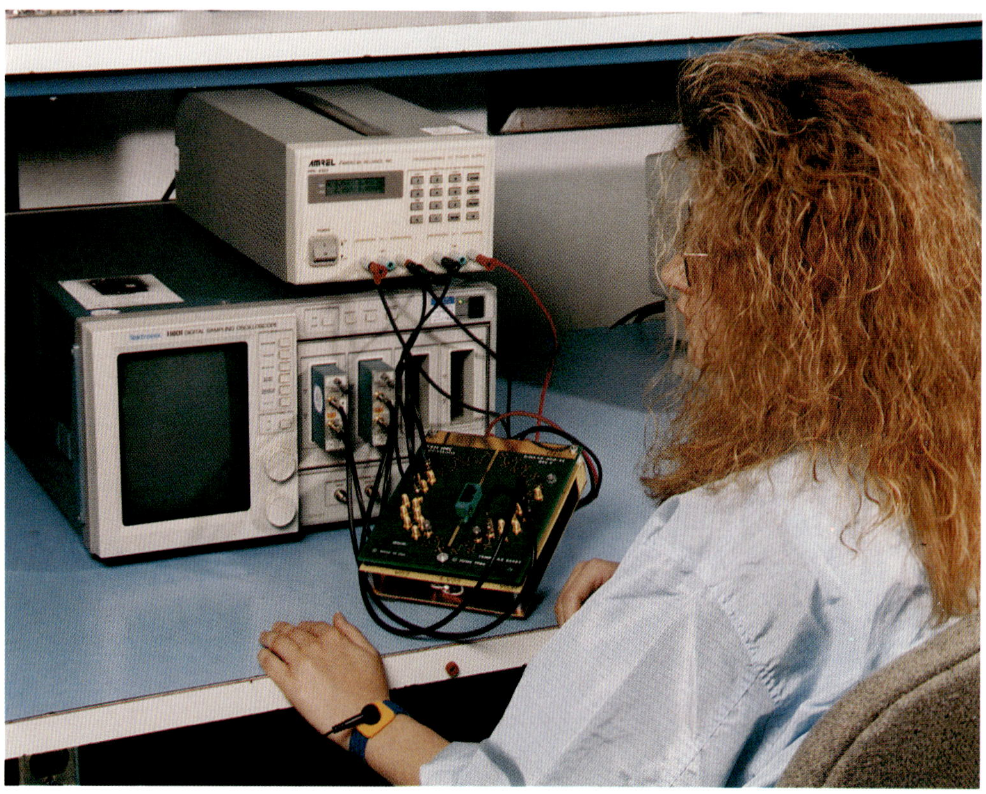

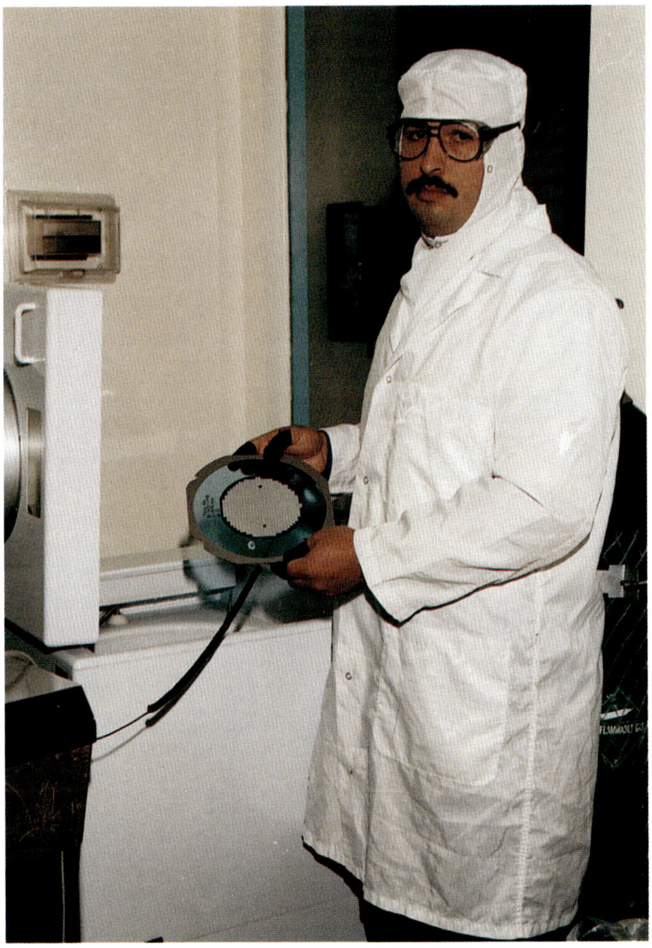

A Minco Technology technician places a semiconductor tape-mounted wafer-washing machine. Photo by Michael Rafferty

'team member.' We've always worked as a team," Coker says.

Minco's management style was the subject of a case study by the Graduate School of Business at the University of Texas. The student panel described it as "astonishingly open and innovative."

Minco has instituted a full company financial training program based on the premise that full disclosure of financial data creates ownership and fiscal responsibility among employees. A profit-sharing program introduced in 1992 has also added to the atmosphere of teamwork.

The Small Business Administration has honored the company for its management style with Awards for Excellence five times between 1984 and 1992. For her leadership, Coker was honored by the SBA as Texas Business Person of the Year for 1992.

Within the community, Minco has proven itself to be a good corporate neighbor. The company founded the Austin Quality Quorum, a discussion group with representatives from a range of industries aimed at promoting excellence. For this and other work, Minco received the Austin Quality Award for Significant Merit.

Minco's recycling and environmental program has become a model for other Austin businesses. In July 1992 the company reached its goal of becoming completely free of hazardous chemicals.

The high-tech firm provides books and mentors to a local elementary school. Also, executives serve as consultants for the Junior Achievements Program, teaching students about business and free enterprise.

Minco was the first company in Texas to institute drug testing aimed at creating a drug-free workplace. Its 1989 court victory cleared the way for random drug testing in the state. For employees with drug problems, the company offers an employee assistance program. No one has ever been fired because of drug problems.

Coker, who helped pioneer the chip industry as an engineer with Texas Instruments, said being comfortable with change is the only way to survive. "We've adapted very well," she says. "The only constant in our business is change, so our attitude is very good. We're always looking toward change."

Custom-designed LM139 probe test fixture. Photo by Michael Rafferty

With an eye toward the future, the company is exploring business opportunities in Russia and Eastern Europe. Minco is also actively courting more space industry customers, whose specifications are often even more demanding than Minco's military clients. But meeting tough specs doesn't scare Minco's chief executive officer. "We live, eat, and breathe quality," she explains.

An International Energy Leader

DRESSER INDUSTRIES

Founder: Solomon Dresser
Founded: 1880
Principal: John J. Murphy, chairman and CEO

Wherever oil and natural gas are found around the world today, Dallas' Dresser Industries is there providing the services and products that pull these hydrocarbons from the ground and the equipment that processes and converts them into myriad refined products, petrochemicals, and electric power undergirding the modern world.

Dresser's transformation into a global energy leader has occurred in the past decade as it shed more than two dozen other businesses to focus squarely on expanding its historic strengths in oil and gas.

Today Dresser is firmly positioned as an international leader across the energy spectrum, with capabilities encompassing oil field services, hydrocarbon processing, and engineering services. Such a spread is unique in the industry—Dresser's markets span not only "upstream" oil and gas exploration, drilling, production, and transmission, but also "downstream" power generation, gas processing, petrochemical production, petroleum refining, and marketing.

"We are a stronger company than we have ever been," says Dresser chairman and chief executive officer John J. Murphy. "We have become the kind of company we wanted to be, leading in the kinds of industries where we wanted to be."

Dresser's Waukesha Engine Division offers gas-fueled engines and power systems in every region of the world.

Although the benefits of its shift are plainly evident today, changing the firm's direction was a bold move when it began in 1982. Success was far from assured.

Solomon Dresser had launched his venture in 1880 to sell a better well packer for the infant oil industry. Energy-related businesses always remained at its core as it grew, but over the years Dresser burgeoned into a multi-industry conglomerate, also selling products ranging from fire hydrants to life insurance.

It was an unwieldy combination, yet profitable. Dresser in 1981 was an industrial leader, with its non-energy businesses generating $1.5 billion of that year's $4.6 billion in revenue. Net earnings totaled $316.6 million. Deliberately divesting one-third of the company's annual revenue and commensurate profit to concentrate on the volatile energy industry was a tremendous risk, Murphy explains.

Murphy, however, knew Dresser Industries was stagnating because it lacked focus. But even though oil exploration and drilling had already started its decade-long slump and, to many, didn't seem a likely avenue for growth, Murphy believed demand for energy could only increase over time. Furthermore, he and other top company leaders came from an oil equipment and services background. They knew the industry and had forged strong customer relationships over many years: Concentrating on oil and natural gas was in essence a return to Dresser's traditional strength.

Setting the ambitious goal of becoming a leading supplier of highly engineered products and services for the entire hydrocarbon energy industry, Dresser gradually sold or spun off its now-extraneous non-energy businesses—26 operating units in all.

Murphy simultaneously turned to acquisitions, strengthening Dresser's energy capabilities and broadening its operational scope as good buys presented themselves.

Initial acquisitions primarily bolstered Dresser's hydrocarbon processing segment, simply because that is where the best purchases developed as companies stressed by the weak oil market looked for a strong haven. Key purchases included Turbodyne in 1984, followed by Worthington Pump and Masoneilan in 1986.

In 1988, however, Dresser expanded into new territory with the acquisition of M.W. Kellogg Co. Acquiring Kellogg, among the world's leading technology-oriented engineering and construction contractors, extended Dresser's horizons by giving it the ability to design and build refineries as well as petrochemical and liquefied natural gas plants around the world.

Dresser expanded as well through the formation of several joint ventures with Ingersoll-Rand Co. First was IRI International Corp., now 50 percent owned by Dresser, formed in 1985 of the two firms' drilling rigs and related equipment products. In a 1987 joint venture now owned 51 percent by Dresser, the two folded their reciprocating compressor and turbomachinery businesses into Dresser-Rand Co. And in 1992 Ingersoll-Dresser Pump Co., of which Dresser owns 49 percent, was created to combine the companies' pump operations.

Dresser and Halliburton Co. in 1986 combined their drilling fluid businesses to form M-I Drilling Fluids Co., which became 64 percent owned by Dresser. In 1987 Dresser's wireline service business was consolidated with Litton Industries' seismic, core analysis, and other reservoir description services. Formed from this joint venture was Western Atlas, of which Dresser owned 29.5 percent.

The result, says Murphy, was five top international competitors. Dresser-Rand, for example, created "a significant worldwide supplier" in compressors and turbines. Ingersoll-Dresser Pump manufactures, markets, and supports the world's broadest range of pump products and services.

Murphy's vision proved far-sighted. Dresser Industries today, with 97 manufacturing plants in 50 countries around the globe, is the world's third-largest oil field services company and is unparalleled in its ability to help customers produce, process, and market oil and gas. Its $5 billion in annual revenues surpasses earlier levels, with nearly all stemming from Dresser's breadth of energy-related businesses. Dresser ranks in the top quarter of the latest *Fortune* 500 company listings.

The Ingersoll-Dresser Pump joint venture manufactures, markets, and supports the world's broadest range of pump products.

As a result of Murphy's efforts to broaden Dresser's reach, the company's overall portfolio is slightly weighted to businesses serving downstream industries. That conscious design helped insulate Dresser from the inherent boom-and-bust volatility of the oil and gas exploration and production business.

"It's the nature of the industry that some segments will be hurting at the same time others are performing beautifully," Murphy explains. "But because Dresser is involved at every level, we can

A broad array of gauges is produced by Dresser's Instrument Division for pressure and temperature measurement and control.

concentrate our efforts where we'll get the best return."

The same principle applies as well to Dresser's international operations. Industries maturing in one part of the world often are expanding in others. With plants and operations in nearly every significant oil- and natural gas-producing center worldwide, the company can lead in opening new markets.

Dresser furthered its transformation into a totally energy-focused company in 1992 with the spin-off of its remaining industrial product companies under the name INDRESCO. But Dresser is continuing to fortify and balance its energy portfolio, concentrating in recent acquisitions on upstream growth and international leadership.

M.W. Kellogg, a Dresser division, designs, builds, and procures equipment for major energy-processing complexes throughout the world.

M.W. Kellogg has a strong position in the U.S. and international markets modernizing refineries and other energy plants.

Dresser's three key acquisitions in 1993 gave the organization new capabilities to serve the world's oil and gas fields. Bredero Price, based in England, holds nearly 60 percent of the pipe-coating business in its international markets. TK Valve, a major global supplier of pipeline ball valves for the oil, gas, and petrochemical industries, significantly builds Dresser's upstream product line, according to Murphy.

Although the Bredero Price and TK Valve purchases were important, industry observers say Dresser achieved a coup with its recent acquisition of Houston-based Baroid Corp. Baroid's strengths in oil and gas exploration and production went far in solidifying Dresser's position as a global competitor. Analysts at the time noted that the acquisition also brought Dresser leadership in the rapidly growing fields of horizontal and directional drilling, plus offshore oil and gas exploration and production.

"The acquisition of Baroid Corp. is integral to our upstream game plan," Murphy declares. "It makes us as complete a player upstream as we are downstream. Nobody else matches our scope and depth as a global oil field services supplier. We have no product gaps."

Shortly after the announced acquisiton of Baroid, Dresser decided to sell its minority interest in Western Atlas for $558 million. Murphy explains, "There was significant hidden value in our noncontrolling interest that we have unlocked. It gives Dresser and its shareowners substantial flexibility for the future."

Dresser also divested its 64 percent interest in M-I Drilling Fluids to comply with the terms of an agreement with the U.S. Justice Department regarding the Baroid acquisition.

Dresser Industries' coming of age in world energy markets happened at the right time to participate in vast new opportunities arising in Third World nations, a number of which have large untapped oil and gas reserves. In fact, the World Bank projects that developing nations will account for 56 percent of the decade's global energy investment, with countries in Asia and the Pacific (not considering Japan) expected to glean more than a third of that investment.

Dresser currently is active in several successor states of the former Soviet Union, the Peoples Republic of China,

and other emerging markets along the Pacific Rim, Indonesia, and various countries in South America and Africa. But Murphy is particularly pleased with the recent explosion of new opportunities in China and the countries of the former Soviet Union. The executive says both areas "could be immense markets for exploration, drilling, and production as well as transmission. Dresser is proceeding on a number of upstream and downstream fronts in both regions."

Experts predict that China may develop its energy potential sooner than the Soviet Union's successor Commonwealth of Independent States because of China's relatively greater political stability. Many economists have predicted that China will sustain average growth rates of at least 7 percent over the next 10 years, which would double its gross domestic product by early in the coming century and perhaps even make China an economic powerhouse. Dresser's experience to date reflects this trend as well, with key operations M.W. Kellogg, Bredero Price, and Dresser-Rand already in the Peoples Republic.

The long-term potential is great in the CIS, however; many geologists think unexplored CIS reserves may be far larger than the sea of oil underlying Saudi Arabia. Noting that Dresser has done business in Russia since the 1930s, Murphy is especially optimistic about its prospects there, once the political and economic climate stabilizes. "Logic tells you that if you've known people over many years and developed a business relationship, you may have an edge over companies new on the scene," he explains.

In an early joint venture that Murphy says has tremendous possibilities, Dresser-Rand will help Russia's state gas industry, Gazprom, convert a military plant to make turbine compressor sets for oil and gas transmission. It will also help revamp gas pipeline compressors in Western Siberia. M.W. Kellogg has signed a letter of intent to design and build a gas injection condensate recovery system in Uzbekistan. Bredero Price is working in Azerbaijan and Western Siberia, and the DMD Division has a Russian joint venture for the manufacture of gas meters. Baroid subsidiaries are also very active in these developing markets.

While Murphy is convinced there are more opportunities long-term in the international arena, Dresser is not ignoring the domestic market. Economic recovery in the United States means more demand for natural gas, boosting drilling and Dresser's products and service prospects along with it. Increasing environmental regulations open a path for more sophisticated products, such as Baroid's new environmentally friendly Petrofree drilling fluid. Expanding environmental safeguards also create engineering and construction opportunities for M.W. Kellogg.

Above: Dresser's Security/DBS operations provide both roller-cone and PDC drill bits to efficiently penetrate oil and gas formations throughout the world.

Top left: Dresser's Masoneilan valves are utilized globally in process, power, and other energy-related markets.

IRI International, 50 percent owned by Dresser, is a leading manufacturer of drilling and workover rigs.

Dresser Industries is confident about its future. "Virtually every aspect of modern civilization is affected by oil and gas, which places us in the forefront of future economic activity," Murphy points out. "Also, we have a global economy now in many industries, and certainly in oil and gas. The companies that will do well in the future are those that are globally competitive. Wherever the business is tomorrow, that's where Dresser Industries will be."

Committed Concern for the Environment

GEO-MARINE, INC.

Founded: 1972
President and CEO: Ruben G. Garza

In 1972 three former Texas Instrument employees decided to put some action behind the talk of two years. They sat down together, with their wives present, and stated the risks clearly. Starting a business was not easy. They would need equipment. Could they get a bank loan? There were many factors to consider. But each partner was ready to take on the task of building a business—one of the first service-oriented companies to enter a new industry—the environmental industry. And ever since then, Geo-Marine has been providing its clients with high-quality services while maintaining a commitment for the intelligent management of our natural resources.

Ruben G. Garza, one of the original principals and current chief executive officer of Geo-Marine, remembers the early days of taking out the office trash, going without pay, and working 15- to 16-hour days in order to position the company toward a rapidly changing society.

In response to the concerns of many newly formed environmental groups, general public awareness of current or potential environmental problems grew. As public awareness grew, both government and private industry became federally mandated to look at their actions' effects upon the environment, with particular emphasis on sensitive ecosystems.

Initially, Geo-Marine targeted as potential clients both municipalities and private utility companies throughout the country. During the firm's early days, many of the projects were in Texas where all but one lake is manmade. Although most Texans view their handy boating and fishing lake as a recreational spot, many were planned specifically to facilitate the needs of electrical utility companies.

In order for the utilities to obtain the now more restrictive government permits, studies had to be done that identified changes in water temperatures and potential pollutants being discharged into a body of water or aquifer. In addition, they had to produce findings of "no harm to fish, marine fauna, and plankton," explains Garza.

Gradually, services offered by Geo-Marine expanded to include the services of biologists, anthropologists, economists, geologists, engineers,

Above: A GMI biologist reads an aerial photo for delineation of a plant community.

Right: Hazardous waste site testing.

planners, and many other scientists and field workers who contribute to the company's interdisciplinary work, allowing Geo-Marine to address a wide range of environmental issues.

With a multitude of federal and state laws and regulations in place, virtually any property transaction or construction activity could require intensive environmental studies. Whether a company is planning a property transfer or significant construction activity, it must know whether there are present or potential soil or water contaminants, archeological sites, endangered species or fauna, wetland areas, or if asbestos exists in any structures on site. "Not knowing the facts before a deal is made," says Garza, "can be costly."

Despite an erratic economy and the waxing and waning of political correctness concerning environmental issues, Geo-Marine today has over 125 employees with its corporate office in Plano (Dallas), Texas, and additional offices in Baton Rouge, Louisiana; Norfolk, Virginia; Oak Ridge, Tennessee; and San Antonio, Texas. Its clients include the U.S. Army Corps of Engineers, the U.S. Navy and Air Force, and private clients such as Batelle and Martin-Marietta with work sites ranging from Baltimore to San Diego and from Canada to Mexico. Having already worked in Venezuela, Pakistan, and Iran, Geo-Marine is also expanding its international market in places such as Mexico and South America.

Today Geo-Marine specializes in the preparation of environmental studies, environmental assessments, environmental impact statements, and hazardous materials management for both private and governmental clients. Geo-Marine has staff qualified and experienced in the preparation of environmental impact analyses for virtually any category required. All of Geo-Marine's environmental assessments address typical environmental attributes including air quality, noise, surface and groundwater resources, socioeconomics, geology and soils, biological resources, and cultural resources.

As an example of its diverse environmental and research experience, GMI was contracted in 1993 by the U.S. Air Force to develop a bird avoidance model for risk assessment of bird aircraft strike hazard at Dare County Bombing Range in North Carolina. The U.S. Air Force suffers approximately 3,000 bird strikes per year with an average cost of $45 million; more important, some lives have been lost as a result of bird aircraft strikes. The methodologies and technology developed by GMI will be used for conservation management and bird aircraft strike hazard reduction at Air Force bases throughout the world.

Geo-Marine's Engineering Department specializes in the conduct of sanitary sewer infiltration/inflow analyses, sewer system evaluation surveys, treatment plant analyses and effluent discharge plume studies, final clarifier short-circuit and solids distribution analyses, and disinfectant contact time studies for water treatment plants, as well as other similar associated engineering evaluations. GMI has the field equipment required to conduct rainfall measurement, flow monitoring, physical system inspection, smoke testing, dyed-water infiltration and night flow isolation studies, solids distribution sampling and analysis, and fluorometric dye dispersion sampling and analysis.

Additionally, Geo-Marine provides hazardous waste site evaluation and remediation planning, Resource Conservation and Recovery Act (RCRA) investigations, groundwater pollution monitoring and modeling, and underground storage tank (UST) evaluations and remediation planning.

"It's always our goal to be totally unbiased and objective when doing environmental

assessments or impact statements," says Garza. But he quickly adds that Geo-Marine is not the world's environmental police squad. "We're here to know the latest environmental laws and regulations. We offer detailed and accurate work, done on time and within budget. And we provide the experience and expertise private companies and governmental agencies are seeking by giving them solutions while meeting the highest environmental standards."

Teddy Roosevelt, back in 1903, made note of the peril the colonial nesting birds faced along the eastern shore and established Florida's Pelican Island as a refuge. It was the beginning of the refuge system for fish, fowl, and wildlife. And during the past 90 years much has been done to create a "safe haven" for natural habitats and their inhabitants. But only in the past two decades has man looked at his effect upon a fragile ecosystem. We have come to understand that for every action upon the environment, there is a reaction, some planned, some totally unexpected. By adding to the understanding of how the environment and technology can work together for a better world, Geo-Marine remains a leader in the field of environmental and engineering services.

Above: A Geo-Marine archeologist measuring artifacts recovered from a site near Houston.

Top: A GMI staff member hand-digitizing a wetlands map for development of a GIS Data Base.

A Key Player in Scientific Research and Development

TEXAS RESEARCH INTERNATIONAL, INC.

Founder: Dr. J. Scott Thornton
Founded: 1975
Officers: Dr. J. Scott Thornton, president and chairman; Julia Maloukis, corporate vice president and business manager; Alice Short, corporate secretary

In Tom Clancy's *The Hunt for Red October*, Navy sonar experts put their submarine detection technology to the test against a stealthy Soviet sub.

Scott Thornton has done his share of development and testing of sonar technology. His company, Texas Research International, Inc., has been a key player in submarine sonar technology for the United States Navy. TRI has also tested suspension bridge cables and protective clothing for firefighters, done environmental engineering, and more.

"The question, 'What do you do for a living?' is a stumper for me," says Thornton, president and chairman of TRI. "It's hard to know where to begin."

For TRI the beginning was 1975 in Austin. Originally called the Texas Research Institute, Thornton founded TRI as a spin-off from Tracor Inc., where he was manager of applied sciences. He continues his founding mission of applied sciences and development services on a contract basis to the government and to business.

"The wonderful thing about working for the government is that the government is more of a risk taker than commercial clients, because it will fund advanced state-of-the-art projects. This means we can get very challenging projects," Thornton explains. "The commercial client wants service, he wants it now, he wants the best, and he doesn't want to pay for the learning curve. We've been successful at taking what we've learned from the high-risk government work and translating that into cost-effective but profitable commercial work."

Texas Research International, Inc., is actually an umbrella company for three independent subsidiary businesses: TRI/Austin, Inc., TRI/Environmental, Inc., and TRI/TESSCO, Inc. Though independent businesses, the subsidiaries cooperate on projects of mutual interest and share personnel and resources, as well as operating and management systems.

TRI/Austin, Inc., under the direction of Dr. Alan Bray, is TRI's flagship company and conducts materials research and development projects. It offers nondestructive testing and evaluation, polymer science and composite materials development, failure analysis, laboratory testing services,

Above: A TRI technician conducting material testing on an Instron machine.

Right: The firm's corporate headquarters, located in the rolling hills west of Austin, Texas.

and reliability engineering services for both commercial and government clients.

Established to address health, safety, and environmental concerns, TRI/Environmental, Inc., under the technical direction of Dr. Ed Golla, focuses on protective clothing evaluation, development, and certification; analytical chemistry testing services; materials testing and characterization; biological testing; and compressed air testing. The firm also works with geosynthetics, which are engineered materials designed to enhance or alter the behavior of soils. TRI/Environmental's customer base is primarily commercial.

TRI/TESSCO, Inc., provides on-site technical and engineering support services for governmental clients. The parent company manages TRI/TESSCO from its Austin headquarters, keeping overhead low and cost-effectiveness high. TRI/TESSCO's future was recently enhanced with the 1994 award of a $16-million contract with the Naval Command Control and Ocean Surveillance Center in San Diego.

TRI's first profitable breakthrough was with compressed air testing. In 1977 the company patented a kit for collecting air samples from tanks used by divers, firefighters, and hazardous materials workers. Even today, compressed air testing is one of TRI's most profitable services.

In 1984 the government turned to TRI to help improve sonar systems used in submarines. TRI and the University of Washington were the only nongovernmental participants in the Sonar Transducer Reliability Improvement Program (STRIP). STRIP combined reliability engineering and materials development for the improvement of sonar for submarines. The program led to generations of improved sonar systems, as well as insight into the thermodynamics of the oceans. Stephen Reitz, one of TRI/TESSCO's chief engineers and a former Navy sonar expert, is now applying TRI's sonar research to a project studying ocean temperatures for evidence of global warming.

In 1989 the Department of Defense awarded the company a $12-million contract to operate the Nondestructive Testing Information Analysis Center, a DoD facility for information analysis of critical defense-related technology. The center, under the direction of Dr. George Matzkanin, gives TRI opportunities to gather, compile, and distribute information to governmental and commercial clients.

TRI has also made inroads into creating adhesives for construction. The Federal Highway Administration awarded it a one-million-dollar contract in 1992 to develop adhesives for bonding parts on bridges and other highway structures. "The commercial spin-off possibilities for this kind of project are enormous," Thornton says.

Texas Research International has been cited for excellence by several technical journals. For example, *Research & Development* magazine gave the firm its first R&D 100 Award in 1989 for a robot designed to inspect heavy cables such as those used on bridges. In 1993 TRI, in conjunction with the Naval Post Graduate School at Monterey, California, received its second R&D Award for developments in thermoacoustics.

Today TRI employs about 130 personnel in offices and laboratories located from San Diego to Orlando—impressive for a business that began in 1975 with Thornton as the only employee. But Thornton is modest about his accomplishments. "This company is about its people, not its founder," he explains. "My main job is to find the best people and then stay out of the way."

In the future, Dr. Thornton says he would like to see TRI create its own customers by spinning off new technology companies, just as TRI was a spin-off from Tracor. "It's like putting a little model sailboat into the water, and giving it a shove. Then you let it go and see what it can do," Thornton says.

Above: TRI board meeting in progress with key personnel.

Top: An analysis of compounds on a gas chromatograph with an Autosampler.

Innovative Solutions

SYNTRON, INC.

Founder: Richard F. Miles, president and CEO
Founded: 1973 in Houston

Syntron, Inc.
A Tech-Sym Company

Houston has long been synonymous with the oil business, making it the natural home for the headquarters of Syntron, a company at the cutting edge of technology in the petroleum industry. As the search for oil and gas grows more complicated, Syntron is at the forefront in the development, production, and deployment of the sophisticated tools required for that exploration.

In a classic American success story, Syntron began in 1973 in the garage of an inventor, who left his employer to improve on his invention of a cable leveler. Syntron was created, appropriately named from the combination of SYNergy and elecTRONics. From that humble beginning, the company has grown into an international operation and industry leader.

Home to this state-of-the-art research, development, and manufacturing enterprise is an unassuming brick building on the city's west side. The 75,000 square feet of light and comfortable work space yield the superior products used by marine seismic exploration firms and oil field service companies.

Syntron, Inc., corporate headquarters in Houston.

This is where Syntron puts together its three-dimensional seismic survey systems, which have changed the exploration process and increased the success of discovery. In essence, the systems are comprised of from one to eight arrays that are towed behind a seismic vessel and contain hydrophone sensors, conductors, and electronic modules. The data on acoustic energy emitted in deep-water and coastal areas is relayed to the vessel. On board are the related computer systems that record, display, and analyze the data acquired.

Syntron's products include the Bay Cable System, used to gather data in shallow water and transitional zones. The new Multi*TRAK*™ system works in conjunction with a digital telemetry system, attaching to the arrays at intervals. These provide depth control, and exact information that is critical to three-dimensional surveying.

The synergistic acquisition of Tri-Tech Systems, Inc., in 1992 has expanded Syntron's progress in developing systems for the control of subsea drilling operations. Demand for sophisticated control systems should increase as deep-water projects take the lead in exploration.

With the exception of printed circuit boards, Syntron manufactures its entire line of products in-house. This not only ensures the quality control that Syntron demands, but affords its clients the opportunity to custom design their products, to pick and choose from the software required to the actual design and construction of the product.

Syntron's products are designed to operate in the corrosive environment of the deep sea, and as such are made of exotic metals and rare steel and plastics, which require specialized machining processes. All products are subjected to rigorous tests and temperature extremes to ensure reliable field operations. In this competitive market, product reliability and data quality are critical to the end user.

In the computer lab, software applications are tested thoroughly and operations can be simulated here should clients in the field require assistance. Perhaps nowhere is the cutting edge of this technology more visible than in the manufacture of the on-board systems that process the data, including one PC board that can handle 192 million FLPS, or floating points per second.

Syntron has dedicated itself to excellence and pledged its commitment to quality, from the resources and standards used in the manufacture of its products, to the training and skill of the work force responsible for

A SYNTRAK 480 Digital Bay Cable module being manufactured.

their manufacture, to the drive to exceed expectations and guarantee customer satisfaction.

That service-oriented philosophy contributed to the development of international operations. In 1988 Syntron Europe was established to provide the marketing and technical support for the operations in the Middle East, Africa, and Europe. Three years later Syntron Asia was established for the same purpose. Both operations provide custom design, manufacture, and repair for seismic streamer cables, enabling Syntron to move quickly to meet its customers' needs.

Syntron, Inc., is one of six principal subsidiaries of Tech-Sym Corporation, also headquartered in Houston. Tech-Sym is a diversified company that designs, develops, and manufactures products for use in exploration and production in the petroleum industry, as well as radio broadcasting, meteorology, defense, air traffic control, radio and telephone communication, and space exploration.

Premier Real Estate Services

LITTLEFIELD REAL ESTATE COMPANY

Founded: 1984 in Austin
Officers: Jeffrey L. Minch, president of Littlefield Real Estate and managing partner of Norwood Properties; Frank P. Krasovec, chairman of Littlefield Real Estate and senior partner of Norwood Properties

On the edge of downtown Austin, modern office towers of glass and steel stand side by side with older buildings of ornately crafted stone, rising together above a city rich in history. Some structures are relics of prosperous times when money for real estate development seemingly gushed like oil from Spindletop, and of later days when financial institutions ran dry and financial ruin became a common tale of woe for many developers.

Above: The Cameron Centre is a five-building, 94,000-square-foot complex of Class A service space.

Right: Great Hills Plaza, located in the Arboretum, has 140,000 square feet of Class A suburban office space.

But two companies, Norwood Properties and Littlefield Real Estate Company, survived the tough times and went on to thrive. "Here in Texas, if you've been around since the 1970s and you haven't gone broke, that's saying something in the real estate business," says Jeffrey L. Minch, managing partner of Norwood Properties and president of Littlefield Real Estate Company.

Both veterans of an Austin development company called Rust Properties, Minch and partner Frank P. Krasovec struck off on their own in 1984 to form Norwood Properties, a real estate investment company, and later Littlefield Real Estate, a property management business. Krasovec is senior partner of Norwood Properties and chairman of Littlefield Real Estate.

Both companies' names are deeply rooted in Austin's past. Norwood Properties takes its name from Norwood Tower, the first truly modern office building in the city. Built by millionaire bond salesman O.O. Norwood in 1929, the 14-story neo-Gothic structure was among the first in the country with air conditioning and a parking garage. The facility served as the old Capital National Bank Building for 40 years, until purchased by Rust Properties in the late 1970s.

Littlefield Real Estate is named for a building on historic Sixth Street and Congress Avenue constructed by Major George Washington Littlefield in 1912. Wounded on the battlefield fighting for the Confederacy, Littlefield hated the North. So, as with the state capitol and many other buildings erected in the war's wake, the main entrance of the Littlefield Building faces south. Norwood Properties bought it in 1991, and spent $2 million on renovations.

"It's very gratifying to take a building that has historic merit and repair it," Minch explains. "By and large, these buildings are constructed in a way that cannot be duplicated. In most instances, they enjoy locations that were taken 50 or 75 years ago, so odds are they're in the best locations in town."

Minch and Krasovec have been involved in the restoration and adaptive reuse of several old downtown structures, including Norwood Tower as well as the Sampson and Colorado buildings. The idea of taking something with problems and making it better is central to how Norwood Properties and Littlefield Real Estate have survived the tough times.

"Basically, we buy office buildings (both central business district and suburban), apartments, warehouses, and the odd retail center. We're always looking to fix them,

either fix the capital structure, fix the physical plant, reverse a management or marketing failure, and then reposition them to benefit from the recovery in Texas," Minch says. "So we've always been in the business of fixing things up. In Texas we were some of the first people to go into that business, and we've stuck with it."

Sticking with it has paid off. Together, Norwood Properties and Littlefield Real Estate have about $250 million in assets, and annual revenues of more than $30 million. With offices in Austin, Houston, Dallas, and San Antonio, the companies employ about 100 people.

Many other real estate businesses begun in the 1980s aren't so lucky. Massive over-building created by easy access to money during the early part of that decade preceded a wholesale loss of capital in the state as the banking and S&L systems went belly-up. Amateurish developers lost their shirts, but the plagues of bankruptcy, foreclosure, and loan default never befell Minch and Krasovec.

Norwood Properties now owns 6 office buildings in Austin, 10 industrial properties in Austin, Dallas, and San Marcos, and 4,000 apartment units in Austin, Houston, and San Antonio.

"In general, we're very bullish about Texas," Minch says. "Texas is going to have positive job growth and positive population growth."

Above: Park North, a two-building complex at Mopac and Steck, offers 136,000 square feet of Class A suburban office space.

Top left: The Littlefield Building, constructed in 1912 on historic Sixth Street and Congress Avenue, was purchased by Norwood Properties in 1991 and then renovated.

Keying on Image

DATAMARK, Incorporated

Founders: Bill and Becky Holmes
Founded: 1989

Top right: "Keying on Image" software is a DATAMARK product.

Below: Company founders Bill and Becky Holmes.

The computer has created new businesses and industries, changed the speed and expectations of business life, and created paper mountain peaks of hard copy just waiting to be entered.

El Paso-based DATAMARK, Incorporated, has found new ways to scale those paperwork mountains for its customers. During the past five years company founders Bill and Becky Holmes have devised new ways to use low-cost personal computers to transform huge amounts of paper-borne data into private customer databases. But they're proudest of the 450-plus jobs their company has created for El Pasoans.

"The entry-level experience is fundamental to a career," says Becky Holmes. "We are very much aware of the number of entry-level jobs that have moved 'offshore'—just a few miles away. And too often, El Paso high school and college students can't find work during the hours they're not in class. We offer them opportunities in keyboarding and data processing, with flexible working shifts to fit their schedules."

After successful work in the United States and South Africa, the Holmeses came to El Paso in 1982 and started DATAMARK in 1989. The couple had worked in data processing since the mid-1960s—he in marketing hardware and software worldwide, she in management of domestic and overseas word-processing staffs.

"In late 1989 we were looking for opportunities," he explains. "We were briefly involved with an offshore data-entry company, and from that we saw an opportunity to create jobs in El Paso instead of offshore. Becky brought with her experience in word processing and data entry and began to structure training courses. I utilized my marketing background to find clients and set up the computer systems."

At the end of 1989 the company was incorporated and sought work from Federal Express. The overnight shipper gave DATAMARK 60 days to be up and running, tested, and certified. Holmes immediately bought a file server, 15

Right: Data-entry specialist DATAMARK brought all operations into this building at 43 Butterfield Circle, El Paso, during 1994.

The firm's busy production center.

work stations, software, configured the programming language, and trained new employees to use the system. DATAMARK beat the deadline, receiving certification and its first batch of production documents.

In less than five years DATAMARK's client list has grown to include more forms for Federal Express, Pennsylvania's EDS Federal Services Group, Massachusetts' Response Technology, Connecticut's survey firm of Willard & Shullman, the GAGE Marketing Group of Minnesota, California's First Source International, Houston Central Appraisers, Virginia's SIGNET Bank Credit Card Division, and others. That translates into more than 150,000 to 200,000 documents each day, and the percolating roar from the keyboards in DATAMARK's airport-area office tends to obscure jet noise. Measured another way—25 million keystrokes in 24 hours, inducting the customers' paper records into DATAMARK's 20-gigabyte online storage capacity.

Understood in the most meaningful terms, DATAMARK's February 1990 payroll included about 25 people. The January 1994 payroll covered more than 450 people.

DATAMARK keyers type their own raises and bonuses. "When the employee hits certain levels of production, he or she gets so-much-an-hour more," says Becky Holmes, adding that keyboarding skills are never wasted. "No matter what job you're going to get, the faster and more accurately you can deal with the computer, the better it is for you."

How could Total Quality Management be applied to this labor-intensive business? DATAMARK researched and responded with physical and psychological answers. "We all work to see results," adds Becky Holmes, "and the keyers continue to amaze us. We post results—personal results, group results, company results. Sharing the results gives everyone a sense of accomplishment."

The median goal is 14,000 keystrokes per hour. That's the average output per person; some keyers roar through at 24,000 keystrokes per hour. Potential employees who lack accuracy or speed get free training classes to practice their skills. Another innovation—DATAMARK's Quality Control Council—oversees the hiring, training, and monitoring of new and veteran employees. The QCC is comprised of management, supervisors, programmers, instructors, and keyers.

While quality is the first consideration, efficiency demands that companies find faster ways of doing the same job. Paper itself is the problem, and Holmes and his programmers are cutting out the paper with high-quality document scanners and lightning-fast telephone lines. "Keying on Image" is a joint product of DATAMARK and Awaretech's new network-supported PC software that lets keyers capture information from an electronically scanned document from anywhere in the world—format, edit, insert data, and return the information to the customer via high-speed data lines.

Yet another division of DATAMARK makes computer-generated labels for mass mailings and Universal Product Code labels for manufacturing and distributing customers. It's one of the few southwestern companies doing this work.

DATAMARK is one of the few domestic companies doing free-lance data entry. "America cannot—certainly this region right here—afford to allow all our entry-level jobs to go offshore," says Bill Holmes. "We can't deprive our young people of those opportunities to learn a good work ethic." As Becky Holmes puts it, "We are training the future workers of America."

Helping to Overcome Adversity

HEALTHSOUTH REHABILITATION HOSPITAL OF AUSTIN

Founded: 1990 in Austin
Officers: Mike Munnerlyn, chief executive officer; Ava Falk, assistant administrator

Patients of Rehabilitation Hospital of Austin receive care from highly skilled professionals.

Some people come in wheelchairs. Others who arrive can walk. It's a cruel reality, but when an accident, injury, or illness occurs, life changes. Fortunately, there are people who can help.

HEALTHSOUTH Rehabilitation Hospital of Austin is dedicated to assisting people who've experienced a traumatic injury or illness find new ways to accomplish activities of daily living such as walking, dressing, communicating, or operating a car. Founded in July 1990, the hospital has become a respected pioneer in rehabilitation. The hospital has 80 beds, four therapeutic gyms with state-of-the-art equipment, and a therapeutic pool. Each of the four floors is structured and equipped to serve a specific population. HEALTHSOUTH Rehabilitation Hospital of Austin has programs in brain injury, spinal cord injury, orthopedic rehabilitation, restorative neurology, chronic pain management, and amputee and pediatric rehabilitation. People with spinal cord and brain injuries are among many who come from across Texas, attracted by the hospital's experienced and compassionate staff.

These patients receive care from highly skilled professionals who work together as a team. Physical, occupational, and speech therapists work side by side with specialized doctors and nurses to help patients learn to function as independently as possible.

The hospital offers a continuum of care, from total supervision to community reentry. The hospital also advocates family involvement and provides education and training to family members.

The Starbright Pediatric Rehabilitation Institute, which occupies the hospital's third floor, works with children affected by birth defects, traumatic injuries, neurological disorders, and other medical conditions. Starbright is the only comprehensive pediatric rehabilitation center in Central Texas. Located next door to Brackenridge Hospital and the Children's Hospital of Austin at Brackenridge, Starbright can take children into the program early in the recovery process.

HEALTHSOUTH Rehabilitation Hospital of Austin has a community-based vocational reentry program for people with mild brain injury. The goal of this program, Living in Functional Environment, is to help people return to work. There is also a driving program to teach people how to get back behind the wheel. When patients no longer need 24-hour supervision, they can receive intensive outpatient care from the same team of therapists through the day hospital program.

For patients who are slow to recover, or who are not able to go through a full day of therapy, the hospital is developing an innovative subacute rehabilitation program. Also in the works is a gait-analysis laboratory, where doctors can determine treatment for persons with mobility impairment by studying how they walk.

The hospital has 80 beds, four therapeutic gyms with state-of-the-art equipment, and a therapeutic pool.

Driven by the desire to serve and the commitment to excellence, the staff of HEALTHSOUTH Rehabilitation Hospital of Austin is teaching people challenged by a traumatic injury or illness how to make the most of life—physically, mentally, and socially.

The Pipeline of Choice Serving the Southwest

El Paso Natural Gas Company founder Paul Kayser.

EL PASO NATURAL GAS COMPANY

Founder: Paul Kayser
Founded: 1929
Principal: William A. Wise, chairman, president, and CEO

In 1929 El Paso was the only big Texas town without natural gas service. More than 200 miles of rugged, dusty terrain separated it from the Texas-New Mexico Permian Basin.

Young Houston attorney Paul Kayser had been helping H.G. Frost buy oil and gas leases in Texas and Louisiana. Both understood the high financial and physical risks of finding, capturing, and piping natural gas. Kayser and Frost persuaded the El Paso City Council to give their untested El Paso Gas Utilities Corporation a franchise to sell natural gas to the city. The wellheads were at tiny Jal, New Mexico—204 miles east of El Paso. The challenge required that a 16-inch welded steel pipeline stretch west to provide "sweet" low-sulfur natural gas within six months.

With the legendary innovations and leadership of engineer A.L. Forbes and Hugh Steen—the wildcatter who eventually became company president—EPG's pipeliners found new ways to ditch, lay, and weld the miles of conduit in the southwestern desert, mountains, and riverbeds.

The first gas loaded into the new pipeline was sweet, but days later the flow turned sour; it contained far too much sulfur, making it useless. Within a matter of days Forbes and a California engineering firm had devised a process and makeshift equipment to remove the unwanted sulfur. Good gas flowed into El Paso almost 30 days *before* the deal's deadline.

But mountains, rocks, and rattlesnakes weren't the only obstacles. The Great Depression almost wiped out the company, but it struggled and survived.

Between 1983 and 1992 El Paso Natural Gas was a subsidiary of Burlington Northern, Inc., and then of Burlington Resources, Inc. In June 1992 Burlington Resources spun off EPG and the company regained its independence as a separate, stand-alone operation traded on the New York Stock Exchange under the symbol EPG. In its second stint as an independent firm, EPG's stock value doubled.

El Paso Natural Gas has emerged as one of the major transporters of natural gas in the United States. EPG's pipeline system has the capacity to deliver more than four billion cubic feet of gas daily. It has 17,000 miles of pipe, connecting the San Juan, Permian, and Anadarko basins to customers in West Texas, New Mexico, Arizona, southern Nevada, Oklahoma, Colorado, California, and the growing Mexican market. Half the natural gas used in California is supplied by EPG.

But EPG delivers more than natural gas. The company's 24-hour-a-day, 365-day-a-year "Passport Gold" electronic bulletin board gives customers access to a large store of scheduling, accounting, and volume delivery information.

El Paso Natural Gas—2,500 employees strong, with 1,400 in the El Paso area—is still a pioneer. Says today's chairman, president, and chief executive officer William A. Wise: "Our strategic objective is to remain the lowest-cost transporter of natural gas in the Southwest."

Reading meters at EPG's Topock facility.

Specializing in Preengineered Superstructures

ARCHER BUILDING COMPANY

Founded: 1984
President: Robin Archer

The deserts and distances of the Middle East and of North and West Africa offer their own special set of challenges to habitation. Robin Archer found out—after spending years overseas engineering airports and other major construction projects, that if you can build it there...

His desk is a combination desk and plan table in a midtown El Paso office. Windows look southward to Interstate 10 and Juarez, Chihuahua, Mexico—and opportunity. The border trend, says Archer, is away from the traditional construction process to design/build construction management.

"Ten years ago I decided that an owner/client did not have to face the unpleasant task of redesigning the project, rebidding, and/or raising additional financing. Our *team* concept of owner, architect, engineer, general contractor, and experienced subcontractors is the most efficient and effective system, and it's especially useful in Mexico."

This tall, blond native of Morenci, Arizona, is a graduate engineer from Arizona State University. He started the firm in 1984 with "broad experience, support from my wife and family—and no means to capitalize a company."

The milestone came in 1989, when his firm became a Butler Builder. "Their 50-year success with preengineered building materials and methods has contributed greatly to our success." Archer employs about 25 management, procurement, and construction experts in El Paso for projects all over the Southwest.

"With preengineered buildings, we often shorten construction time by 25 percent." Archer says his computer-generated program "costs out" a building to the last bolt, so the customer knows exactly what he's buying. There's a certain Japanese restaurant that Archer won't forget. "A few years ago, the heads of two major Japanese automotive companies were scheduled to visit their border operations. We were asked to do the impossible. Our client was scheduled to host a meal for them. We found we could design and build a restaurant *in 30 days*—one-third the normal time. One month later, the chairman and 30 VIPs enjoyed a dinner in the restaurant."

Archer's specialty is preengineered superstructures for office, warehouse, and manufacturing facilities. Designs can have a variety of outside finishes—so much that a basic building doesn't look plain or prefabricated. "The architect and the client can 'skin' it however they want—with glass, concrete, brick, or stucco. We make sure there's a strong structure underneath and overhead, and we get the building completed on time and within budget." But today's challenge is Mexico. Archer's company is working with a client to design and build sturdy structures in El Paso's sister city of Juarez, Chihuahua, Mexico.

Good engineering, planning, and management are crucial to any successful construction project. Archer's firm pulls the physical and fiscal management teams together under one roof. A standing seam roof, of course—over a reinforced concrete foundation—designed and built by the Archer team.

Right: Robin Archer, Archer Building Company.

Below: Archer built this distinguished structure in Ruidoso, New Mexico.

GM—Texas' Vehicle for Success

GENERAL MOTORS

Founder: William C. Durant
Founded: September 1908

Without a doubt, the word "big" and the state of Texas are synonyms.

General Motors Corporation—with more than 20 Texas staff, divisional, and subsidiary operations stretching from Wichita Falls to Brownsville and El Paso—has a Lone Star presence to match its size as the world's largest industrial corporation. Thousands of GM Texans build, store, and finance transportation products ranging from automotive components to midsize cars to advanced aircraft simulators. But GM's biggest Texas operation isn't part of the car business. Information technology giant Electronic Data Systems employs 13,000 Texans throughout the state.

GM's Midsize Car Division is anchored in Arlington—between Dallas and Fort Worth—and employs more than 3,400 skilled workers and managers who produce automobiles for Buick, Chevrolet, and Cadillac divisions. Originally constructed in 1952, the Arlington plant has been expanded and modernized to cover 2.3 million square feet of space.

Wichita Falls is the Texas home of an AC Rochester Division plant. Built in 1978, the 482,000-square-foot facility produces exhaust oxygen sensors, fuel-injection filters, fuel pumps, and fuel pump parts. More than 54.5 million sensors have been shipped from the Wichita Falls operation since 1979, and today's payroll lists more than 465 people.

When consumers and car dealers need credit to buy cars and trucks, they get it from the 23 General Motors Acceptance Corporation and Motors Insurance Corporation operations in the Lone Star State. GMAC serves more than 400,000 retail accounts and provides financial services to more than 500 car and truck dealers.

Need a General Motors part? Chances are it passed through the hands of some of the 575 people in Fort Worth's Service Parts Operations, a parts distribution center that serves General Motors' retail dealers.

Just as there are hundreds of components in today's GM car, there are hundreds of component parts in today's Texas operations. GM divisions in Texas perform a variety of support, sales, and warehouse services for GM operations throughout the world. GM's Packard Electric Division has warehousing and administrative offices in El Paso and Laredo that support the Mexican Operations' final assembly work.

Other General Motors operations in Texas include Inland-Fisher-Guide, AC Delco, Delco Remy, Delco Chassis, Delco Electronics, Chevrolet, Buick, Pontiac, Oldsmobile, Cadillac, GMC Truck, Motors Holding, and Argonaut Realty.

Beyond the car business, the Hughes Aircraft subsidiary, located in Arlington, produces military, industrial, locomotive, and entertainment simulators. Hughes Training, Inc., shows military aviators how to fly at Mach 1 and to maneuver—without even leaving the tarmac. The subsidiary GM Hughes Electronics Corporation is a major player in automotive electronics, commercial technologies, telecommunication, and space and defense electronics.

The Lone Star State—the only mainland state that at one time was a sovereign nation—has long been a center of international commerce. General Motors, with its Texas divisions and subsidiaries, is the horsepower behind much of Texas' economic success.

Global Leadership

AMERICAN AIRLINES

Founded: April 15, 1926

American Airlines gives life to the saying that everything is bigger in Texas. It has certainly proven true for American, which has grown into one of the world's largest airlines while headquartered in Dallas-Fort Worth.

Above: During the 1920s early forerunners of American Airlines flew the U.S. mail using aircraft such as the Pitcairn Super Mailwing, shown here.

Right: The American Airlines hub at DFW International Airport.

American and its regional counterpart, American Eagle, now fly more than 900 planes, with some 4,000 daily flights. In 1993 they flew nearly 93 million people to 355 cities in the United States and around the world. Of the 116,000 employees of American's parent company, AMR Corp., 30,000 work in Texas, making the firm one of the largest employers in the state.

Airline officials say it is Texas' pro-business attitude and its central location that make such growth possible.

"Texas is a preferential place to do business. It isn't accidental we expanded here," says Ted Tedesco, vice president of corporate affairs. "We believe very deeply also that a critical factor in our success over the past 15 years has been having our headquarters at the heart of our route system. We can better manage the business from here than anywhere else."

It's not surprising the state had such an effect on American, whose Texas heritage reaches to the beginning of commercial aviation. "Some don't see us as native Texans because we relocated our headquarters here in 1979 from New York," Tedesco acknowledges. "But we really are a Texas company. Our roots go all the way back to Texas Air Transport in the 1920s, and we've been serving Texas continuously ever since."

Out of Texas Air Transport emerged C.R. Smith, the Texan who led American Airlines until 1968 and who pioneered many innovations that became industry standards. Smith was born in 1899 in the small Texas town of Minerva. Vice president of Texas Air Transport, and later Southern Air Transport, by his late twenties, Smith became vice president of American's southern division after Southern was purchased by AA. He was named president in 1934.

The East Coast was then the business and travel hub of the nation, so it made good sense to base the young airline in New York City. From the beginning, American led the industry with numerous "firsts."

American, for example, pioneered domestic cargo service, first let passengers fly on credit, flew the first nonstop coast-to-coast trip, introduced jets to domestic service, launched the first computerized reservations system, created the original frequent flyer program in AAdvantage®, and invented Super Saver fares.

Yet even as American grew to become one of the nation's leading air carriers, it established vital new links to Texas.

American established its Southern Reservations Office in the Dallas-Fort Worth area to serve the southern tier of its route system. The area was chosen in 1957 for American's

Stewardess College, the world's first specialized training school for flight attendants (today known as the Learning Center). Dallas-Fort Worth also was selected for American's Flight Academy, recognized as one of the world's finest pilot training facilities.

Texas' central location, good flying weather year-round, and favorable business climate made it American's choice when the airline decided to leave Manhattan in the late 1970s. Its existing facilities in the Dallas-Fort Worth area helped seal the decision.

American was certainly a major airline in New York, but Tedesco explains it was only after the move to Texas that it took the lead, more than doubling its size. Texas' can-do attitude perfectly matched American's desire to develop the new business opportunities presented by airline deregulation.

In the new wide-open atmosphere, American realigned its route system around six hubs, into which feed flights from dozens of other cities. DFW became AA's first hub in 1981, followed by Chicago, San Juan, Miami, Nashville, and Raleigh-Durham. American Eagle, a network of regional airlines fully integrated into American's domestic system, was introduced in 1984.

The airline also began international expansion. Today American flies throughout Europe, Central and South America, Canada, the Caribbean, and on to Tokyo, 68 international points in all.

Determined to remain commercial aviation's leader, parent AMR Corp. has now adopted a transition plan to strengthen airline operations while boosting investment in its non-airline businesses. American will reduce or drop uncompetitive services and transfer those planes and people to expand service in areas—like Texas— where growth potential is brighter.

Meanwhile, AMR will invest more in its highly successful non-airline operations that serve other airlines and related businesses, including SABRE Decision Technologies, SABRE Travel Information Network, and other SABRE Group Businesses, AMR Investment Services, AMR Services Corp., and AMR Training and Consulting Group.

"Our transition plan is strengthening the company for the long-term future," Tedesco says. "We want to be among the finest transportation and technology companies in the world."

As part of its transition plan, American will strengthen its hubs at Dallas-Fort Worth, Chicago, Miami, and San Juan while continuing to build its Nashville and Raleigh-Durham operations. American Eagle will expand to feed passengers from outlying cities into the hubs. Hopes are also high for more routes to Europe, Latin American, and possibly along the Pacific Rim.

American will be ready when the economy recovers. "We are famous for being highly competitive," Tedesco notes. "We are scrappy and we are perfectionists." Just as they always have, these proud Texas traits inherited from C.R. Smith will see American Airlines through the transition period into continued global leadership.

Above: The Douglas DC-3 "Flagship Knoxville" in front of American Airlines' C.R. Smith Museum.

Top: American Airlines' System Operations Control Center.

Providing a Home for the Business Traveler

CORPORATE LODGING

Founded: 1972
Chairman: Warren Haskin

Accommodation quality at Corporate Lodging exceeds typical suite hotels, at lower cost.

The hardest part of the job for business travelers on assignment to another city is living weeks on end in a small hotel room; even a standard suite hotel soon feels cramped. A vague malaise sets in that can sap work productivity.

Corporations find a comfortable and reasonably priced alternative in Corporate Lodging, an Austin-based hotelier whose guests live in spacious and secure apartments near their work, entertainment, and shopping.

Typical guests are relocating to the community, on long assignments from another city, or in town for training, although Corporate Lodging also serves overnight guests. Rates range from $49 to $129 nightly, depending upon apartment size and length of stay.

"What we provide truly is a home. Clients tell us their employees even finish the job early because there is no stress in daily living," says Warren Haskin, chairman of the 21-year-old company. Haskin, who was inducted to *Oxford's Who's Who* in 1991, is considered the grandfather of the all-suite hotel industry.

Corporate Lodging works by contracting with desirable apartment complexes so it can make arrangements quickly. "We can set up a suite in two days with every detail the client wants, plus we can put people wherever they want in a city," Haskin explains.

Accommodation quality exceeds typical suite hotels, at lower cost. "These aren't scaled-down suites, but full-size one- or two-bedroom apartments," he says. "We offer services beyond a hotel's, matching exactly what the client needs."

Standard amenities include fully equipped kitchens, color television, and videocassette recorder. Many apartments also have big screen televisions, fireplaces, washing machines, and balconies. Corporate Lodging will install a second telephone line if needed, and even equip the apartment with a computer and fax machine.

Corporate Lodging's hospitality staff pampers guests. Hostesses not only keep the apartment clean, but deliver mail and messages, pick up dry cleaning, shop for groceries, and suggest nearby entertainment.

"You aren't just an anonymous person here. You are 'John,' who has a family waiting for you. Our hostesses write each guest a personal note every day so guests know someone is attending to their needs. We want to be our guests' family while they are with us," continues Haskin.

Haskin began Corporate Lodging in 1973, after helping Southwestern Bell with a personnel relocation to Houston. The company currently has properties in Austin, Dallas, and Richardson, and in Columbus, Ohio. Operations expanded to San Antonio and Houston in 1994. Corporate Lodging also is building a 100-unit apartment hotel in Austin.

Future plans include additional building, buying apartment complexes, and national expansion. The company also is launching a new budget apartment concept aimed at families who are relocating.

To arrange accommodations, call Corporate Lodging at 1-800-84-LODGE.

Luxurious Accommodations

An original Tiffany glass dome covers the Camino Real Paso del Norte Hotel's original lobby—now the Dome Bar.

CAMINO REAL PASO DEL NORTE HOTEL

Established: 1912

Billy the Kid *didn't* sleep here. But Pancho Villa and General John "Black Jack" Pershing *did*. The history and elegance of El Paso's legendary Camino Real Paso del Norte Hotel make it the most prestigious hotel providing the best in guest rooms, ballrooms, and meeting facilities on the Rio Grande.

The hotel is on the National Historic Register; famous names appear on the register. Presidents William Howard Taft, Herbert Hoover, Franklin Roosevelt, and Lyndon Johnson and Vice Presidents Richard Nixon and George Bush stayed here. Actresses Gloria Swanson and Rita Moreno, aviators Charles Lindbergh and Amelia Earhart, musicians Enrico Caruso and Benny Goodman, humorists Will Rogers and Mark Russell—all stayed here.

El Paso businessman Zach White—one of the Southwest's true entrepreneurs—saw the old Grand Central Hotel burn in 1896. Intrigued with the idea of building an "elegant, fireproof hotel," White and the Trost & Trost architectural firm designed a $1.5-million terra cotta building with interior walls of fireproof gypsum. White obtained the finest black, green, and pink marble, mahogany, and gold and brass fixtures. The hotel opened on Thanksgiving Day in 1912 and remained in the White family until 1970, when it was bought by an investment firm. After flying the Westin flag for a number of years, the Paso del Norte became part of the Mexican-owned hotels Camino Real group in March 1993.

A $50-million restoration in 1986 added the tower, facilities for nine simultaneous meetings of 100-attendees-plus each, and an 8,000-square-foot grand ballroom. The Dome Bar—named for White's custom-made, 25-foot-wide Tiffany glass dome that still covers the circular bar—and the adjacent Dome Grill provide refreshment and fine dining. The informal Cafe Rio features cuisines of the Southwest.

The grand hotel sits across from the El Paso Convention and Performing Arts Center. It's a prized focus of the city's historic district. After more than 80 years of hospitality, today's Camino Real Paso del Norte Hotel has proven that it and its notable guests have staying power.

The El Paso Civic Center is the picture of contemporary architecture. Photo by James Blank

PATRONS

The following individuals, companies, and organizations have made a valuable commitment to the quality of this publication. Jostens Publishing Group and the Texas Chamber of Commerce gratefully acknowledge their participation in *Texas Chronicles.*

Ainsa, Skipworth, Conde & Martinez
American Airlines*
Archer Building Company*
Azar Nut Company
BFGoodrich Aerospace Component Overhaul & Repair Inc.*
Camino Real Paso del Norte Hotel*
Commercial Real Estate Services
Continental Airlines, Inc.*
Corporate Lodging*
Crossroads Construction, Inc.
DATAMARK, Incorporated*
Dickshire Distributing, Inc.
Dresser Industries*
DuPont*
EDS*
Elcom, Inc.
El Paso Natural Gas Company*
Fisher-Rosemount*
General Motors*
Geo-Marine, Inc.*
HEALTHSOUTH Rehabilitation Hospital of Austin*
Herman-Miles Trucking
Holt, Rinehart and Winston, Inc.*
Innovative Applications Corp.
Keystone International, Inc.*
KVET/KASE*
Lawyer's Title of El Paso
Littlefield Real Estate Company*
Minco Technology Labs Inc.*
Mrs Baird's Bakeries*
National Instruments*
Phelps Dodge Corporation
Progressive Insurance Companies*
Simpson Pasadena Paper Company*
Southwest Engineering Associates
Southwest Texas State University*
State National Bank*
Stone Container Company
Syntron, Inc.*
Texas Research International, Inc.*
University of Texas at El Paso

* "Chronicles of Enterprise" participants. The stories of these companies and organizations appear throughout *Texas Chronicles.*

BIBLIOGRAPHY

BOOKS

Acheson, Sam. *35,000 Days in Texas: A History of the Dallas News and Its Forbears.* New York: The Macmillan Co., 1938.

Christian, Stella, L. *History of the Texas Federation of Women's Clubs.* Houston: Dealy-Adey-Elgin Co., 1919.

Cranfill, J.B. *R.C. Buckner's Life of Faith and Works.* Dallas: Buckner Orphans Home, 1915.

Duke, Cordia S. *6,000 Miles of Fence; Life on the XIT Ranch of Texas.* Austin: University of Texas Press, 1961.

Faulk, Odie B., and Seth S. McKay. *Texas After Spindletop.* Austin: Steck-Vaughn Co., 1965.

Fehrenbach, T.R. *Lone Star: A History of Texas and the Texans.* New York: American Legacy Press, 1983.

Frantz, Joe B. *Texas: A Bicentennial History.* New York: W.W. Norton & Co., 1976.

Gard, Wayne. *The Chisholm Trail.* Norman: Oklahoma University Press, 1954.

—*The First 100 Years of Texas Oil & Gas.* Dallas: Texas Mid-Continent Oil & Gas Association, 1966.

Gross, Ken. *Ross Perot: The Man Behind the Myth.* New York: Random House, 1992.

Haley, J. Evetts. *Charles Goodnight: Cowman and Plainsman.* Norman: Oklahoma University Press, 1949.

Haley, James L. *Texas: An Album of History.* Garden City, NY: Doubleday & Co., 1985.

Handbook of Texas. 2 vols. Austin: The Texas State Historical Association, 1952.

Handbook of Texas. A Supplement. Austin: The Texas State Historical Association, 1976.

Hause, Katherine. *An Historical Study of the First Forty-Five Years of the Houston Post* (M.A. thesis). Nacogdoches, TX: Stephen F. Austin University, 1978.

History of the Cattlemen of Texas: A Brief Resume. Austin: Texas State Historical Association, 1991.

Huff, Richard A. *A Pictorial History of the 36th Division.* Austin: 36th Division Association, 1946.

Knight, Oliver. *Fort Worth: Outpost on the Trinity.* Norman: University of Oklahoma Press, 1953.

Lane, John J. *History of the University of Texas.* Austin: H. Hutchings, 1891.

McCallum, Henry D. *The Wire That Fenced the West.* Norman: Oklahoma University Press, 1965.

McComb, David. *Galveston: A History.* Austin: University of Texas Press, 1986.

McDonald, Archie P. *In Celebration of Texas.* Northridge, CA: Windsor Publications, Inc., 1986.

Miller, Charles, and H.T. Sanders (eds.) *Urban Texas: Politics and Development.* College Station: Texas A&M University Press, 1990.

Nixon, Pat Ireland. *A History of the Texas Medical Association, 1853-1953.* Lancaster, PA: Mollie Bennett Lupe Memorial Fund, 1956.

Patterson, Mike. *Fort Worth: New Frontiers in Excellence.* Chatsworth, CA: Windsor Publications, Inc., 1990.

Payne, Darwin. *Dallas: An Illustrated History.* Woodland Hills, CA: Windsor Publications, Inc., 1982.

Ragsdale, Kenneth. *The Year America Discovered Texas: Centennial '36.* College Station: Texas A&M Press, 1987.

Raines, C.W. *Year Book for Texas, 1901.* Austin: n.p., 1902.

Richardson, Rupert. *Texas: The Lone Star State.* New York: Prentice-Hall, 1943.

—*Texas: The Lone Star State.* 6th ed. Englewood Cliffs, NJ: Prentice-Hall, 1993.

Rister, Carl Coke. *Oil! Titan of the Southwest.* Norman: Oklahoma University Press, 1949.

Sharpe, Ernest. *G.B. Dealey of the Dallas News.* New York: Holt, 1955.

Sonnichsen, C.L. *Roy Bean: Law West of the Pecos.* New York: Macmillan, 1943.

Steen, Ralph. *Twentieth Century Texas: An Economic and Social History.* Austin: The Steck Co., 1942.

Texas Almanac (various years with first edition published in 1857). Dallas: A.H. Belo Corp.

Texas Looks Ahead, The Resources of Texas. Vol. 1. Austin: The University of Texas, 1944.

Timmons, W.H. *El Paso: A Borderlands History.* El Paso: The University of Texas at El Paso, 1990.

Tolbert, Frank X. *Dick Dowling at Sabine Pass.* New York: McGraw-Hill, 1962.

—*The Story of Lyne Taliaferro Barret.* Dallas: Texas Mid-Continent Oil & Gas Association, 1966.

Warner, C. A. *Texas Oil and Gas Since 1543.* Houston: Gulf Publishing Co., 1939.

Welch, June. *Texas: New Perspectives.* Austin: Steck-Vaughn Co., 1972.

WPA Dallas Guide and History. Dallas: University of North Texas Press, 1992.

NEWSPAPERS & PERIODICALS

Dallas, Dallas Morning News, Dallas Times Herald, Dunn's Review, Forbes, Fortune, Life, Look, New Republic, Newsweek, New York Times Magazine, Time, U.S. News & World Report.

MISCELLANEOUS

The Semi-centennial Celebration of the Agricultural and Mechanical College of Texas . . . (program booklet). College Station: Texas A&M, 1926.

ADDITIONAL PHOTO CREDITS

(Article sections only)

CHAPTER ONE

Page 14 Top—Cirker, *Dictionary of American Portraits,* Dover; Bottom—Archives Division, Texas State Library • ***Page 15*** Institute of Texan Cultures • ***Page 16*** Center for American History, University of Texas at Austin (Prints & Photographs Coll.) • ***Page 17*** Top—Center for American History, University of Texas at Austin (Prints & Photographs Coll.); Bottom—Amon Carter Museum, Fort Worth • ***Page 18*** Cirker, *Dictionary of American Portraits,* Dover • ***Page 20*** Top—Larry Sheerin, San Antonio; Bottom—Texas/Dallas History and Archive Division, Dallas Public Library • ***Page 22*** Institute of Texan Cultures (Evelyn Streng Coll.) • ***Page 25*** Houston Metropolitan Research Center, Houston Public Library • ***Page 26*** Top—San Antonio Museum Association • ***Pages 26-27*** Rosenberg Library, Galveston, Texas

CHAPTER TWO

Page 38 Top & Bottom—Institute of Texan Cultures • ***Page 40*** Cirker, *Dictionary of American Portraits,* Dover • ***Page 41*** Top—Center for American History, University of Texas at Austin (Texas Map Coll.); Bottom—Texas/Dallas History and Archive Division, Dallas Public Library • ***Page 42*** Archives Division—Texas State Library • ***Page 43*** Southwest Collection, El Paso Public Library • ***Pages 44-45*** Center for American History, University of Texas at Austin (Ruffini, F.E., Coll.) • ***Page 44*** Bottom—Center for American History, University of Texas at Austin (Prints & Photographs Coll.) • ***Page 46*** Panhandle-Plains Historical Museum, Canyon, Texas • ***Page 47*** Panhandle-Plains Historical Museum, Canyon, Texas • ***Page 48*** Bottom—Cirker, *Dictionary of American Portraits,* Dover • ***Pages 48-49*** Panhandle-Plains Historical Museum, Canyon, Texas • ***Page 50*** Top—Institute of Texan Cultures; Bottom—Permian Historical Society Archival Collection, The University of Texas of the Permian Basin, Odessa, Texas • ***Page 51*** Houston Metropolitan Research Center, Houston Public Library • ***Page 52*** Bottom—San Antonio Museum Association • ***Pages 52-53*** Institute of Texan Cultures

CHAPTER THREE

Page 66 Left—Spindletop/Gladys City Boomtown Museum (photo by Frank Trost); Top Right & Bottom Right—Spindletop/Gladys City Boomtown Museum • ***Page 68*** Cirker, *Dictionary of American Portraits,* Dover • ***Page 69*** The Stockhouse, Inc., Houston (photo by Art Tilley) • ***Pages 70-71*** Archives Division—Texas State Library • ***Page 72*** Top—Houston Metropolitan Research Center, Houston Public Library; Bottom—Texas/Dallas History and Archive Division, Dallas Public Library • ***Page 75*** Texas/Dallas History and Archive Division, Dallas Public Library • ***Pages 74-75*** Institute of Texan Cultures (Marshall Steves Coll.) • ***Page 76*** Top—Center for American History, University of Texas at Austin (Burleson, A.S., Papers); Bottom—Southwest Collection, El Paso Public Library • ***Page 77*** Center for American History, University of Texas at Austin (Ferguson, J.E., Papers) • ***Page 78*** Bottom—Southwest Collection, Texas Tech University • ***Pages 78-79*** Southwest Collection, Texas Tech University • ***Page 79*** Top—Rosenberg Library, Galveston, Texas • ***Pages 80-81*** Houston Metropolitan Research Center, Houston Public Library • ***Page 81*** Top—Southwest Collection, El Paso Public Library • ***Page 82*** Texas/Dallas History and Archive Division, Dallas Public Library • ***Page 83*** Center for American History, University of Texas at Austin (Brown, J.H., Papers)

CHAPTER FOUR

Page 103 Top—Admiral Nimitz Museum, Fredericksburg, Texas; Bottom—Panhandle-Plains Historical Museum, Canyon, Texas • ***Page 104*** Top—U.S. Army Air Force, LBJ Library Collection; Bottom—Southwest Collection, Texas Tech University • ***Page 105*** Center for American History, University of Texas at Austin (Duren, A.M., Papers) • ***Pages 106-107*** UPI/Bettmann Newsphotos • ***Page 107*** Top—Texas/Dallas History and Archive Division, Dallas Public Library • ***Page 108*** NASA • ***Page 109*** Top—El Paso Public Library; Bottom—Rosenberg Library, Galveston, Texas • ***Page 111*** NASA • ***Page 112*** NASA • ***Page 113*** UPI/Bettmann

CHAPTER FIVE

Page 132 Top—David Vinyard/The Stockhouse, Inc., Houston; Middle—Richard Stockton/The Stockhouse, Inc., Houston; Bottom—Kim Todd/The Stockhouse, Inc., Houston • ***Page 133*** Top—FOTOPIC/The Stockhouse, Inc., Houston; Bottom—John Burkholder/The Stockhouse, Inc., Houston • ***Page 134*** Top—UPI/Bettmann; Bottom—UPI/Bettmann Newsphotos • ***Page 135*** UPI/Bettmann Newsphotos • ***Page 136*** UPI/Bettmann • ***Page 137*** Texas/Dallas History and Archive Division, Dallas Public Library • ***Page 138*** Top—Henry A. Kokojan/The Stockhouse, Inc., Houston; Bottom—UPI/Bettmann • ***Page 139*** UPI/Bettmann Newsphotos • ***Page 140*** Kent Knudson/The Stockhouse, Inc., Houston • ***Page 141*** Top—Lawrence Ruggeri/The Stockhouse, Inc., Houston; Bottom—Pete Saloutos/The Stockhouse, Inc., Houston • ***Page 142*** Top—Houston Metropolitan Research Center, Houston Public Library; Bottom—Kent Knudson/The Stockhouse, Inc., Houston • ***Page 143*** The Office of the Governor • ***Page 144*** Larry Kolvoord/TexaStock

"CHRONICLES OF ENTERPRISE" INDEX

GENERAL INDEX

Italicized numbers indicate illustrations.